Freshwater Aquaria:

Their CONSTRUCTION, ARRANGEMENT, and MANAGEMENT,

With descriptions of the most suitable Water-plants and Live Stock, and How to Keep Them.

By Rev. GREGORY C. BATEMAN, A.K.C.

Fifth Edition

PROFUSELY ILLUSTRATED.

PREFACE TO THE FIRST EDITION.

I WAS always fond of Natural History, and while I was a boy I frequently looked forward to one day possessing an aquarium so large that I might collect as many aquatic creatures as I liked from the neighbouring ponds and streams, place them all together in my tank, and then make myself quite happy by watching the habits and the changes of my captives. But, alas! in course of time, I found, as so many find, that the realisation of one's hopes does not always bring with it the anticipated pleasure. For when I did eventually own as big and—as appeared to me at that time—as suitable an aquarium as I could wish for, and when I did stock it with many curious and (to my mind) interesting animals. I was, after all, not very happy, nor even content; far from it. The Sticklebacks and the aquatic Spiders would not build their nests side by side ; the *Dyticus marginalis* absolutely refused to live on anything like friendly terms with the Minnows ; the Snails while crawling over my most valued plants were not able to refrain from devouring them and ruining them ; the water would not keep bright, nor the glass of the tank clear, and my patience was sorely tried. I bought or borrowed whatever books I could upon aquarium and kindred matters, but I was not able to obtain all the information I required. Then I attempted to find out by experiment

that which I could not ascertain by reading. After not
a few failures and disappointments, most of my attempts were
successful, and as I began to have more knowledge of these
things I resolved that I would, at some time or other, try
to write such a book as that I wished for so much
when I was making my first blunders in aquarium
matters. By-and-by an opportunity was afforded me of
contributing to *The Bazaar* a series of articles upon the
fresh-water aquarium. These articles are now re-published
in book form, and so in this way I have kept my resolution
and have written my book; but as I finished looking over the
"proofs" of its last chapter, I confessed, with not a little
mortification, that it fell far short of the volume I had hoped
to write. However, I shall feel very thankful if I can be the
means of saving some keepers of an aquarium from disappointment and many aquatic animals from unnecessary
suffering.

Before or while writing the above-mentioned articles, I read
all or portions of the following books, and to the authors I
am more or less indebted :

"Land and Fresh-Water Shells," by R. Rimmer, F.L.S. ;
"British Beetles," by E. C. Rye; "Manual of British
Beetles," by J. F. Stephens, F.L.S.; "British Wild Flowers,"
by Miss Pratt; "The Aquarium," by J. E. Taylor, Ph.D.,
F.I.S., &c.; "The Fresh and Salt-water Aquarium," by Rev.
J. G. Wood, M.A.; "Lakes and Rivers," by C. O. G. Napier,
F.G.S.; "Ponds and Ditches," by M. C. Cooke, M.A., LL.D.;
"Pond Life — Insects," by E. A. Butler, B.A., B.Sc.;
"Popular History of the Aquarium," by G. B. Sowerby, F.L.S.;
"The Book of the Aquarium," by Shirley Hibberd; "Intro-
duction to Entomology," by Kirby and Spence; "The Natural
History of British Fishes," by F. Buckland; "Land and Fresh-
water Shells of the British Islands," by J. E. Gray, Ph.D.,
F.R.S.; "Popular History of British Crustacea," by Adam
White; "The Microscope," by Jabez Hogg, M.R.C.S., F.R.M.S.;
"The Home Naturalist," by Harland Coultas; "Country Walks,"
by the Rev. H. Houghton, M.A.; "The Badminton Library"
—"Fishing,"—by H. Cholmondeley Pennell; "L'Aquarium,"

J. Rothschild, Editeur. In addition to these books, I have consulted *Science Gossip* and *Cassell's Natural History*. There are other books whose names and authors I have forgotten, but some of the useful information which I obtained from them I remember, and for it I am grateful. But the correctness or inaccuracy of whatever information I have gained from books or articles, I have tried to prove by practical experience.

G. O. B.

Jacobstowe Rectory, North Devon

PREFACE TO THE SECOND EDITION.

THIS Edition represents a complete revision of the original matter. The alterations, except the chapter on the "Breeding of Goldfish," are chiefly in the form of additions in the shape of descriptions and illustrations of those fish, suitable for life in a tank, which were not generally imported into this country at the time of writing the former edition.

G. C. B.

Bratton Clovelly Rectory, Devon.

CONTENTS.

FRESH-WATER AQUARIA

CHAPTER I.

THE AQUARIUM.

F EW things are more interesting and less troublesome than a well cared-for aquarium. It makes no litter to annoy the tidy housewife, and no noise to distract the student. Besides, if properly arranged, it is very ornamental. The aquarium also is exceedingly useful to the naturalist in the prosecution of his studies; and by its help the botanist can conveniently observe aquatic plants as they pass through the various stages of their existence.

Those who intend to keep an aquarium must remember that though few things are less troublesome, still it does require a little care, and that little care should be given regularly and daily. A few minutes at a time will suffice —just long enough to feed the fish, to see that there is no death and no decay, to notice that the light has not been so strong as to cause the confervæ to grow too rapidly, and to take care that the representatives of the Animal Kingdom do not exceed the proper proportion according to the amount of weed provided. The reason for this is that the fish inspire the oxygen held in solution by the water, and expire carbonic-acid gas. The plants, by respiration, consume the carbonic-acid gas supplied by the fish, using the carbon for the construction of their tissues and fibres, and liberating again the oxygen for the use of the animal life within the aq. a ium; or, to put it plainer, the fish breathe out carbonic-acid gas and breathe in oxygen. The snails, which should always be present in the aquarium, find their food in the confervæ and other decaying vegetable matter. They thus not only remove that which otherwise would be injurious to the inmates of the water, but they, as also do the fish, convert a part of what they eat into food for the plants.

FIG. 1.

The proof that this much-desired result is attained is seen in the apparent health and happiness of the animals and the sparkling clearness of the water. But to arrange matters thus will require a little experience. The plants, however numerous they may be in the aquarium, will not alone supply sufficient oxygen. For the principal duty of the vegetation is, as it has been said, to decompose the carbonic-acid gas expired by the animals, absorbing the carbon into their own substance and setting free the oxygen for the use of the fish; but the oxygen must be chiefly drawn from the atmosphere which comes in contact with the surface of the water. Therefore it will be seen that the shape of the aquarium is a very important matter; and that this is the case is proved by a simple experiment. If a wide-mouthed bottle be filled with water, and an equal quantity of water be poured into a shallow dish or pan about 2in. deep, and three or four minnows be placed in each vessel, it will be seen that while the fish in the pan remain apparently well, those in the bottle will, after having ascended to the surface of the water, die.

The reason that the fish in the one case die and in the

other live. is because water is simply a vehicle for holding in solution the oxygen which is necessary to animal life. And the greater the surface of water exposed to the air, the more oxygen will it absorb in proportion to its bulk.

An aquarium of the shape and size of Fig. 1, which would present to the air a surface of water of 32 square inches,

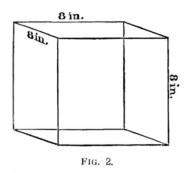

FIG. 2.

would hardly supply the oxygen necessary for the health of three small fish; while one like Fig. 2, having a superficial measurement of 64 square inches, would hold comfortably six small fish; but one of the shape and size of Fig. 3, presenting a surface of 128 square inches, would supply sufficient oxygen for twelve fish. And yet all three aquaria would contain exactly the same quantity of water, viz., 512 cubic inches.

I have kept twenty-six small minnows for a week in an ordinary soup-plate, a little more than half-full of water, and then only one of them died. Further, I have had one pike (9in. long), twenty very small roach (about 1½in. long), nine perch (from 2½in. to 3in. long), and one Great Newt

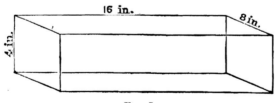

FIG. 3.

(*Molge cristata*) living in perfect health in an aquarium 21in. by 13¾in., but which contained water only 2in. deep—sufficient to cover the dorsal fin of the biggest fish as he swam just clear of the bottom. And these fish lived in this comparatively small quantity of water in apparently the best of health, not only because the water was very shallow in proportion to its superficies, but also because the act of their swimming agitated the surface of the water, thus helping to aërate the whole of it; and for the same reason the twenty-six minnows lived for a week, and would have done so longer, in an ordinary soup-plate half-full of water.

Of course, an aquarium ought not to be so shallow that the water-plants will fail to grow properly. A tank may be of almost any depth, but it must have length and breadth in proportion. To sum up, in order that an aquarium may be a success, it is necessary that it should be of the right

shape; that the representatives of the Animal Kingdom should not be in excess of the minimum amount of weed; and that a little care be taken daily to maintain their balance.

It is almost unnecessary to say that if an aquarium is taken up as a toy, to be fussed over for a few days and then to be neglected for weeks, it will be anything but pleasing and

FIG. 4.

instructive The water in these circumstances will quickly become corrupt and offensive, many of the animals will die, those which are unfortunate enough to survive will be extremely miserable, and the owner and his friends will come to the conclusion that an aquarium is certainly not what I have described it to be—both pleasing and instructive.

There are very many kinds of aquaria, ranging from the simple, flat earthenware pan to the beautiful and expensive combination of plate-glass, slate, fountains, enamel, and gilding. All are more or less useful. The aquarium, of course, most suitable for the fish and the plants is that which most resembles a pond—the light only entering it from above. The great drawback to a tank of this kind is the difficulty of watching closely the movements and ways of its inhabitants, and besides, such a one cannot be said to be ornamental. The commonest aquarium, perhaps, is that often described as an "inverted propagating glass" (Fig. 4). This kind has its advantages and disadvantages. Its advantages are the facility with which the contents can be inspected, its non-leaking character, its cheapness, its portability, and its attractiveness. Its disadvantages are its transparency, which causes much discomfiture to the fish and too great a growth of confervæ; and its proneness apparently to distort its inhabitants as they swim round it. However, the transparency can be partly overcome by judicious shading, the method of which will be explained when "light" is spoken of, and the apparent distortion can be avoided by taking care to choose white and well-blown glasses. In buying an aquarium of this kind, that which is broadest and shallowest should certainly have the preference.

FIG. 5.

Another receptacle for water and fish is the common glass globe (Fig. 5), which has nothing whatever to recommend it, except perhaps to those who delight to hang their

FIG. 6.

unfortunate captives—suspended by a chain from the ceiling—in front of the window; and of course an aquarium which is to be placed in this position—the worst possible—must, on account of its weight, be small; besides, if full, the surface of water exposed to the air must be extremely limited.

The ordinary oblong tank (Fig. 6), containing four glass sides, is both ornamental and useful. However, in order that

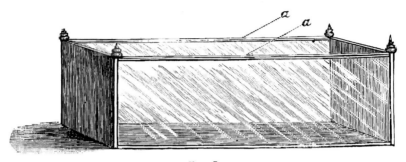

FIG. 7.

the fish may be happy and the vegetation kept within bounds, an arrangement of curtains and the like must be made, which will be explained in due course. This aquarium is made of iron and glass or zinc and glass.

FIG. 8.

A very useful and somewhat easily-made tank is shown at Fig. 7. It is constructed of glass, wood, and slate. The ends and bottom are of wood, the former being lined with thin window-glass, the latter with slate; and the sides are formed of plate-glass.

A more useful aquarium than any yet mentioned is one formed of slate and plate-glass only (Fig. 8). It can be made by an amateur without much difficulty. But perhaps the tank most suitable for its purpose is Fig. 9. One side only is of glass; the others can be made of wood lined with

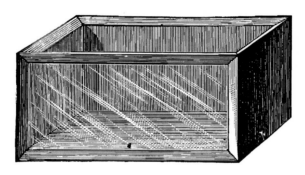

FIG. 9.

glass, or of slate only. The former method is the easier and cheaper to construct, the latter the more serviceable.

Explicit directions for making aquaria similar to those shown at Figs. 6, 7, 8, and 9, are given in Chapter II.

CHAPTER II.

MAKING AQUARIA.

IT appears more difficult to make an aquarium than it really is. Even a tank like Fig. 6, though it is less easy to construct than most of the aquaria mentioned in Chapter I., is not beyond the powers of the ordinary amateur mechanic. Of course it will require some little skill, care, and patience; but when it is properly made

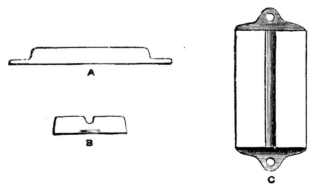

FIG. 10. IRON BLOCK.
A, Side View; B, End View; C, Standing on its End.

it will not only be useful as an aquarium, but also, if wished, it can, at some future time, be turned into either a fernery or a vivarium.

The materials which will be required for its construction are zinc, solder, cement, and plate-glass. The tools necessary are an old tenon-saw, square, hammer, soldering-iron, and a pair of scissors made for cutting sheet metal; but besides these a few blocks must be prepared. The amateur can either make the blocks himself, or he can get them made at a trifling cost. I will describe them in the order in which they will be required.

FIG. 11. STEEL BAR.

Fig. 10 shows an iron block, 6in. long, having a U-shaped groove down its centre. The groove is ⅜in. wide and ¾in. deep. The holes at each end of the block are for the screws which fasten it firmly to the bench. It will not only be useful for the purpose for which it has been made, but at any time it will be serviceable as a small anvil for straightening nails and the like.

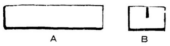

FIG. 12. WOOD BLOCK. A, Side View; B, End View.

Fig. 11 represents a steel bar a little less than ¼in. in diameter, and a little longer than the aquarium is intended to be. Figs. 12 and 13 illustrate blocks made of some hard wood. That in Fig. 12 ought to be not less than 6in. long, and the groove in it should be at least 1in. deep, and just broad enough to receive a double thickness of zinc. The latter has a groove exactly the

FIG. 13. WOOD BLOCK. A, Side View; B, End View.

same size as that in the iron block (Fig. 10). Fig. 14 is made of hard wood, faced with two iron plates. The groove in this block must equal that of the iron block (Fig. 10), and the iron plates should be just far enough apart to receive a double thickness of zinc. Besides these blocks an ordinary mitre-block will be useful, and all of them are more or less necessary, not only for the preparation of the zinc framework of this particular aquarium, but also for other aquaria of a much easier make. The zinc should be moderately stout—that is, about No. 12 gauge.

Having decided upon the dimensions of the tank now about to be made, cut four strips of zinc its exact length, four its

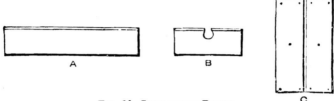

FIG. 14. IRON-FACED BLOCK.
A, Side View; B, End View; C, Face View.

exact breadth, and four its exact height.   Each piece ought to be 2¼in. wide.   Now take a strip of zinc, mark a line down its centre, and place it upon the iron block (Fig. 10), the line marked on the zinc being exactly over the middle of the groove and running lengthwise with it.   Then take the steel bar (Fig. 11) by the handle in the left hand, hold the rod part of it exactly over the line marked on the zinc (and which, of

FIGS 15 AND 16. ZINC STRIP BENT INTO SHAPE AND
METHOD OF PRESSING BY MEANS OF PINCERS.

course, will be over the centre of the groove in the block), and, with the hammer in the right hand, drive the bar and the zinc home into the groove, and about 6in. of the strip of zinc will be bent into the shape of Fig. 15; bend the rest of the strip in this way, then press, by means of a pair o   Fig. 16), the zinc tightly round the steel bar.   When this   done evenly and carefully along the whole length of the strip, put the flat part of the zinc into the narrow groove of the block Fig. 12, the bar not having been withdrawn.

Take the block Fig. 13, place it over the tubing now formed in the zinc, and by striking it (the block) with a hammer rectify any inequality which may have appeared in the moulding. Separate the steel bar from the zinc and slide the latter, tubing downwards, into the iron-faced block (Fig. 14). Then with a chisel or other like tool open the flat portion of the zinc now facing upwards until it forms as nearly as possible a right angle (Fig. 17). When this has been done, withdraw the moulding from the block, and it should now have assumed the shape of Fig. 18. If the edges be found to be not quite straight and true, they may easily be made so by hammering them on a side of the mitre-block.

FIG. 17.

Bend all the other strips in the same way, and then take two of them the length of the proposed aquarium and two of its breadth, and mitre them together. The mitre cuts can readily be made by means of an old tenon-saw and an ordinary mitre-block. Having fixed them in position (Fig. 19), solder the corners neatly and firmly together, taking care to have the flat portions of the moulding perfectly square—that is one edge quite perpendicular and the other perfectly horizontal (Fig. 20). This will be for the bottom of the aquarium.

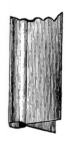

FIG. 18.
SHAPE OF
ZINC
MOULDING

Now take four other pieces of moulding, corresponding to the last four, and repeat exactly the same operation, and then the top of the tank will be formed. Next join the top and bottom together at the corners by means of the remaining four pieces of moulding. Fig. 22 will show the way in which these joints are to be made. Care, of course, should be taken that everything is square and true. The framework of the aquarium will now be complete. It will be, if properly done, very strong.

For a bottom, cut a piece of zinc or slate (the latter being far

preferable) the length and breadth of the tank (inside measure-
ments), place it on the ledge which is running round the lower
part of the frame inside, and solder or cement it there. The
glass for the sides should be ¼in. thick and long enough to go
quite across from end to end. But the glass for the ends ought

FIG. 19. FOUR PIECES OF ZINC MOULDING JOINED TOGETHER, thus forming
either the Top or the Bottom of Frame for Aquarium.

just to touch the glass in the sides, so helping to hold it in its
place. Before putting the glass into the frame its bed ought
to be painted with gold-size and then covered with a thinnish
coating of cement. Recipes for several kinds of cement are
given at the end of this chapter. But, for an aquarium of this

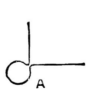

FIG. 20. POSITION OF ZINC
MOULDING WHEN FRAMED.

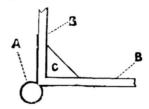

FIG 21. A, ZINC FRAME;
B, GLASS; C, CEMENT.

kind, a mixture of red and white lead is recommended. Now
put the glass in, and press it gently into its place. Put the
sides in first. Paint all the corners with gold-size, and then fill
them in with cement to the depth of about ¼in. (Fig. 21). When
the cement has been roughly put into position, the fixing of it

may be firmly and neatly completed by gently rubbing it with the finger upon the end of which is some gold size.

The tank should now be left to dry for some days; but during this time a stand and covering for it may be prepared. The stand (Fig. 23) can be made of oak, mahogany, or deal;

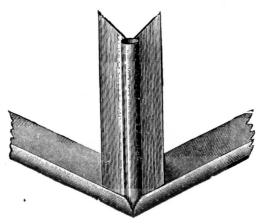

FIG. 22. SHOWING THE JUNCTION OF THE ZINC MOULDING AT THE CORNERS.

this last should be stained and varnished. It ought to be a trifle longer and broader than the aquarium. A groove must be cut in its surface, to receive the beading of the zinc which is at the bottom of the tank. The whole should stand quite firmly. Instead of the heavy-looking covering usually made for such an

FIG. 23. STAND FOR ZINC-FRAMED AQUARIUM.

aquarium as this, a flat piece of glass or of perforated zinc is to be preferred: the former is the better.

At the end of a week the cement will have become somewhat hard; and if red and white lead have been used as the cement, it should now receive two coats of a varnish made of the best sealing-wax dissolved in spirits of wine. With this the zinc bottom ought also to be painted two or three times. Japan black may be used instead of the above varnish, but it will not be so satisfactory. If no varnish at all is used, the aquarium must be filled with water for three weeks or a month before it is stocked with plants and fish, the water being frequently changed during the time. The framework of the aquarium will be much improved in appearance if carefully painted with Brunswick Black or enamel of some suitable colour; if black is used, it may be "picked out" with gold or yellow.

FIG. 24. METHOD OF DOVETAILING CROSSBARS OF AQUARIUM (FIG. 7) INTO UPPER PART OF ENDS.

I have taken it for granted that the maker of such a tank as this has had some little practice in the use of the soldering-iron. But should the reader not know how to solder, and yet wish to attempt to make such an aquarium as this, he cannot do better than purchase one of the many practical manuals in which the subject is dealt with or else write to the Publisher of *The Bazaar,* Windsor House, Bream's Buildings, .E.C. 4, for a number of that journal giving instructions for the work.

It is comparatively easy to make an aquarium to resemble Fig. 7. The ends and bottom are made of 1in. well-seasoned deal, dovetailed together. They are grooved. The grooves run with the grain, and are ⅜in. deep, about the same wide, and ½in. from each edge. The ends are held firmly in their places   .

by two bars at the top of the aquarium (Fig. 7, *a*). These bars
are 2in. broad and 1in. thick. They are dovetailed into their
places (Fig. 24), and have grooves to correspond with those in
the bottom and the ends.

The ends are lined with window-glass and the bottom is lined
with slate. The sides are formed of plate-glass ¼in. thick;
these must be put in their places before the crossbars at the
top of the aquarium are fastened, the grooves into which they
go having previously been half-filled with cement No. 2 (p. 24).
Cover the bottom with a thin layer of the cement just
mentioned, and press the slate firmly and gently into its place.
Fix, in the same way, the glass linings for the ends. Fill up
the corners with a cement of red and white lead to the depth
of ¼in., and when it is somewhat hard put over it a coating of
the cement which was first used. This cement might be
employed throughout; but then, for safety, it must be used a little
more liberally than the other. The junction of the glass
linings with the ends and the dovetailing of the crossbars can
be hidden by four strips of wood, 2½in. wide and ¼in. thick,
neatly mitred together, the corners of which framing may be
decorated with small turned ornaments (as in Fig. 7). The
woodwork will look well either stained, sized, and varnished, or
French-polished. The aquarium should have six little feet
1in. high, screwed to the bottom.

Slate ¾in. or 1in. thick will be required to make a tank like
Fig. 8. It may be procured by the foot at practically any
slate merchant's. The three pieces which will be wanted can
most likely be obtained the size required. The bottom 30in.
long and 16in. wide, and the ends each 16in. by 13in., will
make an aquarium of good dimensions. At 1in. from the
extremity of each end—that is, across the broad part—cut a
groove ½in. deep and 1¼in. broad. This is supposing that slate
1in. thick has been chosen; but if it is only ¾in. thick, then
the groove must be proportionately smaller each way. The
groove may be cut in the following manner : First mark with
an awl the exact place and dimensions of the groove. Then
get two straight-edged pieces of wood some inches longer
than the breadth of the end; place them each side of the line

which is to be cut, and nail them to the bench—they should be just wide enough apart to admit a tenon-saw—and with the saw cut the line to the required depth, ½in. Without some such preparation as this it would be difficult to cut the sides of the grooves with the necessary accuracy. When both lines have been sawn in this way, take a chisel and mallet and cut out the slate which lies between them. But before using the chisel take the precaution to put two or three folds of carpet, or the like, between the slate and the bench to prevent all jarring and the danger of a crack. These grooves are to receive the ends of the bottom.

There is another way of making the cuts for these grooves.

FIG. 25. END OF SLATE AQUARIUM (FIG. 8), showing Grooves for Glass Sides and Slate Bottom and Holes for Bolts.

It is this: Get a piece of hoop-iron, about a foot long, and straighten it. Then for a handle procure 10in. of broomstick, more or less, saw it half through lengthwise, and hammer the hoop-iron into the groove. Mark with an awl the place on the slate where the cut is to be made—and deepen this mark a little by running the point of a three-cornered file a few times carefully up and down. Fill the slight groove thus made with fine white sand, and moisten it with water by means of a wet brush.

Now run to and fro in this sand and water the edge of the tool which has just been made. By continually doing this, always keeping plenty of sand and water under the edge of the iron, the cut will gradually become deep enough. When the cuts have been made, the portion of slate between them may be chiselled out as before directed. As a rule, the slate can be split cleanly out by striking the chisel against the edge and not on the top, and there is less danger of breakage. The latter method of making the cuts is the more satisfactory of the two —the former so quickly blunts the saw.

Now along both sides of the bottom and of each end, cut, at a distance of ¾in. from the edge, grooves ½in. deep and ⅜in.

broad. These grooves are to receive the plate-glass sides, ¼in. thick. After this bore four holes, ¼in. in diameter, right through each end. Two of th ese are to be 1½in. from the edge and ¼in. below the groove which is to receive the end of the bottom, and two 1in. from the top and just within the grooves cut for tho glass (Fig. 25).

The holes are for the bolts which run across from end to end to hold the aquarium together. Bore them with an ordinary brace, and a bit used for metal. The bolts should be made of brass wire; but iron will do. It is a wise precaution to have the thread for the nut a little longer than necessary, for it can easily be shortened when the bolts are in their places, and the long threading is a great convenience in the screwing-up. Before putting the aquarium together, place a little cement in all the grooves. Then raise the bottom on blocks of wood to such a height that it will be level with the grooves cut to receive it in the ends. And when this has been done, put the ends, plate-glass and bolts into position, and screw them all together, turning the nuts of the bolts with only the finger and thumb. Before the nuts are quite screwed home, press the glass gently downward, so that it is forced firmly into its place. Carefully finish filling up the grooves with cement, and the aquarium will be completed. If iron bolts have been used, paint them with Brunswick Black.

An aquarium like Fig. 9 will perhaps be more suitable for its purpose than any yet described, but will not be so ornamental. It makes an excellent tank for marine specimens; and may be made either of wood, slate, and glass, or of slate and glass only. If made on the former plan, the directions given for the construction of an aquarium like Fig. 7 will suffice for the building of this, with the following exeptions: A wooden side lined with window-glass, or roofing-slate, will take the place of a plate-glass side. As the aquarium will be broader than Fig. 7, the grooves in the ends for the glass front must run across the grain, and the bottom must be made the required breadth by clamping and gluing on another piece of wood. The wood work ought to be dovetailed together; but if this cannot conveniently be done, nailing with long French nails will do. The

C

front must be framed as well as the top. A useful size for an aquarium of this description will be 24in. long, 20in. wide, and 10in. deep. If the tank is to be of slate and plate-glass only, the directions given for making an aquarium like Fig. 8

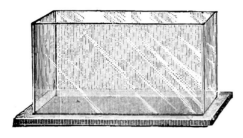

FIG. 26. PORTABLE AQUARIUM.

will be enough, except that in the place of a glass side there will be a slate one, and for this the grooves, instead of being ½in. deep and ⅜in. broad, ought to be ½in. deep and 1⅛in. broad. This is a most useful and durable aquarium.

Fig. 26 represents a very easily and cheaply made aquarium. It is a small tank, chiefly useful for observing the habits of insects and the like. Being of little weight it can conveniently be moved about when full of water. It is deeper and narrower in proportion than an aquarium in which fish are kept ought to be. The foundation is made of 1in. well-seasoned wood (mahogany answers the purpose excellently). Cut a piece 14in. long by 11in. broad. At 1in. from the edge, all round, make a groove ¼in. wide, and the same deep; bend four pieces of zinc moulding according to the instructions already given, 10in. long. Bore a hole ¼in. in diameter at each corner of the grooving in such a

FIG. 27. BOTTOM OF PORTABLE AQUARIUM, showing Grooving for Glass and Zinc Moulding.

way that the square part of the moulding when sunk in the wood will come flush with the outside of the groove; and when this has been done make a cutting with a keyhole-saw to receive the flat portion of the zinc upright (Fig. 27). Drive gently with a mallet each piece of moulding until its end has come flush with the other side of the wood foundation; then by driving a long French nail, *minus* its head, into the side of the wood and through the flat part of the zinc, each upright can be made firm. Now cut two strips of zinc 12in. long, and two 9in. long, all 1in. wide. Mitre them, then join together with solder. When this has been done, take what is made of the aquarium, turn it upside down, place each upright on a corner of this frame, and solder them carefully there. Next get a piece of roofing slate, and with an old saw cut it to fit as a lining for the bottom. The four sides may be of window-glass of a moderate thickness. Use red and white lead as the cement, and paint it, when dry, with two coats of sealing-wax varnish or Aspinall's Bath Enamel. If this cement is not covered in some way, every aquarium in which it is used must be thoroughly soaked before it is stocked; indeed, the soaking of a new aquarium in which cement of any kind has been used should never be omitted. Fill the spaces which may have occurred through inaccurate work, between the outside of the glass and the groove in the wood foundation, with Portland cement or plaster of Paris, and the tank is complete.

If the uprights are not more than 6in. in height, they will need no support at the top. Instead of the groove cut in the wooden foundation, slips of wood may support the glass at the bottom; the slips will save trouble, but will not make the aquarium look so neat as the grooving would. Aquaria made in this way are easily and cheaply constructed, and are not likely to leak.

An arrangement of an aquarium and fernery combined is interesting and ornamental (Fig. 28). This combination is fixed outside a window. The tank should be of slate and plate-glass, like Fig. 8, but it may be similar to either Fig. 7 or Fig. 9. If it be either of the first two shapes, then the stand should be so arranged that there will be a place for ferns beyond the aquarium. The effect of seeing them through the water will be pleasing, and at the same time they will provide suitable shade for the fish. The framework to support and protect the aquarium and fernery may be as

FIG. 28. AQUARIUM AND FERNERY COMBINED.

high as the window—or only half as high—but its breadth
should somewhat exceed that of the window. The reason for
this greater breadth is that the tank may be so long that its

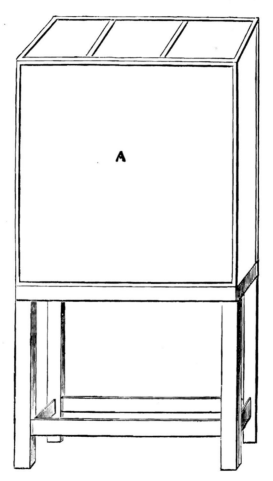

FIG. 29. BACK OF AQUARIUM AND FERNERY COMBINED.

ends will not be exposed to view, the aquarium thus appearing to be larger than it really is. If the tank is made

of slate, according to Fig. 8, only a piece of plate-glass will be seen as its front, no top bar being necessary, which would mar the effect. The whole combination may be supported by a strong wooden stand outside the window (Fig. 30); or if the room to which it is affixed is an upper one. iron brackets let into the wall must be used instead of the stand The frame, back, and sides should be glazed with tinted cathedral glass, especially if the view from the window is unpleasing One large sheet is used for the back (A, Fig. 29); but if it should not be convenient to use only one pane for this purpose, the necessary wood-work for more than one may be tastefully covered inside with cork, with here and there a fern, which may be planted in the following way : Get a small, round tin canister with a few holes punched in the bottom, and sew round it two pieces of sufficiently-curved cork, using thin copper wire for this purpose, and in this contrivance plant the fern. Ferns in suitable baskets may be hung from the roof of the frame, but care should be taken that they are not too heavy, as this roof should be so arranged as to open and shut at pleasure. No fern ought to be hung in such a way that the drip from it would fall inside the aquarium. If anything does hang over the tank, it should be a fern-basket and filter in one, which combina· tion is not difficult to make.

A fountain playing in the aquarium will be a great im· provement, and can, according to circumstances, be more or less easily contrived.

Directions for making fountains and the filter are given in another chapter.

Fig. 30 represents a section of the fernery and aquarium combination. A, window-sill; B, aquarium; C and D, trays for ferns, running the whole length of the aquarium; E, one of the hanging-baskets; F, fountain; G, wooden support; H and I, legs to support aquarium and tray. The trays ought to have holes in their bottoms, to allow for drainage, which should be able to run freely through the floor of the frame-work into the yard or garden outside. Instead of the trays C and D for ferns, one tray, so arranged as to admit of a sloping surface of mould (as shown by the dotted line) may be substituted.

All the aquaria described in this chapter, with one ex-

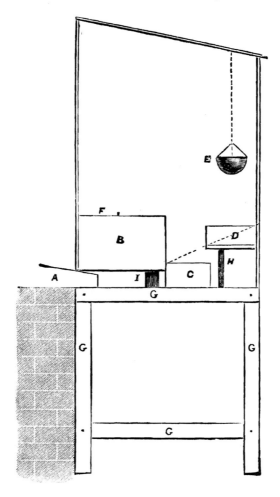

FIG. 30 SECTION OF AQUARIUM AND FERNERY COMBINED.

ception, I have myself made at different times, and the one excepted was made by a friend; therefore it will be seen that their construction is not beyond the powers of an ordinary amateur mechanic.

The following cements have been found useful in the construction of aquaria:

1. Red and white lead—the two being mixed together into a stiff paste. The bed for this cement ought to be painted with gold-size.

2. One pint each of plaster of Paris, litharge, fine white sand, and one-third pint of finely-powdered resin. This (or in this proportion) should be kept in a well-stoppered bottle, and when wanted the necessary quantity should be made into a putty with boiled oil and driers. This is a very quick-drying cement. It becomes, if anything, too hard.

3. The same as No. 2, with the exception of the plaster of Paris and the driers.

4. The best Portland cement.

5. One part pitch and one-fourth part gutta-percha, applied when warm. These should be melted together in an iron ladle over a gas-flame or lamp. This cement is especially useful for an aquarium made of wood.

6. The cement generally sold for fixing solid or cushion india-rubber tyres to bicycles makes a very useful cement for some aquaria. When used it should be melted and made to run by tilting the tank where it is wanted to go. As it soon hardens, the aquaria can be filled with water within an hour after its application. The cement may, with advantage, be placed over red and white lead as soon as this has become a little dry.

In buying an aquarium, care should be taken to choose one which is broad and shallow in proportion to its size. It ought, at the same time, to be neat in appearance and strongly made.

The different aquaria suitable for insects only will be described in another chapter.

CHAPTER III.

THE CABINET AQUARIUM.

AN arrangement called tne "cabinet aquarium" is exceedingly interesting and instructive. It consists of a kind of backless bookcase, upon the shelves of which are placed small aquaria containing such aquatic plants and animals as are unsuitable, owing to various reasons, for the general tank. These shelves should be strong, and so constructed that they will stand quite firmly. They may be made of almost any kind of wood, and in either a plain or an ornamental manner, as the taste of the aquarium-keeper may dictate or his purse allow. They may also be constructed to stand upon the floor, or upon a table. Care should be taken, however, that the shelves are at different distances apart, the greatest space being between the first two shelves, counting from the bottom. Shelves thus arranged will hold vessels of various sizes.

The most suitable position for the cabinet aquarium is about 6ft. from a window, and out of reach of the direct rays of the sun. Then, if the stand has been wisely built, the contents of the aquaria can be easily watched without any inconvenience.

No shelf should be so low as to occasion stooping on the part of the aquarium-keeper, or so high as to necessitate his standing upon a chair or stool. If the stand is required to hold very many vessels, it should be long rather than too

high or too low. A cabinet aquarium, if properly arranged
and cared for, is rather an ornament in a room. It will
impede hardly any light when placed at right angles to a
window.

None but those who have possessed some such arrangement
as a cabinet aquarium can readily understand how much interest and instruction it is able to afford. Some change or
other is always taking place in the various aquaria, and thus
there is continually a fresh lesson to be learnt or a new wonder
whereat to be astonished. As nearly all the little tanks can
be made more or less self-supporting, a very small amount of
trouble will be required in their management. If the shelves
are made to stand upon the floor of the room, and not upon
a table, a small cupboard or a drawer or two may be contrived beneath the lowest shelf, which will be very convenient
for holding siphons, nets, cans, and the like.

An arrangement of a simpler kind than that just described
can be made by placing a piece of strong board lengthwise
across any large tank which has slate or wooden ends. Such
a board will hold several small aquaria. If it be of a fair length,
three small inverted propagating-glasses may be placed upon
it at equal distances apart, the middle glass being a little
larger than the other two, chiefly for the sake of appearance.
The glasses will stand quite firmly if the knob of each is
inserted through a hole made in the board. There may also
be room for other and smaller aquaria between the glasses.
Little oblong tanks might be used, and with advantage, instead
of the propagating-glasses.

The vessels of the cabinet aquarium may be either rectangular
or round—the former shape, for several reasons, being the
more suitable; but whether they are square or round there
should certainly be some uniformity among them. Propagating-
glasses of various sizes can always be used in the cabinet
aquarium by fixing them as just described. A great disadvantage of these glasses is that they so much distort the
objects which they contain; but if they are used it is
wise to have a few common stands at hand for them, which
will be convenient in case the glasses have occasionally to be

moved. The stands can be easily and cheaply made. For instance, a piece of wood about 6in. square, having a hole big enough to receive the knob of the glasses bored in the centre, and also having two strips of wood (1in. thick) nailed across two opposite ends, will be quite as firm as the ordinary turned stand; or a small and strong wooden box, with a hole cut in the middle of the lid, or if there be no lid, through the bottom, will answer the purpose very well. In the latter case, the box must be inverted, of course.

Various cheap glass bottles or jars are useful for the cabinet aquarium—for example, the jam or fruit jars made

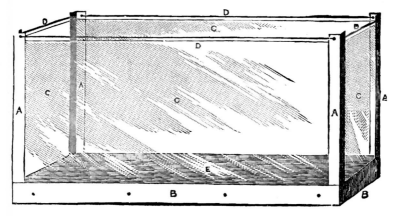

FIG. 31. EASILY AND CHEAPLY-MADE INSECT AQUARIUM.

by many firms in this country. They are of fairly clear glass, wide-mouthed, neckless, neatly shaped, and provided with lids, which, when perforated with small holes, make excellent covers. Of course, there are other vessels equally suitable for the cabinet aquarium, and those specified are only referred to in order that some idea may be given of what kind to use. The long clear glasses used by confectioners for the exhibition of sweetmeats in their windows can be utilised with advantage for such purposes as the cultivation of certain aquatic plants and some animals. There are other bottles, too, generally used also by confectioners for keeping their goods in, but not for showing them. These are made of coarser glass than those just mentioned, and they also possess the disadvantage of having a short neck and a mouth of a much less diameter than the rest of the bottle. The neck and mouth, however, can be cut off by a simple method, which will be explained. There is, nevertheless, a great drawback to all bottles and the like for aquarium purposes, and this is that their depth is much too great in proportion to their width. Still, there are circumstances under which they are more useful than wider and shallower vessels.

Rectangular aquaria are by far the best for the cabinet and other purposes. Small ones, such as that illustrated at Fig. 31, can be easily, cheaply, and quickly made, according to the following directions:

For the bottom (E), procure a piece of well-seasoned board 1in. in thickness of any size up to 16in. long and 12in. wide. No tank which is intended for the cabinet aquarium should be broader than the shelf of the cabinet upon which it is to stand.

Cut four strips of stout zinc 1in. wide, and of any length up to 6in. long.

Bend these four pieces of zinc lengthwise at right angles. This may be done by the help of a carpenter's ordinary vice, or by hammering half of the zinc over the square edge of a hard piece of board. A line should be made down the middle of the strips to guide the bending, which ought to be quite correct.

Make at nearly the extremity of one end, by means of a small awl, two holes, one through each side of the zinc moulding, for the wire as represented at D D.

Before nailing a piece of the moulding to each corner of the board which is intended for the bottom of the aquarium, a small portion of the wood should be cut away so that the zinc-moulding may be let in until it is quite flush with the edge of the board.

Cut a strip of zinc 1¼in. wide and so long that it will go exactly round the edges of the board for the bottom (B B).

Nail one piece of the zinc moulding at each corner of the

board in the place cut for it (A A). See that it is quite upright. Use small French nails, and hammer them well into the zinc. One nail at each side of the moulding will be sufficient.

Nail the piece of zinc, which has been cut 1¼in. wide, quite round the edge of the wood for the bottom. The zinc to the height of ¼in. should come above the board. The nails ought to be put through the centre of the zinc. If the tank is not more than 6in. long, three French nails in each side will be enough; one nail at each end, close to the edge of the uprights, and one in the middle.

Window-glass should now be cut to fit the frame just made, and put in its place (C C). The glass ought just to reach the holes in the zinc made for the wire.

Draw four pieces of thin copper or brass wire tightly through the holes made for it, and fasten it neatly (D). Copper wire must be well stretched before it is used. The wire should then hold the glass sides in their places.

Melt in a tin saucer over a lamp four parts pitch and one part gutta-percha. The pitch and gutta-percha must be well mixed before it is fit for use. It should boil for some little time and be stirred with a small iron spoon. Instead of the pitch and gutta-percha the following cement may be used, viz.: One part pitch, one part resin, and a little boiled oil—this last in the proportion of a tablespoonful to ½lb. pitch. This also must be boiled and well mixed together.

Take what is already made of the aquarium and hold it in the left hand. In the right hand take a spoonful of the boiling cement and allow it to cool a little for a moment or two, or it will crack the glass. Then put the spoonful of cement into one corner of the aquarium, and having returned the spoon to the saucer, with both hands tilt the framework carefully, so that the cement will run just at the junction of two pieces of glass, up to the top of the aquarium and then down again. Continue to do this until the cement ceases to flow. If this be well done the cement will not be seen beyond the edges of the moulding. Treat all the corners in the same way, but do not begin a second corner until the

first is quite firm. This cement sets very quickly. When all
the corners have been cemented, with the spoon pour sufficient
of the mixture on the bottom to cover it, and then the
aquarium, after standing an hour, will be ready for use.

After a little practice, several aquaria, such as the one just
described, can be made in a morning. If carefully constructed
they look very neat, and will not leak, unless perhaps when
placed for a long time within reach of the rays of a very
hot sun—a position which is not fit for any aquarium. Even
in these circumstances probably the tank would not leak
at all, but the pitch would begin to melt. The zinc-work of
these small cabinet aquaria may be painted with Brunswick
Black or with Aspinall's Enamel. Instead of the pitch-cement,

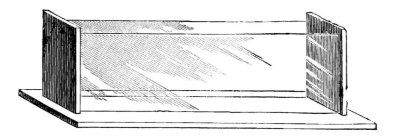

FIG. 32. CHEAPLY-MADE ALL-GLASS AQUARIUM FOR INSECTS.

mixed red and white lead can be substituted, and after it is
quite dry covered with Aspinall's Bath Enamel. When the
red and white lead are used the aquarium must be well
soaked before it is stocked.

Tanks made according to the above directions should not be
of greater dimensions than 16in. long, 12in. wide, and 5in. deep.
Those of the largest size should be placed on the bottom shelf
of the cabinet. In fact, these tanks ought to be constructed
according to the shelves, and should stand at least 2in.
apart when placed in position, in order that they may be
easily moved.

Fig. 32 represents another useful and easily-made little tank
which is very suitable for the cabinet aquarium. This small

vessel is made entirely of glass, of which there are five pieces, fastened together with marine glue. The two sides and the ends are stuck to the bottom at the distance of about ¼in. from its edge all round. The former are ½in. shorter than the bottom. and the latter are nearly if not quite as broad. The sides are put in their places first, and when they are firm the ends are glued to the extremities of the sides. The gluing is done by holding a piece of glue about the size of a pea, attached to the point of an awl, in the flame of a candle until it begins to burn and melt, when it should be gently drawn along a mark which has been made on the glass until the glue at the end of the awl is used. The glue should be placed on the glass quite evenly to the depth of about ⅛in., and the same in breadth. When a line of glue is completed, the edge of the piece of glass which is to be fastened by it should be gently heated, and then pressed carefully into the glue In a minute or two the glass will be quite firm. The gluing should be executed neatly, for any trimming that is required to be done after the aquarium has been put together, tends to weaken it. As soon as the little tank is finished, it may be filled with water, and if the work has been done with care there will be no leaking. Should the vessel, however, be not quite watertight, it may be easily made so by an additional piece of glue, or by running a little of the pitch-cement previously recommended over the weak spot, and, to make matters safer, over every joint. Such an aquarium as the one just described is very useful for small aquatic animals; but it should not be con- structed of greater dimensions than the following, viz., 9in. long, 2in. wide, and 2in. deep. I have made tanks of this kind as large as 1ft. long, 6in. deep, and 6in. wide; but I find that they are liable to give a little when the weather or the room in which they are placed is too hot. Though the joints open sometimes under these circumstances as much as ½in., the glue and pitch together become so elastic that the water is rarely allowed to escape.

The large bottles, which have been already referred to as suitable for the cabinet aquarium, can be cut in half by satu- rating a piece of thick worsted in paraffin, and tying it evenly round the bottle at the proper place and then setting it on fire. As the worsted burns, the glass will crack in the direction of the flame. The rough edges of the shortened bottles may be rubbed off by using a piece of the stone with which scythes are sharpened.

Among other things, clear, thin, plain glass tumblers are very convenient vessels for the upper shelves of the cabinet aquarium; but the habits and wants of the various animals and plants should be considered before they are placed in any of the many different articles which may be converted into aquaria.

Every tank of the cabinet aquarium ought to be provided with a well-fitting glass cover, for the purpose not only of preventing the escape of its inmates, but also of excluding the dust and of lessening, as far as possible, evaporation; and it is wise to gum a strip of white paper along the bottom of the front of each aquarium, in order that a record may be kept of the times when and the places where its contents were obtained, and any other circumstance of interest in connection with them.

When the stand of the cabinet aquarium is completed, and all its shelves are judiciously filled with vessels, some clean and fine river-sand or well-washed bird-sand should be prepared for the purpose of covering the bottoms of the different aquaria. But those tanks which are intended to contain interesting aquatic plants rather than animals ought to be especially prepared for the reception of such subjects by the placing of mud, loam, or anything else they may require, beneath a layer of the gravel The aquaria, however, which are to receive various animals will need for the covering of their bottoms only fine gravel or sand, for in such foundations the very useful American weed (*Anacharis alsinastrum*) will readily grow, and provide all that is required of vegetation in the tank. The most convenient way of planting the Anacharis in the small vessels of the cabinet aquarium is to attach to each spray a small piece of lead and drop it in the water. The spray thus weighted will sink rapidly to the bottom of the vessel, and assume there its proper position. By the help of a penholder or a small stick the lead may be easily pushed beneath the gravel, and thus hidden from sight. The Anacharis, or any other suitable weed thus treated, can be easily placed in or removed from any aquarium without either trouble or disturbance. When this method of planting is adopted, it is advisable to fill the vessel with water before the introduction of the weed. As a rule, the different tanks of the cabinet aquarium should be supplied with water and stocked with weed before the animals which they are to contain are bought or sought for

CHAPTER IV.

COLLECTING EQUIPMENT.

OF course, it adds greatly to the interest of cabinet or other aquaria if the various specimens can be obtained personally from their native waters. Fish generally should be carried from place to place in well-constructed bait-cans; and it is wise, if possible, for this purpose to procure a can which has a mechanical contrivance for aërating the water within it. In such a can, fish may be transported great distances without injury. If, however, a can without such a contrivance is used, it should be so made that the water does not readily splash out of it, and the splashing thus confined within the can goes a long way towards aërating the water and supplying the fish with the necessary oxygen. The can ought not to be more than three-quarters full of water. Of the many very useful bait-cans which have been from time to time invented, two may be referred to here, viz., one recommended by the late Mr. Frank Buckland in his " Natural History of British Fishes," and the other patented some years since by Mr. Basil Field. The former is a German invention, and though Mr. Buckland, while speaking highly of this can, says that he engaged a tinman to construct it, he omits to mention that workman's name and address. The latter can is shown in Fig. 33. The perforated zinc interior (**D**) is lifted whenever a fish is required, and there is obviously no occasion to wet the hands or warm the water by groping in it for the fish. In the handle (A) is a small pair of bellows, worked by merely pressing the knob B. The air passes down the small tube (C), and bubbles up at the bottom of the can. When at the riverside, the perforated interior can be sunk in the water. The ordinary pike-fisher's double live-bait kettle, which can be got at any tackle-maker's, is practically the same thing minus the aërating bellows.

Fig. 33. Patent Aërating Bait-can.

If the aquarium-keeper is unwilling to go to the expense of buying a bait-can, he may easily make one for himself out of an ordinary oblong tin coffee-canister. This is done by soldering the lid of the canister in its place, cutting a new opening in the side of the tin, and covering this opening with a small flap-lid. A handle of strong and rather thick wire is fastened on each side of the aperture by soldering a strip of tin over each end of the wire handle after about 1in. of it has been bent at right angles. The lid is affixed by bending about 1in. of its end over a piece of straight wire cut to such a length

that it projects a short distance on either side of the lid.
When the lid has been put into its place it is fastened
there by soldering a strip of tin over both extremities of the
projecting wire. After this can has been painted with Brunswick
Black or with enamel, very few would be able to see that it
was originally a coffee-canister. I have found such a contrivance as this very convenient, and have carried fish in it
a distance of more than 200 miles by rail.

When the aquarium-keeper intends, during his hunting
expeditions for specimens for his aquaria, to include fish among
his other captives, it is a good plan for him to set out provided with a can in which he has placed one or two short,
wide-mouthed bottles. He will thus be able to sort his prizes
in such a way as will be conducive to both their safety and
their comfort. He ought, however, to prevent all movement
of the bottles within the can by cutting a piece of tin, zinc,
or wood in such a way that it will fit inside the can and
go over the mouths of the bottles. If the holes, which are cut
in whatever material is chosen, fit the tops of the bottles
exactly, the latter cannot move sufficiently to hurt the
fish or anything else in the can. The clear glass jars which
have a lip but no neck, and which are sold containing jam,
are excellent vessels for placing within the bait-can and also
upon the shelves of the cabinet aquarium.

Should it not be the intention to catch fish, however,
the can ought to be left behind and several wide-
mouthed bottles taken in its place. These may be very
conveniently carried by placing, say, three of them side by
side in a narrow and light wooden box or specially constructed wicker basket. Good bottles for this purpose are
those already referred to as for fruit, &c. They are of a portable
size, and their tin covers, which screw on, are very useful
for preventing both the splashing of the water into the
basket or box and the escape of the inmates. If the
receptacle for the bottles is a little deeper than they
are, there will be room above them for forceps, brush,
macintosh, magnifying-glass, and any other small appliance
which the aquarium-keeper may require.

Fig. 34 represents a very useful net for obtaining aquarium specimens. The frame is of strong iron, which is screwed into a stout wooden handle of about 6ft. in length. The material for the net part may be of what is called mosquito-net, or of that light canvas which is sold for straining milk. The net should not be too deep, and be of the shape represented in the engraving. It ought to be—at any rate, the fore part of it—attached to the iron frame by means of small rings, which prevent to a great extent the wearing away of the net by rubbing against the mud, stones, and bottom of the water. Such a net as this, which should be about 3ft. in circumference, with care will last for a long time.

Another, a much smaller net in every way, but made upon the same plan, will be found very convenient in addition to the one just described.

Besides the nets, there should be taken on the hunting expedition, a long piece of strong cord, at the end of which is fastened a kind of hook, made somewhat after the fashion of a tiny anchor. This will be useful for pulling up from the bottoms of ponds, &c., masses of aquatic

FIG. 34. COLLECTING-NET.

plants, among the dripping and muddy tangles of which will be found many very interesting creatures.

A very simple arrangement may be made for obtaining almost any number of Entomostraca and other small aquatic animals. It consists of a wide-mouthed bottle, a small metal funnel, and a small indiarubber or leaden tube. The broad end of the funnel is covered with a piece of very fine muslin—so fine that it will hardly allow anything but the water itself to pass through it—and the narrow part of the funnel is attached to one end of the tube. As long as the funnel will go into the bottle, the broader

it is the better. The funnel should occupy the same position
in the bottle as represented in the illustration (Fig. 35). The
bottle ought to have a piece of strong string tied round its
neck, in order that it may be easily carried—even while water is
running through the siphon—from place to place. Another
bottle should be fastened to the end of a strong walking- or other
stick, so that water may be taken from the pond, ditch, or
stream, both near the edge and some distance from it, and
poured into the bottle possessing the siphon. As soon as the
latter is full of the water, which is supposed to contain the
minute animals required, the siphon is made to run, and by

constant additions of water
is allowed to continue
doing so until sufficient
captives are taken.

When the muslin gets
choked—as it occasionally
will do—with mud and
the like, it may be cleared
by gently striking it once
or twice against the sur-
face of the water within
the bottle. This operation

FIG. 35. BOTTLE AND SIPHON.

will necessitate, of course, the re-starting of the siphon. As the
Entomostraca, which are described in Chapter XV., are attracted
to the surface of the water by the shining of the sun, a fine
rather than a dull day should be chosen for catching them.

Besides the cans, bottles, and nets, the collector of specimens
for the aquarium will find the following articles very useful
during his hunting expeditions: (1) A pair of forceps, (2) a
small brush of camel's-hair, (3) a piece of macintosh, (4) magnifying-glass, (5) wading boots, (6) wire, string, and a pocket-
knife.

The forceps are convenient for quickly and gently picking
certain animals off the weeds, or out of the mud brought to
the banks with the weeds, and placing them into the receptacles
prepared for them. Fig. 36 represents two kinds of forceps.
The steel forceps may be obtained, for a small sum of money, of

a surgical instrument maker. The wooden forceps can be easily made at home by nailing two slender pieces of hard and elastic wood to a small centre block. If the latter pair of forceps are 1ft. long, they may be used also for bringing up objects from the bottom of the smaller aquaria.

The camel's-hair brush is convenient for removing the more delicate animals from the weeds or net, and placing them in the bottles.

The piece of macintosh is useful for three different purposes: for the collector to kneel on while he is examining the weeds or mud which he has taken from the water; for receiving the various animals which fall from those aquatic plants which are shaken over it; and for wrapping up the weeds which are

FIG. 36. WOODEN AND STEEL FORCEPS.

intended to be carried away. It should not be much less than 1yd. square.

The magnifying-glass is often of great help in making a close and careful examination of both plants and animals, and in deciding what are to be left behind and what taken home.

Of course, it goes without saying that a pair of strong boots are almost a *sine quâ non* during the expeditions in search of aquarium specimens; but those boots in which the collector can wade in the water up to his knees, are not only a great convenience, but are also often the means (by reason of the greater range which they give) of making interesting captures.

A piece of string, some thin wire, and a pocket-knife, should never be left behind, for one or other of them is almost sure to be required for something during the day.

If the aquarium-keeper be prudent he will take care not to overburden himself with bottles and nets, for nothing is so likely to mar the pleasure of a hunting expedition as a long walk home, after hard work, with more than one can conveniently carry.

I have many times heard it said that one of the greatest charms of English sport is that one never knows for certain what is going to "get up." This is, in a way, true of hunting for aquarium specimens, for the collector is always wondering what he will fish up next; and after he has begun to use his nets in some well-stocked piece of water, he hardly knows when to leave off or when he has obtained enough prizes. At least, such has generally been my own experience. There are often in ponds, ditches, and streams, what may be called traps. These traps consist of old boots, old hats, pieces of rag, and half-sunk bonnet-boxes or newspapers; and if the collector will take the trouble to examine such things, he will frequently be well rewarded for his pains, for in them or under them a good collection of many and various aquatic animals are often to be found. It is, indeed, a good plan purposely to set these useful traps.

I can easily remember that while I was a small boy I often looked forward to the time when I should be able to possess one very large aquarium in which I could place all the different aquatic animals I might procure; but I have long since learnt by experience that it is impossible for the members of such an interesting (to me) collection to live peaceably together for any length of time—no, not even for one single night. It is wise, therefore, for the collector to return home from his hunting expedition before it be too late, or before he be too tired, to put his prizes into their respective dwelling-places. Should he, however, be indisposed or unable at once finally to assort his captives, he ought to transfer into shallow and well-covered vessels those creatures which he cannot trust, either for their own welfare or for the welfare of their comrades, to remain in the collecting-bottles. The various animals and plants can then be conveniently arranged on the following day.

There is a little net which may be cheaply and easily made,

and which I have found very useful for transferring aquatic specimens from vessel to vessel. The net is constructed out of one of the small wire baskets which are sold for the purpose of hanging on to the ends of teapot-spouts, in order that they may catch those tea-leaves which otherwise would fall into the cups. The wire fastening which is made to go down the spout of the teapot is taken off the basket, and a straight piece of rather thin wire, about 16in. or 18in. long, is wound (at its middle) once round the basket, just below the rim, in such a way that the two ends when twisted together form a handle of nearly 1ft. in length. The teapot-spout basket may be bought at almost every ironmonger's for a few pence.

There is hardly any part of the year which is altogether unsuitable for excursions in search of aquatic animals or plants. I have had successful days even when I have been obliged to break the thin ice which was covering the surface of the water. However, the summer-time is the best season of all for these expeditions.

CHAPTER V.

MANAGEMENT OF THE AQUARIUM.

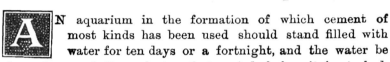

A N aquarium in the formation of which cement of most kinds has been used should stand filled with water for ten days or a fortnight, and the water be changed several times during that period, before it is stocked. The cement will thus have an opportunity of giving off anything which would be likely to injure the inhabitants of the tank. When the aquarium has been sufficiently seasoned in this way, empty it, clean it, and put it into its permanent position, taking care that it stands quite firm and is perfectly level in every direction. After this has been satisfactorily arranged, some sand should be taken from a river or running stream; but if it cannot conveniently be procured from there, ordinary bird-sand will do very well when it has been prepared in the following manner: By means of a fine-meshed sieve all the larger stones should be separated from the rest of the sand. As the sand is riddled it should fall into a bucket of water. When a sufficient quantity has been obtained in this way it ought to be energetically stirred for several minutes with a stick, and the muddy water poured off. The pail should now be filled with boiling water, in which the sand ought to be thoroughly washed, and then the water emptied away. When this operation has been repeated twice or thrice the sand will be ready for the aquarium. River-sand should also undergo the same careful washing. This cleansing of the sand ought never to be neglected, for without it some decaying matter, either vegetable or animal, will certainly be present, and in time may corrupt the water of the tank, and so cause injury to its inmates.

This clean sand should now be placed in the aquarium to a depth of from 2in. to 4in., according to the size of the tank and the character of the plants which are to be introduced. But if the aquarium is bell-shaped, all its lower portion may with advantage be filled with sand until it reaches that part of the vessel where the sides begin to be vertical. This will both lessen the depth of water and increase the rooting-space for vegetation. Over the sand a layer of some fine gravel should be put, which also must be washed perfectly clean. This gravel may be obtained from a river or stream, but that which has been sifted from the bird-sand will do very well. The gravel is chiefly for the purpose of preventing fish and their comrades from turning up the sand and sediment, and thus interfering with the clearness of the water. Charcoal is sometimes buried in the sand—for it has the power to some extent of counteracting putrefaction and preventing unpleasant smells. Its presence, however, in the aquarium has its draw-backs : if allowed to float in the water, it will look unsightly; and if sunk in the sand, there will be a difficulty in renewing it when its efficiency as a deodoriser has gone. A properly-stocked aquarium needs no charcoal.

Among the occupants of an aquarium there will be some which will not care to remain in the water always ; and for their accommodation it will be advisable to erect a kind of rockwork, the top of which ought to rise above the surface of the water. This rockwork will also provide shade for the fish and the other animals which delight in retirement. It can be bought all ready for the aquarium ; but often that which is offered for sale is gaudily coloured, or is in other respects unsuitable. Sometimes it will be found made in the shape of ruins of various kinds. Of course such rockwork is altogether out of place in a well-arranged tank, for no one with any taste at all would care to see a fish, for instance, swimming through the window of a house, or a triton wriggling through the loophole of a castle.

Suitable rockwork can easily be constructed. It should be of small dimensions rather than the reverse, as long as it will answer its purpose; for much rockwork takes up valuable space, and does not look well in an aquarium. Care ought to be taken to so arrange it that, while it will afford the necessary shade to the occupants of the tank, it will not at the same time provide them with retreats into which they can retire altogether from their owner's sight; for, if the animals are able to completely hide themselves, it is very possible that, should they die, their deaths will be undiscovered until the corrupting bodies have done irreparable damage to the whole aquarium.

Rockwork may be made of pumice-stone, coke, melted glass, mica-schist, or other material of a like kind. If the desired shape and size cannot be found in one single piece, two or three pieces may be joined together by means of Portland cement, always remembering that this cement, after it has well set, should be soaked for some days in water before it is placed in its permanent position in the aquarium. Pieces of pumice-stone or coke may be united by means of wooden rivets, each rivet running into the adjoining parts a couple of inches, the holes for which can easily be made with an ordinary awl. Before coke is put in the tank it should be dipped into some liquid Portland cement of about the consistency of ordinary whitewash, keeping the mixture well stirred during the process.

An aquarium like Fig. 9 may have rockwork so arranged as to represent a cave, out of which and into which the fish and other animals seem continually to go and come. To effect this arrangement it will be necessary to get a piece of looking-glass about 5in. square, more or less according to the size of the tank. Paint the back of this two or three times with sealing-wax varnish, japan black, or anything else which will protect it from the action of the water; then, when this is dry, place the aquarium with the glass front upwards, and cover its back, inside, with cement No. 2. Now take the looking-glass and fix it firmly in the centre of the back of the tank, and around it arrange mica-schist in such a way that the glass will represent the mouth of a cave. All the back should be covered with the stone. This plan, however, is more appropriate for a marine than for a fresh-water aquarium. Instead of rockwork, a small island may be constructed for the newts; and upon the island a fern or some semi-aquatic plant can be grown.

Most plants should be put in their places before the aquarium is filled with water. Those which do not require much rooting-space may be planted in the sand and gravel at the bottom of the tank; but those which need greater depth can be set in small flower-pots. These pots can either be hidden by means of a careful arrangement of rockwork, or they themselves may be made to resemble it by covering their sides with small pieces of coke, fastened into position with Portland cement. The whole should be then dipped as before described. There is one great advantage in putting plants into pots, inasmuch that, should occasion require, the aquarium can be emptied without materially interfering with their growth. But wherever plants are placed, whether in pots or at the bottom of the tank, the sand above their roots should be covered with plenty of gravel, as it tends to make the setting firm and permanent. The different aquatic plants suitable for freshwater aquaria will be described in another chapter.

In an aquarium that is properly arranged and cared for, the water should seldom or never need changing. Its character, therefore, is a matter of much importance. The best water for the purpose is that from a river; next, that from a large and very clear pond; next, very clean rain-water; next, that from the "tap"; and last of all, and to be avoided if possible, hard water from the well. When the aquarium has been made quite clean, its glass has been well polished, the sand and the gravel, in the proper proportion, at its bottom have been perfectly washed, the plants have been put in their places, and the rockwork has been placed in position, then—and not till then— should the water be introduced.

There is really only one satisfactory way, so far as I know, of filling an aquarium with water, and that is by means of a very slender siphon. A siphon of large diameter is worse than useless for this purpose; but should the proper-sized siphon not be conveniently at hand, the water may be intro- duced in one of the following ways:

1. Pour it very slowly and carefully, by means of a slender-spouted can, against the sides of the tank.

2. Place a jug in the centre of the aquarium, taking care that it does not stand on any plant, and pour the water gently into it until the tank is full; then remove the pitcher without emptying it.

3. Put the aquarium, if not too large, under a "supply" tap, and regulate the latter so that it allows the water to drip slowly upon a sponge placed on the gravel of the former. The sponge, while being taken out, should not be squeezed.

4. Fill the tank by the help of a watering-can which has a very fine rose.

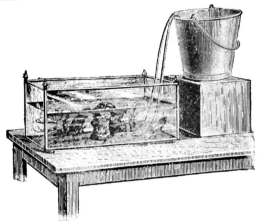

Fig. 37. Correct Method of Filling an Aquarium.

But however carefully the water is introduced into the aquarium in any one of the above four ways, it will be found not to be perfectly clear. A small siphon only will attain that much-desired end. If one siphon does not work quickly enough, two or three may be used at the same time. A slender india-rubber tube of the necessary length, not thicker than the stem of an ordinary clay pipe, will make the siphon. The smaller the tubing in its diameter, the more satisfactorily will it do its work (Fig. 37). The lower end of the siphon should rest on the gravel of the aquarium or upon the rockwork.

When the aquarium has been properly filled in the way just described, it is a good plan, if patience will allow, to postpone the introduction of any animals for at least ten days or a fortnight—the longer the better. During this time the plants ought to commence to grow and give off oxygen. At first only a few occupants should be introduced—say, a newt, three or four small fish, and a few snails—and if these do well, one or two more may be added, and so on. When the plants are fairly established, the aquarium will support much more life than when they are only just beginning to grow. If the fish swim near the surface of the water tails downwards and mouths upwards, there are too many in the tank, and unless some are speedily removed, many will die. There should always be too few inmates in an aquarium rather than too many; but if the tank is properly arranged, it is really surprising how much animal life it will support. For instance, I have at the time of writing in a bell-glass aquarium, 19in. in diameter, one gold-fish, one silver-fish, one carp, about a dozen snails (*Planorbis corneus*), and at the least forty small minnows (*Cyprinus phoxinus*). All these fish are seemingly in perfect health, and have been so for about ten months. The plants in this aquarium are *Vallisneria spiralis* and the Cape Fragrant Water Lily (*Aponogeton distachyon*).

The water of an aquarium that is properly balanced and cared for, should never require changing, as a rule; but circumstances do occasionally arise in which it is necessary to empty the tank. For instance, the water may have become corrupted by an undiscovered dead body; the plants may need renewing, or the rockwork re-arranging; perhaps the aquarium has sprung a leak, or it is necessary to remove it to some other position. Any one of these circumstances would require the emptying away of the water. This can easily be done by means of a piece of india-rubber tubing, of about $\frac{1}{2}$in. in diameter, used as a siphon (Fig. 38.) Before the commencement of the withdrawal of the water, as many of the fish and other inhabitants of the aquarium as possible should be transferred elsewhere. However, it is not probable that all will be caught, for some will hide themselves in the weeds or under the rockwork; and to

prevent their being sucked up, the end of the siphon which is
to go in the aquarium should be covered with a piece of mosquito
net or similar material.

The position of an aquarium is an important matter, for very
much depends upon the regulation of the light. Light is
necessary to the growth of the plants, and to the production
of oxygen. But too much light will encourage the development
of the freshwater Algæ commonly called Conferva. This con-

FIG. 38. METHOD OF EMPTYING AN AQUARIUM.

ferva is a vegetable growth which appears upon the inside of
the glass of the aquarium, depriving it of its transparency. It
grows also upon the plants, interfering with their welfare,
and it will quickly spread, if unchecked, throughout the
water, making it thick, green, and unsightly. Care is there
fore necessary to guard against both too much, and too little
light. The latter is much to be preferred to the former. The
rays of the sun should never fall directly upon an aquarium.

for, if they do, not only will the growth of the conferva be encouraged, but the temperature of the water will quickly rise too high. The higher the temperature of the water, the fewer animals will it be able to contain; besides which, water in this condition very readily becomes impure. The average temperature of an aquarium ought to be about 50deg., and, if possible, it should never be allowed to vary more than 10deg. either way. It may be reduced by covering the tank with a woollen cloth, the lower end of which is standing in some water.

As a rule, aquaria are placed near a window—a position conducive to the growth of the plants, but not to the happiness of the fish. Indeed, it is positively cruel to put fish in an all-glass aquarium and allow the sun to shine upon it during the hottest part of the day. Since an aquarium, however, will most likely be put close to a window, let it be one facing the north if possible. An eastern aspect is not at all unsuitable, but it will be advisable to cover the tank at night, so that it will not get the early morning sun.

There are many ways of shading aquaria so that they shall not be unduly influenced by light and sun. If the aquarium is round, a sheet of green paper or a piece of American cloth, hung by means of small wire hooks to the edge of the glass, will answer the purpose. This can easily be removed for the inspection of the contents of the aquarium. Of course, such a screen cannot be called ornamental, but it is effective. Flowers or ferns placed between the aquarium and the window will supply not a little shade. If the tank is rectangular, and all four sides made of glass, the same kind of shading will do, or cardboard may be cut to exactly fit three of the sides, instead. A little protection from too much light and sun may be obtained by having three of the sides made of ground-glass, or by covering these sides (externally, of course), with whitening dabbed on with a sponge, in imitation of ground-glass; or the confervæ may be allowed to grow upon the three sides, and the fourth kept clear by using, when necessary, a piece of flannel tied to the end of a short cane. A good piece of looking-glass, cut the exact length and depth of the aquarium, and placed

E

behind it, will give both shade and effect. The back of the
mirror must, in some way or other, be protected from the action
of the sun.

It has been already mentioned that the water of an aquarium
should obtain the necessary oxygen, not only directly from
the atmosphere above it, but also from the vegetation growing
within it; but there are circumstances under which artificial
means of aëration should be resorted to. For instance, the
tank may be overstocked with fish, and their owner, un-
wisely, be reluctant to part with any of them; or the
temperature of the water, from some cause or other, may
suddenly have risen too high. I think, therefore, that a short
description of some of the instruments by which the water of
an aquarium may be artificially aërated, will not be out of
place here.

A fountain is very useful for this purpose, and is also, if
properly arranged, ornamental. Fig. 39 represents one which
may be easily and inexpensively constructed. A is a tank,
made of wood, slate, or zinc; but if made of the last-named
material, its interior should be protected from the action of
the water by Japan-black, or something of the like kind. This
tank has a spout and a tap at the bottom of one end. It is
placed upon the top of a bookcase or some other convenient
elevation, and should be hidden there if possible. B is a deal
table, over which there is a cover reaching down to the floor
of the room. C is an easily-lifted can, capable of holding
about three gallons of water. D is a leaden or indiarubber
tube, joined at the upper end to the spout of the tank A, and
at the lower to E, which is a leaden pipe running under the
table and through its centre, and through that of the bottom
of the aquarium. The hole in the tank to receive E should
be rather larger than the pipe. When the pipe has been
inserted into the hole, it can be fastened in its place by
means of little wooden wedges, and all the interstices left
between the wedges, the pipe, and the bottom of the tank,
should be tightly filled up with red and white lead. F is a
leaden waste-pipe, the lower end of which runs just through
the table in order that it may be inserted into the indiarubber

tubing (H), which will connect it with the can (C). F is fixed in the bottom of the aquarium in the same way as E has been; its length within the tank will of course regulate the

FIG. 39.   AQUARIUM CONTAINING AN EASILY-ARRANGED FOUNTAIN.

height of the water there.   If the aquarium is made of slate, there may be an overflow pipe at G (instead of F), fixed in the side of the tank as high as the water is intended to rise.

Should there be an objection to cut the table and its cover,
the longer part of the pipe (E) can be fastened by means of
brackets to the bottom of the aquarium instead of the inside
of the top of the table; and the tubing (H) which is affixed
to F may run round the farther edge of the table, and so into
the can (C) beneath it. H should be long enough to reach
the bottom of the can (C), and so the noise of trickling water
will be prevented. The tubing (D) might be brought quite
down to the floor, and thence up under the table to its connection with E, whether the latter is fastened to the bottom
of the aquarium or not. However, there should be an en-
deavour to hide from sight the tank, the tubing, and the over-
flow-can.

There are various ways of forming the jet (I). The easiest,
perhaps, is to cut the end of the pipe off square with a pair
of cutting pincers (this will press the edges of the pipe closely
together); then, with a point of a pin, make the hole or holes
required. The object is to procure the flowing upward of the
least amount of water with the greatest effect. No more water
should be placed in the tank (A) than the can (C) is able to
hold, or some time or other there is certain to be a flood
in the room. The top of the overflow-pipe (F) should be protected with a little cap made of finely-perforated zinc; this
will prevent insects and pieces of weed from being sucked down,
and so causing death and stoppage.

The pipes within the aquarium should be hidden by well-
arranged rockwork. A good way to do this is to get a piece
of slate about 3in. or 4in. wide, and long enough, when standing
on the bottom of the tank touching the front glass, to reach
just above the jet (I). It should rest against the overflow-pipe
and not on the fountain, or it will interfere with the upward
flow of the water; and for this purpose the former might be bent
a little to the front. Care should be taken that the jet points
perfectly upright. Pieces of coke can be fastened by means
of Portland cement to the slate just mentioned. All one
side should be covered with the coke, and an inch or so from
each edge of the other side ; the edges also being hidden in the
same way. The whole ought then to be dipped in some liquid

Portland cement of the consistency of cream, and then left to dry. When it is quite dry, it must be well soaked before it is put in the aquarium. In constructing the above rockwork, and anything else of the kind, care should of course be taken that all formality of arrangement is avoided. This movable rock-work is very convenient in case a missing animal has to be searched for. Rockwork could be built against the pipes by the help of cement with perhaps better effect, but then it must be a fixture.

Such a fountain contrivance as this just described I have found a great success, and very little trouble. All that is required is to take the can (C) full of the overflow water every morning, empty it, while standing on a chair, into the tank (A), and return the can to its place under the table. If the fountain is cared for by a lady, the can (C) should be smaller, and perhaps emptied twice a day instead of once.

Instead of having the supply tank in the room, the fountain may be connected by means of a leaden siphon to the cistern at the top of the house. I have at present a fountain in an aquarium, worked by a siphon connected with an outside cistern, which is a great success, and when once started is no trouble at all. The two pipes — overflow and supply — run through one hole at the bottom of the window-sash. The aquarium, its slate framework covered with cork, stands on the sill of a staircase window, making an interesting ornament.

A syringe is a useful instrument for supplying oxygen arti-ficially to the water of an aquarium. It may be of glass, or such a one as is commonly found in a greenhouse, and con-structed of metal. To use the syringe, it must first be filled with water from the tank, and then, being held at a good height, made forcibly to return the water. This operation should be repeated several times.

A pair of ordinary kitchen bellows will also do for the purpose of aëration, but it is clumsy and rather tiring to work. A smaller and more suitable pair may be generally bought at a toy-shop, or can easily be made at home. The wood for the construction of the bellows should be about $\frac{3}{8}$in. thick, so that it will not break when they are worked with the necessary force, and will not split when the leather or American cloth is being nailed to its edge. Fig. 40 will show how such bellows may be made to work with a spring instead of the ordinary handles. A, the bellows ready for use, to the nozzle of which (j) is attached a prepared indiarubber tube (h); B, the lower side, to which the spring (d) is fastened; C, the upper side, having a round hole (f) not more than $\frac{1}{2}$in. in diameter. To this hole inside is nailed the usual leather trap-door (i) which opens to receive the air and closes to expel it through the nozzle of the bellows. The nozzle

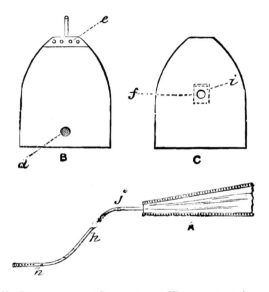

FIG. 40. BELLOWS FOR AËRATING THE WATER OF AN AQUARIUM

should be about $\frac{1}{4}$in. in diameter, and made of some metal; a piece of small gas-piping will do. It is fixed in the centre of a slip of hard wood, $\frac{1}{2}$in. thick, and this is screwed across the narrow end of B at e. The spring is made by twisting a piece of elastic and stiff wire round the end of a broomstick or something of a like nature, and when made is fastened in the centre of the broad part of B at d. The two sides are joined together by nailing to their edges a piece of leather or American cloth, cut the desired shape (for which see A). The little nails or upholstering pins are placed very closely together, so that the bellows are made perfectly air-tight; and the indiarubber tubing should be just large enough to fix securely over the end of the nozzle (j). The other end of the tubing must be stopped with a cork, which should be tied firmly in its place. At the cork end of the tubing there are ten or fifteen little holes, which have been made with a strong pin, and so arranged that they are all point upwards when the tubing is at the bottom of the tank, and the bellows are resting upon the stand or table which the aquarium is on. When the instrument is completed and put in the position just described, press the bellows forcibly with one hand, and immediately several small bubbles of air will be seen to rise in the water and ascend to its surface. This contrivance will be found very useful, not only for aërating an aquarium, but also for supplying air to fish which are being taken a long distance by rail or by road.

Fig. 41 represents a useful instrument for aërating the water of an aquarium. It is a small pump or syringe made of indiarubber, and can be bought for a few shillings. It can also be made at home by inserting two pieces of small indiarubber tubing into opposite sides of an indiarubber ball. I have found that sound uncovered tennis-balls will answer the purpose. The pieces of tubing, one longer than the other (Fig. 41), are put into holes just large enough to receive them. These holes can be made by means of a hot piece of thick wire. The tubing and the ball are firmly united by covering the junction (Fig. 37, a) of the two several times with pure indiarubber, this having been dissolved in bisulphide of carbon or chloroform. The carbon or chloroform soon evaporates, and leaves the indiarubber dry and firm. A second coat of this solution must not be applied until the first has become hard. At the end of the longer piece of tubing a kind of trap must be fixed, so that the water can be drawn in there, but cannot be expelled by the way it entered. This trap may be made out of about 1¼in. of lead piping, the diameter of the indiarubber tubing. The bore of one end of the lead piping should be enlarged a little (Fig. 46, B and C). This enlargement can be made with a sharp, square-pointed bradawl, a little larger than the hole in the piping. While being used for this purpose the awl must be steadily turned round and round. The plug (c) can be made of india-rubber cork, or leather; and it must be made so that it will close the smaller bore in the pipe perfectly, but not the larger. This plug is kept in position by a pin (d), which should be a black one, run through the centre of the plug, and turned

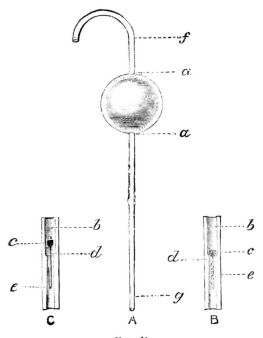

FIG. 41.

A, Pump for Aërating the Water of an Aquarium; C and B, Sections of Traps which are inserted in A at *f* and *g*.

ᵣound another pin, running right through the pipe at *e*. C and B (Fig. 41) show the section of the trap. The former represents the plug raised for the purpose of allowing the water to be drawn into the pump; the latter illustrates the plug driven home, and so preventing the water from escaping by the way it entered. Two of these traps ought to be prepared, one to be inserted in the tubing of the pump at *g*, and the other at *f*. If there is a difficulty in putting a trap so far down the tubing as *f*, the latter must be cut through at that point, and joined again by placing each extremity of the cut part over opposite ends of the trap. When this has been done, the junction should be made quite secure by covering it three or four times with the indiarubber solution. When this pump is used, the longer tubing is put 2in. or 3in. deep in the water, while the shorter is held over it; and as the ball is repeatedly and vigorously squeezed, an almost continuous stream of water will run out of and back into the aquarium.

The trouble of making the traps may be prevented by substituting two of the glass tubes which are made for babies' feeding-bottles. These tubes are trapped.

A piece of sponge fixed in the hole of a flower-pot will make a kind of filter. The sponge should be so tightly packed as to allow the water to run through the hole slowly in drops only. This simple contrivance can be either suspended over the aquarium or placed on two strips of wood resting on the top of it at the centre. It may also stand on the cover of the tank if that be strong enough.

FIG. 42. TOP OF FLOWER-POT FILTER, showing Wire Frame for holding in position Pot containing Plant.

Of course, if the cover is glass, a hole must be cut through it, to allow the water to run from the filter into the tank. Should the flower-pot be something better than a common one, and another, in which some pretty semi-aquatic plant is growing, is placed inside it, the arrangement will be both useful and ornamental. A little water, taken occasionally out of the aquarium by means of a small siphon and put into the filter, will cause an almost constant drip of water into the aquarium. The pot containing the plant is kept in its position in that which is acting as a filter by means of a small wire frame.

(Fig. 42). Occasionally the sponge will get clogged, and require taking out and cleansing.

Other simple means of aërating the water of an aquarium will readily suggest themselves to the reader, such as violently agitating the water for a few minutes with a short, slender stick—a penholder, for instance—by taking a small portion of water from the aquarium and returning it again through the fine rose of a watering-can, or by using an ordinary bicycle pump.

CHAPTER VI.

WATER-PLANTS.

IT has already been explained why aquatic plants of some kind or other should always be present in an aquarium ; and in this chapter a few hints are given as to the choice and management of such vegetation. Half the pleasure of owning and caring for an aquarium would be gone if no plants were necessary: they give to the tank nearly all its beauty.

Almost every aquatic plant can be grown in the still water of an aquarium, and be made more or less useful there. Some may be introduced chiefly for their beauty, others for their utility; but for both beauty and utility none is superior to the Italian Water-weed *Vallisneria spiralis*. This plant has for many years been a great favourite with those who keep an aquarium; for besides being ornamental and useful it is also exceedingly interesting, inasmuch as it possesses a peculiar method of reproduction, and in its graceful grass-like leaves the cyclosis, or circulation of the sap, may be readily seen by the help of a microscope, just as one may observe the circulation of the blood in a frog's foot or in a tadpole's tail.

Vallisneria spiralis belongs to the natural order Hydrocharideæ, of which there are only three species native in Britain, viz., the Frog-bit (*Hydrocharis morsus-ranæ*), the Water-Soldier (*Stratiotes aloides*), and the Canadian Water-weed (*Anacharis alsinastrum*).

The Vallisneria comes from the South of Europe, and is named in honour of an Italian botanist, Antonio Vallisneri. This weed is diœcious, that is, its female flowers grow on one individual plant (Fig. 43), and its male flowers on another (Fig. 44). The female flowers are borne at the end of long spiral

FIG. 43. ITALIAN WATER-WEED, (ALLISNERIA SPIRALIS (FEMALE PLANT).

stalks, giving to the plant its specific name. These stalks, which increase in length very rapidly, are able to adapt them-selves to the depth of the water in which they are growing, so that their flowers can readily reach its surface. The male flowers are produced at the base of their own plants, and after

a time become detached, rise to the top of the water, and float
there until they fertilise the female flowers with their pollen.
After the fertilisation the latter sink to ripen and to grow.

The Vallisneria also increases by runners, somewhat similar
to the common strawberry. These offshoots run along the
bottom of the water until they begin to strike root in the soil.

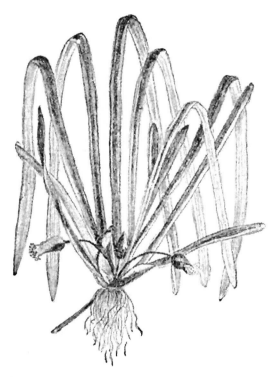

Fig. 44. Italian Water-weed, Vallisneria spiralis (Male Plant).

and so a new plant is formed. This weed grows fairly well
in the sand at the bottom of an aquarium; it will grow better
in pots in which there is some 4in. or 5in. of a good loam
covered by a layer of fine gravel; but it will grow best of all in
a tank prepared for the purpose, and kept in a cool greenhouse.

This tank should be oblong, with four glass sides, and its bottom ought to be covered to a depth of at least 4in. with rich garden mould, over which there must be about an inch of gravel. In this about a dozen plants should be carefully set, and the vessel properly filled with clean soft water, of not too cold a temperature. The glass sides ought to be shaded with four pieces of board or slate, to prevent the light from causing an excess of confervæ. The object of having transparent sides is, that the growth of the Vallisneria may be easily seen by removing the shading; and thus anything that is wrong may be readily discovered, and quickly put right before much damage has been done. The top of the tank should be covered with a piece of glass, raised ½in. above the edge by means of two wooden slips. Many years ago I bought twelve plants through the medium of *The Bazaar*, growing them in the manner just described, and though there lived in the tank a large favourite old carp, the Vallisneria grew to profusion; and notwithstanding that, from time to time, I took a great deal out with which to stock other tanks or to give to friends, the supply was always equal to the demand.

The following precautions should be taken in regard to the cultivation of *Vallisneria spiralis*, and indeed almost any kind of water-plant :

1. Do not place it in too little light, or it will not flourish; nor in too much, or it will be choked with confervæ.

2. Do not chill it by putting it in water any colder than that from which it has been taken.

3. Do not let any rusty leaves remain on the plants, but cut them off close to the roots.

4. Do not stock the aquarium with any animals until the Vallisneria has begun to grow ; and when the tank is stocked, be careful to remove those creatures which show a disposition to feed upon this particular plant.

The Vallisneria is one of the best of all water-weeds for producing oxygen, therefore it is well worth careful management. The female plant seems to be much commoner than the male, but it is not necessary to have the latter in cultivation, as the former will readily increase by means of offshoots.

The Frog-bit (*Hydrocharis morsus-rance*) is a very pretty and suitable plant for the aquarium (Fig. 45). It is easily cultivated and very hardy. Its beautifully-veined leaves, growing on rather long stalks, are kidney-shaped, and its three-petalled flowers are white; and when seen in masses upon the surface of

FIG. 45. FROG-BIT (HYDROCHARIS MORSUS-RANÆ).

some pond, it will be readily conceded that the plant has been well named Hydrocharis (a beautiful aquatic). The Frog-bit is a floating plant, its roots never entering the soil. Like *Vallisneria spiralis*, it sends out runners; but these, instead of taking root, put forth small buds, soon to develop into new plants. As the winter comes on, the parent plants decay, leaving their buds and seeds to sink to the bottom, where they remain dormant until the spring, then rising to the surface and taking the place and functions of their predecessors of

FIG. 46. WATER-SOLDIER (STRATIOTES ALOIDES).

the previous summer. One drawback to the presence of this plant in an aquarium is that the snails are very fond of feeding upon it, especially any of the Limnæidæ; and the Great Water-beetle (*Hydrophilus piceus*) is quite capable of doing con

siderable damage in a meal or two. This plant does not grow
in all ponds and other suitable pieces of water, but where it does
grow it is generally to be found in profusion. However, it can,
as a rule, be procured in a healthy condition, during the summer
months, from dealers in aquarium necessaries.

The Water-Soldier (*Stratiotes aloides*) (Fig. 46) is chiefly
found in Lincolnshire, Cambridgeshire, and Norfolk, but hardly
anywhere else without having been specially introduced. Sometimes it grows in such quantities in these counties as to become
quite a nuisance to fishermen. Its leaves are numerous, long,
narrow, pointed, and serrated; and it bears a rather large pretty
white flower at the end of a stalk about 5in. or 6in. long. This
plant, like the Vallisneria and Frog-bit, increases by both offshoots and seeds, generally the former. Its roots penetrate the
muddy soil at the bottom of the water, and the whole plant
remains submerged during the greater part of the year, only
rising to the surface for a short time during the flowering
season. The Water-Soldier, so named from its sword-shaped
leaves, grows readily in an aquarium, and is very ornamental
there. It will flourish either planted in the sand or floating
upon the surface of the water. In either position it will
produce new plants. If it is allowed to float, it will require to
be taken out occasionally and carefully trimmed of all dying
leaves and decaying matter. When the little plants, which it
will bear at the end of long stalks, are of a fair size, they may
be separated from the parent and floated in the water, or
planted at the bottom of the tank. This plant does not seem
to be a great producer of oxygen, but as it is ornamental,
unusual in appearance, and a furnisher of shade, it is decidedly
worth cultivating in an aquarium.

The Canadian Water-weed (*Anacharis alsinastrum*) (Fig. 47)
is remarkable both for its history in this country and for the
manner and great rapidity of its growth. It was first discovered in Britain about the year 1842, and from that date it
has extended to nearly every part of England and Scotland,
growing in some localities in such profusion as to choke the
watercourses, endanger the swimmer by entangling his limbs,
and exhaust even the patience of good fishermen. However,

F

the aquarium-keeper, as far as he is concerned, ought to be grateful for its appearance here, for not only is it one of the very best plants for the tank, but also in its tangled masses, much interesting animal life is almost sure to be found. Its leaves, varying from dark to light green, according to age, are three or four in a whorl. They are minutely serrated, and are

to be found in shape from roundly ovate to oval-oblong; and in them the cyclosis may easily be seen under the microscope. In this country the plant—as the female flower is only found as a rule—increases chiefly by budding and not by seed. The male flower has been discovered, it is said, growing on long tubes somewhat similar to the spiral stalks of the female flower of the Vallisneria. The stem of the Anacharis is long, round, transparent, and very brittle, the smallest portion of which, as long as it contains a whorl of leaves, will send out roots and grow, in a comparatively short time, into an entire mass. It will flourish either floating in the water or planted in the soil at its bottom ; however, its specific gravity is so great that it very frequently sinks

FIG. 47. CANADIAN WATER-WEED
(ANACHARIS ALSINASTRUM).

from its own weight. From what has already been said, it will be readily gathered that the Canadian Water-weed is very hardy, and an excellent producer of oxygen. It will never die if it is carefully pruned of all decaying branches. The snails and some of the fish will eat it ; and swans and even horses are said to be fond of it. Indeed, the birds are useful in checking its undue growth in streams and ponds. In an aquarium it should not be allowed to float, for it will make the water look untidy; small pieces ought to be planted at the bottom. If the tank has been filled with water before the introduction of this plant, a small stone may be tied to the end of a short spray and sunk where it is intended to grow, and it will quickly take root; but it must be watched, lest it occupy, through its rapid increase, more than its share in the tank.

In concluding my remarks on the Anacharis, I will venture to remind the aquarium-keeper that he should be exceedingly careful not to be the cause of the introduction of this plant into the streams and ponds of his neighbourhood. All that he does not require ought to be completely destroyed, and not thrown carelessly away; for the smallest portion of this most vigorous weed, being conveyed either by accident or otherwise to any permanent piece of water, may quickly become quite a nuisance there.

The Mare's-tail (*Hippuris vulgaris*) (Fig. 48) is only useful and ornamental in an aquarium until after it has flowered, when it sinks to the bottom, and should be removed. It ought to be planted in a pot containing loam mixed with

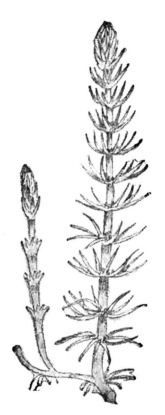

FIG. 48. MARE'S-TAIL (HIPPURIS VULGARIS).

silver sand and covered with a layer of gravel; the weed can then be easily taken away, when its duty has been done, without disarranging the aquarium. As this plant rises several inches above the surface of the water, it should not be introduced into a tank which has a covering. The

Mare's-tail is rather common, especially in the ditches of Lincolnshire. It is a ready producer of oxygen, and should be obtained as young as possible.

FIG. 49. SPIKED WATER MILFOIL (MYRIOPHYLLUM SPICATUM).

The Spiked Water Milfoil (*Myriophyllum spicatum*) (Fig. 49) has long been a favourite with keepers of aquaria. It is common in stagnant water, where it is entirely submerged with the exception of the flowers, which rise a few inches above the surface. Water animals of many different kinds are fond of making the tangled masses of the Milfoil their head-quarters. In the aquarium it looks and grows well, and gives off oxygen freely. The greenish flowers grow in whorls, forming a leafless spike about 3in. or 4in. long; its leaves also grow in whorls of four, and are finely divided into hair-like segments. Most appropriately is it named the

FIG. 50. VERNAL WATER STARWORT (CALLITRICHE VERNA).

Milfoil (the myriad-leaved). It flowers in July and August. A portion (not a bunch) of this plant may be tied to a stone and sunk in the aquarium: it will quickly take root and grow.

The Vernal Water Starwort (*Callitriche verna*) (Fig. 50) grows in both slowly-running and stagnant water. The leaves grow in pairs, and are narrower when found in a stream than in a pond. It is a very pretty plant, its leaves forming a mass of emerald-green stars on the surface of the water; hence its common name. It is entirely submerged, with the exception of the little green flowers which rise above the water in June and July. If this plant is examined it will be readily seen that it takes its generic name (*Callitriche*) from its beautiful hair-like roots, some of which slightly enter the soil at the bottom

of the water; so slightly, indeed, that a small plant, with a little care, may be easily pulled up without the breakage of any of the slender stems. The Vernal Starwort is a great favourite with both female newts and freshwater shrimps (*Gammarus fluviatilis*), for the former wrap their eggs carefully in the narrow leaves, while the latter find lurking-places in its tangles. There are various opinions concerning the suitability of this plant for the aquarium. Some keepers of aquaria declare that it is useless, as it dies so quickly; while others assert that it is a ready grower, and consequently a good producer of oxygen. There is truth in both these statements, for if it is tied in a bunch to a

Fig. 51. Autumnal Water Starwort (Callitriche autumnalis).

stone (as it so often is) and sunk in the water of a tank, the lower part of it will soon die, its leaves turning a sickly-looking yellow; but if, on the other hand, 3in. or 4in. of the top of each healthy spray is broken off and simply floated in the water, it will quickly put forth some hair-like roots and grow. In these circumstances it will supply a fair quantity of oxygen, and by its utility and beauty will earn a place in the aquarium.

The Autumnal Water Starwort (*Callitriche autumnalis*) is decidedly a rare plant compared to the Vernal Starwort. It grows in similar situations, but it does not, like that plant, ever rise above the surface of the water. Its leaves are narrower (Fig. 51) and of a darker green. *C. autumnalis* is occasionally found in the neighbourhood of London, and in some of the northern lakes. A few inches of the top of a healthy spray

FIG. 52. WATER CROWFOOT (RANUNCULUS AQUATILIS).

may be tied to a small stone and sunk in the water of the aquarium. No two sprays should be tied together.

The Water Crowfoot (*Ranunculus aquatilis*) (Fig. 52) is an excellent plant for the aquarium, and one very easily procured, as it is common almost everywhere. It grows in streams and ponds, sometimes nearly covering the latter with its beautiful green leaves and its pretty flowers. The leaves of this plant are of two different shapes : the upper leaves are three-lobed, with rounded notches, and float upon the surface of the water; the lower ones are divided into numerous hair-like segments, and are always submerged. In quickly-running streams the floating leaves are generally wanting. The rather large flowers are white, with many yellow stamens, very like strawberry blossom, and are borne from May to September. The Water Crowfoot is a most useful plant to the owner of an aquarium , for it will grow extremely well in a tank, and in its masses under water much interesting animal life is almost certain to be found. If a healthy portion of this plant is cut off, so that it is just long enough to allow the flowers and the lobed leaves to float on the surface of the water while the severed end touches the bottom, and is then tied to a stone and sunk in the aquarium, it will quickly take root and grow; indeed, so rapidly will it increase that care must be taken lest it usurp the entire tank.

The Ivy-leaved Crowfoot (*Ranunculus hederaceus*) is a very useful little plant for the aquarium, especially for those which are not deep. In some neighbourhoods this weed is very common, and is to be found growing in shallow water, on the sloping margins of ponds, and on those places from which the water has lately retired. This plant is not nearly so large as the Water Crowfoot, and its flowers are very small. It has a creeping, submerged stem, throwing out roots, and its leaves are roundly lobed, rising on rather long stalks some little distance above the surface of the water. Any portion of the stem having leaves attached will grow and blossom freely in an aquarium.

Water Lobelia (*Lobelia Dortmannii*) is a very pretty and suitable plant for the aquarium, but it is not readily to be procured, as it is almost confined to the northern lakes, where it grows in thick masses at the bottom of the water. Its flowers are light blue, and grow droopingly upon long stalks, which rise above the surface of the water, and its leaves are long and narrow and almost cylindrical. This plant may be set in the sand and gravel of the aquarium.

The Nymphæa-like Villarsia (*Villarsia nymphæoides*) (Fig. 53), named in honour of M. de Villars, a French botanist, is a very lovely and rare water-plant. It is found in still waters in the neighbourhood of the Thames and in some slow Yorkshire rivers. Its nearly round though almost heart-shaped leaves float at the end of long stalks on the surface of the water. The stem is long and branched. The five-petalled flowers are rather large, yellow, and fringed. It is very hardy, and is easily

FIG. 53. NYMPHÆA-LIKE VILLARSIA (VILLARSIA NYMPHÆOIDES).

cultivated in the aquarium, but it should be planted in a pot containing good loam mixed with silver sand. The Villarsia can be propagated either by seed or by division of the root, and is a rapid grower. Though this plant is so rare it can generally be bought from some London florists for quite a reasonable sum, and I think the aquarium-keeper will never regret the purchase.

The Buck-bean (*Menyanthes trifoliata*) perhaps can hardly be called an aquarium weed, because it prefers to grow in very damp, boggy soil rather than altogether in water; still, its exceeding beauty tempts one to place it in the tank if possible, and there it will certainly succeed well if properly situated. Few British flowers are so beautiful as those which this plant

FIG. 54. FORGET-ME-NOT (MYOSOTIS PALUSTRIS).

bears. It should be planted in as large a pot as convenient, and so hidden among the rockwork that the lower part of the pot is in the water. A small plant ought to be chosen. It is a trefoil, that is, three leaflets grow on a common stalk, and "each leaf-stalk has a sheathing base, opposite to one of which rises the beautiful cluster of blossoms." The buds are a bright rose colour, and the open flowers are covered with a white silken fringe, well said to resemble plush. It blossoms during June and July. The Buck-bean is found growing on spongy bogs, and sometimes in stagnant water. Though there may be difficulty occasionally in finding this plant growing wild, it

FIG. 55. BROOKLIME (VERONICA BECCABUNGA).

can generally be bought cheaply enough from some of the larger London florists.

The Forget-me-not (*Myosotis palustris*) (Fig. 54) is placed in the aquarium chiefly for its beauty. It is rather common, and is in flower from June until the end of September. This plant has a creeping stem, and bright green and rather rough leaves. The flowers, which grow on leafless stalks. are pale blue, with yellow centres. The buds before they expand are pink, and are coiled up in such a way at the top of the flower-stalk as to give to this plant and its relations the name of Scorpion Grass. The Myosotis should be set in a pot, and placed among the rockwork of an aquarium. This weed is also called the Creeping Water Scorpion Grass, and is said to be the true Forget-me-not, though this romantic title has been often claimed for other plants.

The Brooklime (*Veronica beccabunga*) (Fig. 55) is very hardy, and grows rapidly in an aquarium. Its bright green leaves are oval and roundly notched on their margins. They grow opposite one another, in twos, on a creeping stem, which sends out small roots. The flowers blossom from May to September, and are generally of a deep blue colour; but occasionally they are flesh-coloured. The Brooklime is a great favourite with keepers of aquaria, for it is very pretty, common, and useful. A small portion of the plant, containing a short piece of the stem, will begin to grow almost directly it is planted in the sand and gravel at the bottom of the tank. This weed is often found growing in the company of watercress, with which it is sometimes eaten, though the flavour is rather pungent.

The Water-mint (*Mentha sylvestris*) is one of the most ornamental of water-plants. It is fairly common, and is found growing either in or on the edges of shallow streams, often in dense masses. The leaves are egg-shaped and serrated. The flowers, which are a pale lilac, grow on the upper part of a stem in thick whorls, the top flower of all forming a kind of head. The Water-mint will grow well in an aquarium, and may be planted in a pot, or in rather deep sand and gravel at the bottom of the tank. It flowers from July to September, and emits rather a strong scent, which is pleasing or unpleasing according to individual tastes.

The Common Hornwort (*Ceratophyllum demersum*) (Fig. 56) grows in slow-running streams and ditches. It is not by any means a rare plant; indeed, in some counties it is very common. There is no difficulty in recognising this weed, its appearance is so different from any other. It has narrow bristle-like leaves growing round a stem in whorls. Each leaf is divided in forks, three or four times, so making a rather dense mass. The green flowers are also whorled, and grow in the axils of the leaves. The fruit has two horns near the base. The Hornwort is useful in an aquarium, and will do

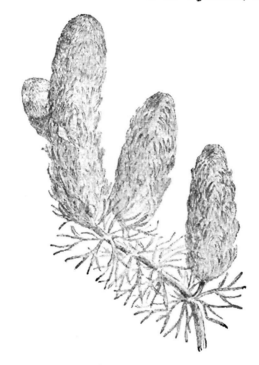

Fig. 56. Common Hornwort (Ceratophyllum demersum).

well if a small portion is tied to a stone and sunk to the bottom. It grows entirely under water, and flowers in July.

The Bladderwort (*Utricularia vulgaris*) (Fig. 57) is a rare and very interesting plant. It is found in some of the ponds and slow-running rivers of the southern and eastern counties of England. Its leaves are divided into hair-like segments, to which are attached numerous small bladders of a purplish or pinkish colour. The bladders are for the purpose of so buoying up the

plant that its flowers may have the air and light which are
necessary to their development, and partly for the purpose of
catching food for the plant in the shape of aquatic insects.   The
bladders, therefore, are not only buoys, but traps : veritable
insect-traps formed on the same principle as many a rat- or
mouse-trap.   The way in is as easy as the way out is difficult.
If the bladders of one of these very interesting insect-feeding
plants were examined during the flowering season, it would be

FIG. 57. BLADDERWORT (UTRICULARIA VULGARIS).

found that nearly every bladder contained its prey in the shape
of one or more aquatic insects, upon which the plant was either
feeding or upon which it would feed.   Dr. Taylor in his book,
" The Sagacity and Morality of Plants," describes the entrance
of these traps as being "set with bristles or stiff plant hairs, and
which point inwards, so that insects easily get in, but cannot get
out."   When the flowering season is over, the bladders fill with
water and the whole plant sinks to the bottom of the river or
pond.   The rather large yellow flowers grow in clusters of six

or seven upon the upper part of the stalk, which is raised several inches above the surface of the water. Towards the end of the year the greater portion of the plant decays, leaving the hardish, oblong terminal buds, about the size of a pea, to lie dormant during the winter at the bottom of the water. In the spring these buds rise to the surface and grow into new plants. The buds may be obtained from the bottom of those ponds

FIG. 58. WATER VIOLET (HOTTONIA PALUSTRIS).

where the plants are known to grow, by means of a fine muslin net; or they may be taken as soon as they rise to the surface, in the spring. When procured, they should be placed in the aquarium, where they will soon become interesting, ornamental, and useful.

U. neglecta, a very rare and interesting water-plant, found in Essex, Gloucestershire, and perhaps other counties of England, has the bladders upon both the stem and its thread-like leaves; while *U. vulgaris,* as implied above, possesses them only on its leaves

The Water Violet (*Hottonia palustris*) (Fig. 58) is named after Professor Hotton, of Leyden. In some respects it is like the Water Crowfoot, though it certainly has the advantage of the comparison. It is by no means a common plant, but it is found plentifully enough in the ponds and ditches of Norfolk and Suffolk Dealers in aquarium necessaries are generally able to supply this weed during the season. It will grow well in a tank, but it should not be tied in a bunch and sunk by a stone to the bottom, according to a common practice; it ought to be planted separately, a piece of the creeping root being attached. *H. palustris* has feathery leaves, which grow in tufts under the water, only the upper part of the flower-stalk rising a few inches above the surface. The five-petalled flowers are rather large, and vary in colour from pink and yellow to almost white.

FIG. 59. FLOWERING RUSH
(BUTOMUS UMBELLATUS).

Amphibious Persicaria (*Polygonum amphibium*) is a handsome plant, and will grow readily in an aquarium. It is not uncommon, and is found either in still water or upon marshy land; but when living in the former it assumes a different shape from that which it has when growing upon the latter; indeed, the difference is so great that the varieties might be taken for two distinct species. In the one case, the leaves are broad and smooth, and float at the end of long stalks; in the other, the stem is short and the leaves are narrow and rough. The flowers are rose-coloured. A portion of this plant having a piece of the creeping stem attached (which stem ought to be sending out roots at a joint or two) should be set in the sand at the bottom of the aquarium.

The Flowering Rush (*Butomus umbellatus*) (Fig. 59) is an exceedingly pretty water-plant. It has narrow, three-cornered leaves, which spring from the root, and its beautiful pink or purple flowers grow in a bunch upon the top of a long and circular stem. This plant is found in ponds and slow-running rivers, and blossoms from June to September. The Flowering Rush will grow very well in an aquarium if a small plant (having its tuberous root) is placed in a pot containing rich garden mould, covered with plenty of well-washed gravel.

The Great Water Plantain (*Alisma plantago*) (Fig. 60) is a very good weed indeed for the aquarium. Its leaves are of two different shapes : those which grow above the water are of a bright green colour, and something like those of the Common Plantain, while those which remain entirely under water are long and narrow. The lilac-coloured flowers grow on long three-sided stalks, which rise some distance above the surface. This plant is more or less common in ponds and ditches all over England. It can easily

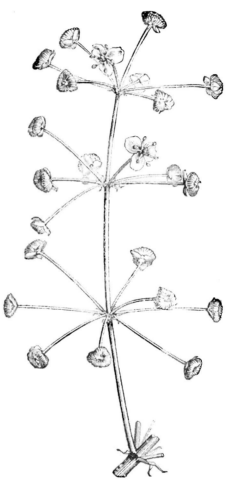

FIG. 60. GREAT WATER PLANTAIN
(ALISMA PLANTAGO).

be cultivated in the aquarium, where it is both ornamental and useful. There are very few plants, I think, which so soon begin to grow after having been introduced in the tank. Small

G

plants should be chosen for the purpose : such can generally
be found growing very near a large one. They ought to be
taken with as much of their native soil clinging to their roots
as possible, and then planted in a convenient-sized pot containing loam and gravel.

The Common Arrow-head (*Sagittaria sagittifolia*) (Fig. 61) is

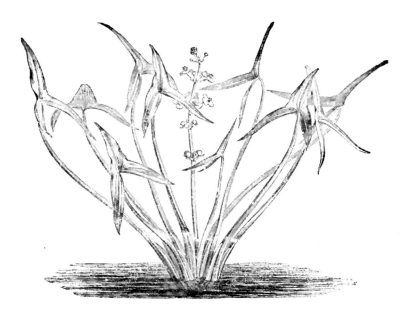

FIG. 61. COMMON ARROWHEAD (SAGITTARIA SAGITTIFOLIA).

very hardy, and will grow well in the aquarium. The arrow-
head-shaped leaves of this plant will easily lead to its recog-
nition. Its flowers have three white petals, and grow in whorls
on stalks which rise about 6in. above the water. This plant
sends out runners ending in tuberous roots. The Arrow-head is
rather common in lakes, ponds, and ditches, and is often found
in the company of the Water Plantain. It should be placed in
the tank according to the directions given for the setting of the
latter plant.

The Branched Bur-reed (*Sparganium ramosum*) (Fig. 62) is ornamental in a large tank. Its fruit, which resembles burs, and its long wavy leaves, cause it to be readily recognised. The flowers grow on long, branched stalks, which sometimes rise

FIG. 62. BRANCHED BUR-REED (SPARGANIUM RAMOSUM).

as high as 3ft. above the water. It should be planted in a pot containing loam.

The Sweet Flag (*Acorus calamus*) (Fig. 63) is an interesting plant, and may be grown in a pot immersed in the water of an aquarium, where it will be ornamental. It is something like

a large grass or sedge in its habit, but it may be easily distinguished by its curious spadix, which is 2in. or 3in. long,

and of a light brown colour.
The whole plant gives out a
very pleasant aromatic scent,
and for this reason it was
frequently used many years
ago (and is, I believe, even now
sometimes) for covering the
floors of churches and houses.
This plant is common in Norfolk and Suffolk.

The Broad-leaved Pond-weed
(*Potamogeton natans*) (Fig. 64)
is common in ponds and ditches,
but more so in the former than
in the latter. The only drawback that I know of to the
presence of this plant in the
aquarium is the liability of

FIG. 63. SWEET FLAG
(ACORUS CALAMUS).

some of the leaves to premature decay: in other respects it is most
suitable for a tank, as it is both ornamental and a good producer
of oxygen. *P. natans* has, as a rule, particularly in deep water,
two sets of leaves : the upper ones float upon the surface at
the end of long stalks, which are able to adjust themselves to
the depth of the pond or ditch in which they are growing ; the
lower ones are often absent in shallow water. The floating
leaves are ovate, and 2in. or 3in. long; the submerged ones are
somewhat similar to long grass. The green flowers grow on
small spikes just above the water. This weed may be planted
in a pot containing loam and silver sand.

The Close-leaved Pond-weed (*Potamogeton densum*) is quite
as useful and beautiful a plant for the aquarium as *P. natans*.
With some people it has the preference for this purpose.
Its tapering-pointed leaves are of a lighter green, and, as its
specific name implies, are closely placed together. It is, if
anything, a freer grower than the Broad-leaved Pond-weed,
and is consequently a good producer of oxygen. When an

occupant of the tank, it should be treated in the same way as has been recommended for *P. natans.*

The Cape Fragrant Water Lily (*Aponogeton distachyon*) (Fig. 65) grows exceedingly well in an aquarium, and is very graceful, having bright green, ovate, floating leaves on very long stalks. The groups of white flowers are forked, and float upon the water : they remain in perfection for a long time, and give out

FIG. 64. BROAD-LEAVED POND-WEED (POTAMOGETON NATANS).

a strong, pleasant smell. This plant may be propagated by division of the root, and can always be bought for a small sum ranging from 1s. 6d. to 3s. It should be planted in a pot containing loam and silver sand mixed. It is a rapid grower and a useful and ornamental plant for the tank. I have found that it will not flower well unless it can have as much sunlight as is compatible with the welfare of the rest of the aquarium.

The Water Chestnut (*Trapa natans*) (Fig. 66), though not a native of England, is a great favourite with some aquarium-keepers. It is a floating plant, common in the lakes and slow-

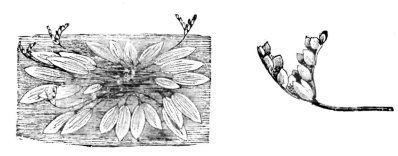

FIG. 65. CAPE FRAGRANT WATER LILY (APONOGETON DISTACHYON).

running rivers of some parts of Europe. The flowers are a reddish-white. The fruit is large, black, and armed with four

FIG. 66. WATER CHESTNUT (TRAPA NATANS).

spines (Fig. 67). The seeds are good to eat, and are sometimes used in soup: they are said to have a taste similar to that of the chestnut, hence the common name. This plant can often be bought in London for a moderate sum: but perhaps the seed might be obtained more readily.

The Water Awlwort (*Subularia aquatica*) (Fig. 68) has been strongly recommended as a plant suitable for an aquarium, but I have never been fortunate enough to obtain a specimen. It is only, as a rule, found in mountain lakes. The leaves, awl-like in shape, grow from the root, which is composed of long white fibres. The flowers are small, and sometimes are borne under water.

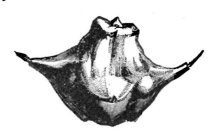

FIG. 67. FRUIT OF TRAPA NATANS.

Though almost everyone knows the duckweed when he sees it, yet very few, comparatively, know what an interesting plant it really is. Four species of duckweed are found in Great Britain, and all are useful and pleasing in the aquarium, for they keep the water shaded at the surface, they form hiding-places for the smallest animals, they are introduced without trouble, they grow well, and their presence has a pleasing effect. Only a few plants should be placed in a tank at a time, as they multiply rapidly. They increase by offshoots at the edges

FIG. 68. WATER AWLWORT (SUBULARIA AQUATICA).

of the fronds. The duckweeds are the smallest of all flowering plants, but they blossom very rarely—the Greater Duckweeds not at all in Britain. In winter they sink to the bottom of the water.

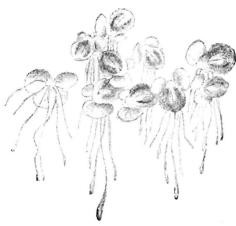

FIG. 69. GREATER DUCKWEED (LEMNA POLYRHIZA).

The Greater Duckweed (*Lemna polyrhiza*) (Fig. 69) is rather larger than the rest of the duckweeds. Its fronds or leaves are nearly round, about ½in. in diameter, thickish, dark green above and purple below, each frond having a number of little roots or fibres growing from beneath. This is a rare plant.

The Thick Duckweed (*Lemna gibba*) (Fig. 70) has fronds almost round, about ½in. in diameter, bright green in colour, flat above and round beneath. The fronds have only one fibre each. This plant is occasionally found growing with other duckweeds upon still water.

The Lesser Duckweed (*Lemna minor*) (Fig. 71) is the commonest of all: the fronds are small, ovate, light green above and a lighter green below, with one rootlet to each frond.

The Ivy-leaved Duckweed (*Lemna trisulca*) (Fig. 72) is fairly common on lakes and ponds. It is about ½in. long, elliptical, thin, serrated near one end, and of a light green colour. The young fronds grow at right angles to the old ones, and each frond has one fibre

FIG. 70. THICK DUCKWEED (LEMNA GIBBA).

The *Characeæ* are divided into two genera—*Chara* and *Nitella* (Fig. 73)—both of which are very useful and ornamental in aquaria, but particularly in those which contain only very small animals. These plants are too fragile to be placed within the reach of large fish. There are many species of the *Characeæ* in Britain, some of them being common. They grow in ponds and ditches where the water is clear. They have neither true leaves nor true flowers, but they have instead sub-divided branches and a curious kind of fruit.

FIG. 71. LESSER DUCKWEED (LEMNA MINOR).

The principal difference between the Chara and the Nitella is that the former has a compound stem, and the latter a simple one. These plants, especially the *Nitella trans-lucens*, do not require much light for their development, growing far better when placed at some distance from the window than when cultivated in close proximity to it. A small portion of each plant should be sunk by the help of a small stone to the bottom of the aquarium. Both the Chara and the Nitella succeed much more satisfactorily when planted in this way than when simply thrown into the water. They grow very quickly, and will in a short time fill the receptacle in which they are placed.

FIG. 72. IVY-LEAVED DUCKWEED (LEMNA TRISULCA).

These plants are also very interesting on account of the ease with which the circulation of the sap in their stems may be seen under a good microscope.

Willow Moss (*Fontinalis antipyretica*) (Fig. 74) is found growing on stones, and altogether submerged in rapid streams and rivers. It can be easily seen through the clear water waving up and down under the action of the current. The plant itself is of a dark green colour, but its new shoots or terminal buds are light green. It is a beautiful and hardy plant, and very useful in the tank. It is also of the greatest utility to the aquarium-keeper, for its tangled masses are full of numerous kinds of animal life. A small and suitable-shaped stone covered with a short growth of the Fontinalis should be placed in the aquarium.

The Crystalworts (*Riccia fluitans* (Fig. 75) and *Riccia natans* (Fig. 76) are also very useful little plants in an aquarium. They are sometimes found growing upon the surface of still water amongst duckweeds. *Riccia fluitans* is about 1 in. long, and light green. Its leaves or fronds are repeatedly forked, each segment having at the

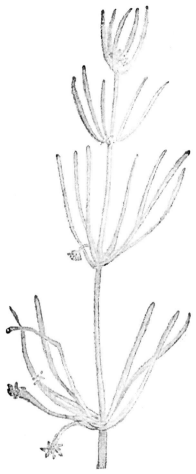

FIG. 73. NITELLA TRANSLUCENS.

end a small notch. Like the Greater Duckweed, it has several rootlets or fibres growing from beneath and hanging down in the water. *Riccia natans* is about ½in. long, heart-shaped, and light green. It also has several root-like fibres.

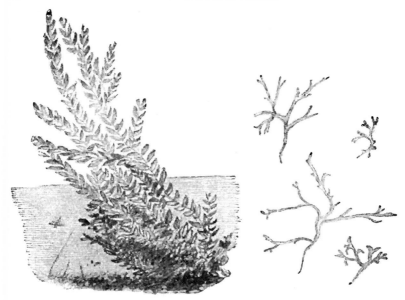

FIG. 74. WILLOW MOSS
(FONTINALIS ANTIPYRETICA).

FIG. 75. CRYSTALWORT
(RICCIA FLUITANS).

Besides the water-plants thus briefly described in this chapter, there are of course others which would also be both useful and ornamental in aquaria; but enough has been said, I hope, to give the novice in aquarium matters an idea of what kinds of plants to look for, where they may be found, and how they may be introduced into his tanks.*

FIG. 76. CRYSTALWORT (RICCIA NATANS).

* At the time this article appeared in *The Bazaar* the Editor of that paper appended the following note : "At Green's Conservatory, Covent Garden, we saw the other day a small Water Selaginella, which was very pretty. It was exactly like fragments of a small variety of Selaginella or Club Moss, and grew freely on the surface of the water, like duckweed." I have tried this plant, and can speak favourably of it.

CHAPTER VII.

AMPHIBIANS.

IN a large aquarium, which contains an island of some kind, various interesting amphibians may be kept. Indeed, so interesting are many of these animals that it is worth the while and expense to provide tanks entirely for their use, particularly in the case of those reptiles which would be likely to prey upon the usual inmates of an ordinary aquarium. For instance, a fresh-water Tortoise, unless it is very small, will not be likely to live for any length of time among fish and beetles without devouring many of them. This lesson I learnt somewhat unpleasantly several years ago. I had placed a Tortoise in a large tank, properly arranged, as I thought, for his comfort. When he became tame enough (as he quickly did) not to take a header from his island into the water on my approaching the aquarium, I used to feed him by placing small worms or tiny minnows as near to him as I could. He would crawl close to his food, suddenly seize it in the curious manner peculiar to these reptiles, and after tearing it with his sharp claws swallow it in a very dog-like fashion. I soon got fond of the Emys, and thought him a most interesting addition to the tank. However, it was not very long before I had cause to qualify my opinion, for one morning I noticed some curious things upon the water, which upon closer inspection I found to be the air-bags of fish. He had eaten, as Tortoises so often do, all his prey except the tell-tale bladder. Of course, he was banished to another tank, and a mate was purchased to share it with him. This and other experiences taught me that, though very small Tortoises will live peaceably with fish, rather large ones will not. Those Emydes whose carapaces, or back plates, are not more than two inches across will be quite harmless among the ordinary inhabitants of an aquarium—at least, such I have found to be the case.

Fresh-water Tortoises are carnivorous : the smaller ones will feed upon little worms, bluebottle flies, small pieces of meat, and the fry of fish; while the larger ones, in addition to these

FIG. 77. MUD TORTOISE (EMYS LUTARIA).

things, will devour birds, frogs, and mice. They should be fed regularly and sparingly, in order that they will not be so satiated with one day's food as to refuse that of the next. This regularity of feeding will tend to prevent neglect, for when anything has to be attended to every second or third day, it runs a very great risk of being forgotten. The Tortoises will not eat much during winter, nor will they often enter the water. Besides the *Emys lutaria* (Fig. 77) there are other fresh-water Tortoises which will live well in the tank, such as the *Emys reticulata* and the *Chelodina longicollis;* indeed, I believe any small fresh-water Tortoises will thrive in an aquarium. As all the Terrapins are pretty good climbers, their tanks should be covered.

The metamorphoses of the Frog (Fig. 78) and toad are most interesting, and can easily be observed by the help of the aquarium. The spawn of either the Frog or the toad may be obtained during the early part of the year, from almost every ditch and pond. In the South of England it is sometimes found in January, and frequently in February. The speed of the development of the tadpole from the egg depends

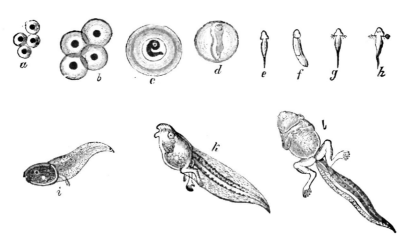

FIG. 78. METAMORPHOSES OF THE FROG, showing the growth of the Embryo, from the Egg to the Four-legged Tadpole.

greatly upon light and heat. The spawn of Frogs may be readily distinguished from that of toads, for the former is found in shapeless masses, while the latter is deposited in strings of two rows each, placed alternately and regularly. These strings vary greatly in length. Eggs of toads are also smaller and rather darker than those of frogs. The spawn of either, when first laid, consists of small globular bodies surrounded by a glutinous envelope (Fig. 78, *a*), into which a large quantity of water is quickly absorbed (*b*). The whole then has somewhat the appearance of small shot embedded in jelly. The development of the embryo can be easily seen through its almost transparent covering, and the following

stages may be observed: (1) the round egg becomes
elongated; (2) furrows appear; (3) head, tail, and clingers or
claspers partly distinguishable; (4) branchiæ may be seen
on each side of head; (5) a little movement observable;
(6) the nostrils can be detected; (7) branchiæ more distinct
and lobed, and in which the circulation of the blood may be
watched under the microscope (c); (8) jerkings from a curved
into an almost straight position (d) until the envelope is
broken and the tadpole is free (e and f). The branchiæ (g)
now grow until they arrive at their full size (h), and then
they begin to decrease, soon becoming altogether hidden by
the operculum, and after being absorbed are replaced by
lungs. The little animal begins to take the true tadpole
shape (i); the eyes are more distinct, and the mouth
appears at the extremity of the head. After a time, short
or long according to circumstances, the hind legs bud and
grow (k), and these are followed by the forelegs (l). When
all the legs have appeared, the tail, beginning at the tip,
becomes gradually absorbed. It used to be gravely asserted
that the tails fell off. The creature is now able and willing
to leave the water and live almost entirely upon land. Young
tadpoles at first feed upon vegetable matter and afterwards
upon animal. They are capital scavengers in the aquarium,
living there for many months in the tadpole state. I had one
in the middle of September which, I think, was hatched
early in March, and it had not then obtained its fore-legs. In
October, I have caught tadpoles with no legs developed, and
sometimes they will live for a whole year in a tadpole condition. This tardy development into the Frog or toad is due,
I suppose, to an insufficiency of animal food.

The spawn when first obtained should be placed in some
shallow vessel, the bottom of which is covered with well-
washed river sand. If a rapid development of the embryo
is required, the eggs must have both light and heat. As soon
as the tadpoles, after becoming free, have consumed that
portion of the spawn which they will eat, they should be
removed to a larger vessel, especially if their number is at all
great; and when moved they should be provided, in small

quantities, with two or three different kinds of waterweeds. They are very fond of confervæ. As they grow they will begin to prefer animal food to vegetable, and small pieces of meat may be given sparingly, as a very little will satisfy a great many tadpoles. All that is not eaten must be removed, or it will corrupt the water. I find that tadpoles, if not kept in too large a number, are very hardy little creatures. They will not die should they be given no animal food, but they will remain for a very long time in the tadpole state.

When the tadpoles have absorbed their tails and have become young Frogs, they should be allowed their liberty in the garden, where they will be very useful; for at that time of their life it is a difficult matter to provide them with the necessary food, consisting as it does of minute insects. They will not be worth the trouble, as Frogs of a size suited to the aquarium can readily be obtained.

The Edible Frog (*Rana esculenta*) is larger than the Common Frog (*Rana temporaria*), and more likely to adapt itself to a life in the tank. It is a great lover of water, and rarely comes to land. It may easily be distinguished from the Common Frog (Fig. 79) by the absence of the black band which runs from behind the eye of the latter to the shoulder. Though the Edible Frog is not indigenous to this country, it can be found in Cambridgeshire and in some other parts of England. As it is a very handsome animal, it is well worth the extra trouble of procuring instead of the common kind.

The Frog feeds upon insects, worms, slugs, and the like, and its manner of feeding is interesting and peculiar. The prey is captured by the help of the tongue, which is a very curious member, being, unlike most tongues, fixed in front and free behind, and capable, therefore, of a great reach. The tongue is also covered with a very sticky secretion, which enables it to withdraw every insect it touches into the mouth.

Frogs, though they possess lungs, have at the same time the power of cutaneous respiration : that is, they are able to breathe, as it were, through the skin. Hence they can live for a considerable time under water. This cutaneous respiration is also necessary to assist the pulmonary respiration, or respiration by means of the lungs, but it cannot take place unless the exterior of the skin is moist. It can readily, then, be seen how essential it is that the skin should be continually moist. But as the Frog cannot always have access to water, it has been provided with a kind of portable reservoir which contains pure and tasteless water, and by means of which the animal is able to keep its skin, even in dry places, in the

Fig. 79. Common Frog (Rana temporaria).

necessary state of dampness. The Frog when captured will often discharge the contents of this reservoir.

When the aquarium-keeper has carefully watched the development of the egg into the tadpole, and the tadpole into the perfect batrachian; when he has noticed its curious tongue and its manner of feeding; and when he has knowledge of its cutaneous respiration and portable reservoir, he will come to the conclusion that the common and often despised Frog is indeed a very interesting and extraordinary animal. The tanks in which Frogs are kept should be covered.

Newts are very interesting and suitable animals for the
aquarium. They are handsome, intelligent, easily tamed, and
their presence in the tank adds very much to its attractiveness.
Their colours are pleasing and variable, and their movements
when swimming are very graceful, indeed, as much so as
those of fish. As the animals go in and out among the weeds
or climb the rockwork, or fight with one another over
some portion of food, one is reminded, by a slight
stretch of imagination, of alligators, or even of the "fabled
dragons."

There are three species of Newts in Britain, viz. :

(1) The Great Crested Newt (*Molge cristata*).

(2) The Common Smooth Newt (*Molge vulgaris*).

(3) The Palmated Newt (*Molge palmata*).

The first two are common almost everywhere, while the last
is somewhat rare.

The Great Newt is the best adapted of them all for a life
in the aquarium, as it is a lover of water and does not
often venture upon land. The males of all the Newts are
distinguished during the spring and early summer by large
crests which run along their backs and tails. The crest of
the Great Newt (*Molge cristata*) (Fig. 80) is serrated and is

FIG. 80. MALE GREAT CRESTED NEWT (MOLGE CRISTATA).

divided at the junction of the tail and body, while that of
the Smooth Water Newt (*Molge vulgaris*) is wavy at the
edge and continuous throughout. The females of both are
crestless. These crests, being absorbed, disappear during the

autumn and winter, and there is little then to distinguish the sexes—except, perhaps, in the case of the Great Newt, for the orange of the lower part of the body of the male does not extend to the tip of the tail as does that of the female.

The colouring of Newts varies considerably, but the following are the approximate markings of the different species: the upper part of the body of the male of the Great Molge is a dark brown, with here and there darker spots; the sides are spotted with white, and the sides of the tail are white; the crest is almost black; the female of the Great Newt (Fig. 81) is marked something similar to the male, the upper

FIG. 81. FEMALE GREAT NEWT (MOLGE CRISTATA).

part of the body being dark brown, the lower orange with black spots; the sides are speckled with white. The *Molge cristata* is often more than 6in. in length, and its body is covered with warty tubercles: these tubercles are supposed to be for the purpose not only of defence, as they are capable of discharging bitter secretions, but also of supplying moisture to the skin when the animal is out of the reach of water.

The upper part of the body of the male of the Smooth Newt (*Molge vulgaris*) is greenish-brown; the sides are bluish-white, speckled with black or dark brown spots: the under-part of the body is orange; the edges of the crest are red; the whole body is more or less covered with spots. The female of the Smooth Newt (Fig. 82) is very similar to the male in her markings.

The Great Newt is shyer than the Smooth Newt.

The Palmated Smooth Newt (*Molge palmata*) is smaller than the *M. vulgaris*. The fingers and toes of the male, during the breeding season, are webbed. The upper part of the body is

FIG. 82. FEMALE SMOOTH NEWT (MOLGE VULGARIS).

of an olive-colour, and the upper part of the head is a dark brown. The sides of the body are light brown, speckled with round black spots. The tail of the male is truncate and ends in a filament about three lines in length.

The Newts, comparatively recently, have been given the generic title of *Molge*, a Greek word meaning *slow*. These batrachians certainly seem to deserve this name, for they are slow in their development and slow in their movements, particularly while on land.

Newts may nearly always be found in ponds and ditches. They can easily be caught either by fishing with a worm or by using a small hand-net. The fishing apparatus is very simple, and consists of a walking-stick, a piece of thin string, and a lively worm. One end of the string should be tied round the centre of the worm and the other to the stick. If the water is clear and a Newt can be seen, the bait should be dropped as close to the nose of the animal as possible, and when he has taken the worm as far as the string by which it is tied, the batrachian may be gently lifted upon the land. When the water is thick the fisherman must watch the movement of the string. The hand-net, if a Newt cannot be seen, must be passed along the bottom of the water and among the weed until the desired capture is made. The best time to obtain Newts is during the early part of the spring : they will all then have returned to the water, and have developed their most striking colours, and in the case of the males, their crests.

Newts take readily to a life in the tank; and, if they are provided with an island, proper food, and suitable weed, the females will soon begin to lay their eggs. During their breeding season they are very lively, continually moving gracefully to and fro in the aquarium, or coming up to the surface of the water for a fresh draught of air, often making as they do so a "popping" noise ; and besides being lively, they are extremely inquisitive, apparently taking notice of all that goes on both within and outside their tank.

It is very interesting to watch the female Newt lay her eggs. She generally wraps them carefully, as they are laid, in the leaves of some waterweed. But should the desired plants not be within her reach, she will deposit the eggs upon stones, or between two leaves which are not pliant enough to bend, or she will fold them in the leaves of the willow should any be dipping in the water, or in blades of grass. The plants which she prefers for the protection and hiding of her eggs are the Starwort (*Callitriche verna*), the Anacharis, and the Water Crowfoot (*Ranunculus aquatilis*).

FIG. 83. LEAVES OF VERNAL GREATER STARWORT ENFOLDING EGGS OF NEWT IN VARIOUS STAGES OF DEVELOPMENT.

The egg-laying is spread over several days, and may take place during the months of April, May, and June. The Newt, when wishing to lay, hunts about for a suitable leaf. She seems to be very particular, and appears to test its suitability by smelling and bending it. When she has obtained one to her taste she will fold it with her hind legs and carefully lay the egg within the fold, gently pressing the leaf upon the egg until the former is firmly stuck around the latter. Sometimes, to make the matter surer, she will take the leaf and egg within her mouth, and thus give them a final pressure. The egg is very small, and is surrounded with a glutinous substance. The leaf gradually unfolds as the embryo of the future *Molge* begins to grow. Fig. 83 represents the eggs in various stages of development, and laid in the leaves of the Vernal Starwort. As soon as

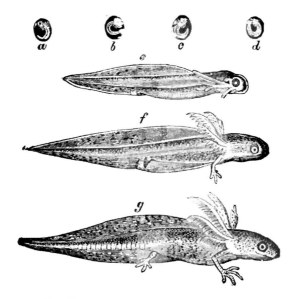

FIG. 84. METAMORPHOSES OF THE NEWT.

the eggs are deposited they should be collected and placed in a shallow aquarium or earthenware dish—the latter the better. The vessel ought to be covered with a piece of glass and put near a sunny window. The speed of hatching depends upon light and temperature. Sometimes, under favourable circumstances, the young tadpoles will be free within twelve days after the eggs have been laid. It should be arranged that the eggs have the heat of the sun without receiving its direct rays. The eggs of the Great Newt take longer to hatch than those of the Smooth Triton.

The young tadpole's growth (Fig. 84, *a, b, c, d*) can be observed while it is within the egg. The embryo for the first three or four days is globular, and then begins to lengthen out gradually. At the end of the first week the head and tail can be distinguished, and soon after this the branchiæ appear. The little animal at this stage looks more like a fish than a Newt. The circulation of the blood may now be seen under the microscope. This sight is most interesting, and well worth the trouble necessary for the observation. As the tadpole grows it changes its position in the egg, and finally becomes rather fidgety, until by its struggles it forces itself free. The egg collapses as the young Newt leaves it.

The *Molge* tadpole just after it is hatched (Fig. 84, *e*) is not very easy to find, even in a very small aquarium. When it is discovered, that which will attract attention most is the brilliancy of its golden-looking eyes. It does not move much at this period of its life, except to dart away rapidly on being disturbed. As it has no legs yet, Nature has provided it, as the frog tadpole, with two small claspers, but these disappear upon the development of the forelegs (Fig. 84, *f*). The speed of growth of the small batrachian depends very much upon its food, which at first should be, if possible, very small water-insects, Water-Fleas (*Daphnia pulex*), Cyclops, and the like; and as it increases in size it will eat the larvæ of the gnat and similar prey, until it grows big enough to devour small portions of tiny garden worms.

The animal is so transparent until it is about three months old (Fig. 84, *g*) that a glance will tell whether it has been able to satisfy its appetite or not. In time (how long depends upon food and temperature) the gills, shortly after the appearance of the hind legs, will be absorbed, and the young Newt will be obliged to come to the surface of the water to breathe. Unlike the frog tadpole, the fore-legs are produced before the others. This batrachian sloughs very frequently, some-times as often as once in ten days. Occasionally the skin comes off in one piece, not even excepting the toes; and if the aquarium-keeper will skilfully remove it from the water by the help of a small camel-hair brush, and place it carefully upon a sheet of white paper, he will find that it makes a very interesting object: the skin will readily adhere to the paper When the Newt is about to change its skin, it will, as a rule, become sluggish, and lose its appetite. It assists the operation by crawling between the weeds and rockwork. Sometimes the *Molge* will imitate the toad, and make a meal of its late covering.

As the autumn approaches, the Newts, especially the Smooth ones, will attempt to leave the aquarium. Their colouring at this time becomes dull, and they lose a great deal of their activity and inquisitiveness. The island in the aquarium should be provided with some hiding-places, which at this season of the year will be taken possession of by the Newts. In captivity they begin to hybernate about November. After wintering in the aquarium, and as spring approaches, the batrachians will slowly become active, and the males will gradually develop their crests.

Newts while in confinement may be fed upon the Water-Louse (*Asellus aquaticus*), tadpoles of frogs or toads, garden worms, or pieces of meat either cooked or raw. The meat should be cut in narrow slips. The Newt is sometimes guilty of cannibalism, especially when the Great Newt is kept in the tank with the Smooth one, and when the tadpoles of any species of *Molge* are allowed to remain with their parents and older relatives.

Newts, in common with lobsters and other animals, have the power of reproducing lost limbs. A Great Newt of mine once climbed out of his own tank and fell into that containing two young pike. When I found him in the company of the fish I discovered that he had lost one of his hind legs. I said I was sorry for him; but I do not think I was very unhappy, for I had long been desirous of seeing the reproduction of limbs, of which I had read and heard. I placed the poor fellow in a small tank by himself, fed him carefully, and watched him attentively. In a short time I was rewarded for my care by seeing a new limb gradually grow until it became nearly as large as the other hind leg. I believe (I cannot be sure, for this happened many years ago) the new leg from the first was perfectly shaped. However, I was glad to prove the truth of report without having been cruel enough to make an amputation.

FIG. 85. MEXICAN AXOLOTL OR LARVA OF AMBLYSTOMA TIGRINUM.

The tanks in which Newts are kept should be carefully covered, or the animals will be certain to escape and perhaps cause some annoyance to the ladies of the household.

There is a peculiar kind of batrachian—found principally in the lake close to the city of Mexico—which is of unusual interest, not only in the aquarium, but to all who have any liking for natural history. The strange animal is commonly called the Mexican Axolotl (Fig. 85). In shape it is something similar to the three-month-old Newt; that is, a young *Molge* which has developed all its legs but which still retains its branchiæ.

The Axolotl may be described as the tadpole of the Amblystome (*Amblystoma tigrinum*) (Fig. 86); but for a long time it was considered to be an animal which retained its branchiæ throughout its existence, like the Siren or Proteus, and was therefore placed among the *Perenni-branchiata* or retainers of branchiæ through life.   The Axolotl when full grown is about 9in. or 10in. long, and rather stoutly built.   It is generally of a very dark slate-colour, covered with black spots, and in the earlier part of its existence it is not ungraceful either in form or in movement.   There are also albinos; these do not differ in shape from the type, but are white,

FIG. 86.   AMBLYSTOME (AMBLYSTOMA TIGRINUM).

save for a yellowish tinge about the tail, and have pink eyes and gills.   It is provided with lungs as well as gills, and is therefore able to breathe both below and above water.   The tail of the Axolotl is finned like that of the *Molge*.   The head is flat and broad, and the muzzle blunt   The eyes are small and the mouth wide.   There are four digits on the front feet, and five on the hind.

The Axolotl, or Siredon as it is sometimes called, lives apparently very happily in the aquarium, soon becoming tame enough to take food from its master's fingers.   It is not necessary to provide it with an island, as it prefers to remain in some shady retreat at the bottom of the tank.   Occasionally, however, it comes to the surface of the water for atmospheric air (desiring, I suppose, a change of air), making as it does so the same "popping" noise as the newt under like circumstances; and sometimes it remains stationary in mid-water in an almost perpendicular attitude, head pointing upwards.   The Axolotl has a very good appetite and will live upon finely cut-up raw meat, earthworms, water-insects, and tadpoles. It is also quite ready to make a meal of a small fish or a young newt. One day, for instance, I placed two young newts, about four months old, in a tank which contained a pair of Axolotls, and a little while afterwards on looking for the former to remove them I could only find one. I hunted under every piece of weed and behind the rockwork in vain for the other, and was about to give the search up when I caught sight of the tip of the tail of the missing animal just protruding out of the mouth of one of the Axolotls. And as I watched that tip, every moment ex-pecting it to disappear altogether, the animal, much to my surprise, suddenly disgorged its captive, which immediately swam about the aquarium, apparently none the worse for its late rather awkward predicament. An Axolotl will eat almost any amount of frog and toad tadpoles, and I have seen one swallow a young minnow with the greatest possible ease. The fish swam near the reptile, there was a sudden dash on the Axolotl's part, and the fish had disappeared.

The Axolotl, curiously enough, though not the perfect animal, will reproduce its own species even in an aquarium. It affixes its eggs to the water-plants, preferring the *Vallisneria spiralis* for this purpose, or to the rockwork, or to the sides of the tank. The young are released from the eggs in fifteen to thirty days, according to the temperature in which they are placed. As soon as the eggs are deposited they should be removed, if possible, to a rather large aquarium which contains plenty of well-established water-weed, and also much small (no large) animal life, such as Water-Fleas, Cyclops, and the like. The eggs then will be undisturbed until they are hatched, and the young Axolotls will have plenty of proper food before they are old enough to eat tiny garden worms. From the first they are provided, of course, with branchiæ, but no feet. In nine or ten days the fore-feet appear, and these are followed some time afterwards by the hind ones. When first hatched the young tadpoles are of a greenish colour, and covered with little dark spots. The length of time which will elapse before the Axolotl becomes the perfect Amblystome depends upon circumstances: sometimes it will lose its branchiæ and develop into the air-breathing animal within twelve months, and sometimes it will remain an Axolotl for three or four years. However, by far the greater number of Axolotls never develop into the perfect batrachian. The Amblystome will also reproduce by laying eggs.

The Axolotls, like the newts and other animals, have, as I have seen proved, the power of reproducing lost limbs. Though these animals are generally of the colour described above, frequently they are white. These white specimens used to be rare, but now they can be bought for a few shillings in Covent Garden and elsewhere.

These animals seem to prefer to seize their food before it reaches the bottom of the water. If they do not take it as it falls the first time, it is a good plan to withdraw it and let it drop again, as close to their noses as possible. Some aquarium-keepers **feed** their Axolotls only once a week, and others every second or third day; but I think that it must be better to **feed** them regularly every morning, and this I do, and always find them ready for their food. They seem to know their feeding hour, for they swim towards me as I go near the tank. Axolotls will soon learn to eat raw meat, which need not be so carefully cut as for the newts, for they have wide mouths and take their food at one gulp.

Though the Axolotls will grow, under favourable circumstances, almost as large as the water-vole (water-rat), it is not necessary for that reason to keep them in a proportionately large aquarium. Four full-grown animals might be kept in a tank 2ft. 6in. long by 1ft. broad and 8in. deep. If they are well and regularly fed they will not attack fish of a fair size; but if, on the other hand, they are neglected, they will attempt to devour not only the fish, but even one another. In Mexico, Axolotls are eaten by the natives; they are prepared and cooked in the same way that eels are prepared and cooked in this country. If anyone wishes to see the Axolotl develop into the Amblystome, he will have the best chance of doing so by allowing all the water of the tank in which he keeps it gradually to evaporate. Should he be fortunate in his enterprise, he will observe the gills of the Axolotl gradually being absorbed until their openings are closed, and the large dorsal and caudal fins slowly disappear until the tail has assumed the appearance of that of the ordinary Salamander; the toes lose their appendages, and yellow spots come upon the skin. Finally the animal will breathe entirely by means of its lungs, and leave the water altogether.

Axolotls can be bought in London and other large towns of the principal dealers in aquarium requisites.

The Proteus (*Proteus anguineus*), or Olm, as it is frequently called, is an interesting and very curious batrachian well adapted to a life in the tank. For more than two centuries it has been of great interest to naturalists. The creature is a native of the subterranean waters of the Alps in Carniola. It is much more snake-like, as its specific name implies, than its near and only relative of the family (Proteidæ) to which it belongs. The Olm's body is furnished with two pairs (very far apart) of legs, the front legs possessing three toes each, and the hind ones two. There are twenty-six or twenty-seven costal grooves, corresponding to the ribs beneath. The skin is flesh-coloured, and the branchiæ, which are present throughout the creature's life, are red. The head is long, the mouth being small and protected by thick lips. The eyes are minute, and placed beneath the skin. The sight, though exceedingly feeble, enables the animal to find the darkest part of the water in which it lives. The Olm is slender and nearly a foot in length : the tail being fairly short, compressed, and finned.

This batrachian, though a permanently-gilled Salamander, has the power of breathing by means of its lungs, hence the tank in which it lives need not be large, but it should be well shaded as the creature shrinks from light.

The Proteus' food, while in captivity, should consist of garden worms, river worms (*Tubifex rivulorum*), aquatic larvæ, and the like.

The Austrian peasants, during flood time, catch this batrachian and sell it to tourists. It may occasionally be bought in England at a sum ranging from 7s. 6d. to 12s.

CHAPTER VIII.

FISHES.

IT is almost unnecessary to say that there are no more interesting and attractive inhabitants of an aquarium than fish. Fish are both intelligent and, to a certain degree, affectionate. No one ought for a moment to doubt their possession of intelligence when he calls to mind the time, thought, patience, and skill, which must often be expended before the devices of man can overcome the craftiness of some fish; when he comes to remember how apt they are to profit by experience, and how ready they are to take advantage of the least clumsiness or carelessness on his own part when, having hooked them, he is attempting to land them; and when he reads (and believes) that certain fish have been known to come to their feeding-places in the lake in which they live upon the sounding of a gong, and that others (sticklebacks in an aquarium) have been trained to ring a bell when they were wanting food. Nor is it unreasonable to suppose that fish possess affection when sharks hunt in twos; when pike pair, and if one of them should be captured, the other haunts the spot waiting for the return of his mate; when sticklebacks carefully build their nests and fight in the defence of their young; and when bullheads constantly watch and guard their little ones until the latter are able to take care of themselves.

Most fish in captivity will grow quite tame, learn to know

their owner, and come to the side of the tank on his approach.

By the help of the aquarium we are able to learn very much concerning the habits and characteristics of fish, which knowledge, without its assistance, we should fail to obtain. It is very pleasant to see healthy fish in a tank when the water is bright and clear, the plants are green and growing, and everything is quite clean. But, on the other hand, it is distressing to see fish swimming with their noses close to the surface of thick, unwholesome-looking water, vainly endeavouring to get a sufficiency of oxygen; to see plants partly dead and decaying, and fungus growing upon food which, in excess, has been carelessly thrown into the aquarium and left there until it has introduced disease. To see a miserable bird in a dirty cage is bad enough; but it is far worse, I think, to see dying fish in foul water. There are few pets which require such little care as fish, but it is absolutely necessary that they should have some attention, and he who keeps fish and neglects them is just as much guilty of cruelty as he who is summoned for working a horse with sore shoulders.

If the aquarium-owner would keep his fish in a healthy and happy condition, he ought to carefully observe the following rules :

(1) Provide shade for the fish.

(2) Never let the sun shine for any length of time upon the water in which fish live.

(3) Never keep more fish than the aquarium can contain in comfort.*

(4) Never put large fish in a small tank. Prefer small fish.

(5) Never forget to feed regularly, and on suitable food.

(6) Never allow discarded food to remain in the water.

(7) Remove diseased fish at once, and never introduce strange ones about whose health there is any doubt. Keep them in quarantine for a short time.

---

* There are too many fish in an aquarium when they swim with their noses close to the surface of the water.

(8) Never permit the presence of armed and bullying fish with unarmed and timid ones—*e.g.*, sticklebacks with small goldfish.

(9) Never allow the water-plants in their luxuriant growth to fill the whole aquarium, and so interfere with the free movements of the fish.

(10) Always remove dead and dying weeds, or dead and dying animals of any kind, at once.

There are no fish more commonly seen in the aquarium than the Gold-fish (*Carassius auratus*) (Fig. 87), and few are more suited to a life there than they are. They are

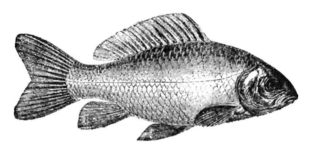

FIG. 87. GOLDEN CARP (CARASSIUS AURATUS).

very hardy, not too active, handsome, of various colours, and easily tamed. Not only do these fish vary in their colour, but also in their fins: some fins are double, others are entirely wanting. Occasionally one fish has two or three tails. I had a Silver-fish in my possession for some years whose tail looked, from behind, like an inverted capital Y This fish was perfectly healthy and very handsome, his scales glistening like mother-of-pearl.

It is a long time since Gold-fish were first introduced into England, and when is a matter of doubt; probably, however, about the year 1611. They originally came from China.

A great many Golden Carp are now annually bred in this country, especially in those tanks which receive the waste hot water from some of the great manufactories in the

North of England. For the aquarium, "cold-water" fish
should always be chosen—that is, those which have been
born in ponds uninfluenced by artificial heat: they are much
hardier than the "hot-water" ones. Not seldom the latter
will be found on their backs in the tank gasping for breath
and apparently dying. When this is the case, they may be
revived by placing them in running water, under a tap for
instance, or by dropping a very little brandy down their
throats, or by putting them for some time in fairly warm
water (about 90deg.). This last remedy—the simplest—is
perhaps the most effectual.

"Cold-water" fish, if properly managed, hardly ever suffer
from illness, and rarely die except from accident or old age;
indeed, I have found that the mortality of fish (not Gold-fish
only) in an aquarium is very far less than that of birds in
an aviary. Mr. T. H. Jones, of Woolwich, has told me, and
has kindly allowed me to mention the fact, that he placed a
Silver-fish in his aquarium on 20th May, 1853, and that it
lived there until 11th April, 1883, a period of thirty years all
but about six weeks. This fish was fed during that time
upon raw meat (beef or mutton), cut into narrow pieces
to resemble worms. The food was given about thrice a
week. Once while I was in a bird-dealer's a lady
came in and asked for some Gold-fish, adding the remark
that she could never get hers to live more than about
half a year. On hearing this I ventured to ask, as
politely as I could, whether she fed her fish. "Oh, no,"
she replied, "I never give them anything to eat." As
she said this the shopkeeper exclaimed: "Never feed your
fish if you want 'em to live." That lady's fish had
died the very painful death of slow starvation. And her
fish, alas! I fear, are not the only ones which so die. The
fish this man sold were healthy "cold-water" fish, and this I
knew, for I had bought several of him, which had lived in my
aquarium for years, and were alive and well then. Some
of my friends also had bought fish of him, with the same
satisfactory result. And this lady's fish died, not because
they were unfitted to live in confinement, but because they

were improperly cared for. And those people who so often complain that their Gold-fish die, may depend upon it that, as a rule, the fault is not in the fish or in the seller of the fish, but in their own mismanagement. Fish, however healthy, must of course be regularly fed.

A good food for Gold-fish is finely-crushed vermicelli. This should be thrown sparingly into the water, and as it sinks the fish will soon learn to take it eagerly. Never give them more than they will eat at the time of feeding. Besides this food, the fish will eat the eggs and fry of the water-snails (which should always be present in the tank). A little raw meat, some ants' eggs, and a few garden or water worms, will be good for them as a change.

Golden Carp, in common with all the Cyprinidæ, have the power of living for a considerable time out of water. The reason of this is that the covers of their gills, having bony supports, can be opened by the action of the muscles, and so the fish are able as it were to breathe the atmospheric air. Aquarium-keepers have often recorded instances in which Golden Carp have jumped out of their tank on to the floor, have remained there for several hours before they have been discovered, and then, on being returned to the water, have quickly regained their former health and spirits. A convenient way of carrying these fish a long distance is to wrap them up in damp moss. The late Mr. Frank Buckland says, that once having a dozen Gold-fish given to him, he placed them in wet grass and then in a cloth in his carpet bag. " There they remained all night." On his arrival in town, during the afternoon of the following day, he placed them in water, and found that six of them were still alive after having been kept a night and half a day in his carpet bag. When first placed in the aquarium they rolled about as if intoxicated, but they soon recovered from the effects of their journey.

When Gold-fish, by accident, have been allowed to remain for a long time out of water, they may frequently be revived by administering a little brandy, even if they are apparently quite dead.

Gold-fish will breed in a large aquarium: they deposit their spawn among the water-weeds there, to which it adheres. The spawn as soon as deposited should be removed to another tank, or the old fish will eat either it or the fry which are hatched from it. The young fish are hatched, according to the water's temperature, in from four to seven days. They should be provided at first with the smallest animal life for food, such as water-fleas and Cyclops. When about six months old they may be returned to the aquarium, for they will then be quite able to take care of themselves. The young fish at first are very dark, almost black, but gradually as they grow they become either golden or silvery in colour.

Gold-fish can be more easily bred in a small pond in the garden than in an aquarium. The pond for this purpose need not be more than 8ft. or 9ft. in diameter and about 3ft. deep. The sides of the pond ought to slope gradually from the edge, so that the young fry will be able to get out of the reach of those old Gold-fish which pursue them with cannibalistic intentions. The pond may be made perfectly watertight by means of a mixture of Portland cement and sand. Before any fish are introduced into the pond it should be filled with water, which ought to be frequently changed during a period of six weeks or two months. The Portland cement will then be deprived of any poisonous properties which would be likely to injure the fish. When the pond has been properly soaked, its bottom should be covered with well-washed river sand to the depth of about 6in., and in this sand some Water Lobelia ought to be planted. When the Lobelia has taken root, and made a fair amount of growth, the fish may be introduced—say, eight male Gold-fish and six females. These in favourable circumstances will increase with great rapidity: one carp alone will sometimes deposit about half-a-million eggs: luckily, however, only a small portion of these hatch. The fish during their breeding season should be fed on meat and garden worms as well as vermicelli. The pond ought to be so situated that as little dust and as few dead leaves as possible can enter it.   The Lobelia must be watched, lest it make too luxuriant a growth, and thus prevent the free movement of the fish. About six dozen water-snails (*Planorbis corneus*) should be put into the pond with the fish; their eggs and little ones will help to supply the young fish with food. No frogs or sticklebacks must be allowed with the Gold-fish; indeed, it is better to put no other fish at all into the pond if the Gold-fish are wished to breed. Such a pond as this might be made very profitable.

There is certainly no more suitable fish for the aquarium than the Common Carp (*Cyprinus carpio*) (Fig. 88), for it is

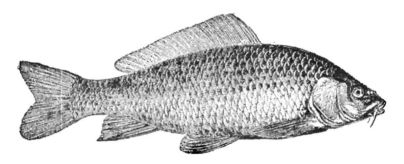

FIG. 88. COMMON CARP (CYPRINUS CARPIO).

very handsome when in good health, its scales looking—as it has been well said by Pope—as if "bedropp'd with gold." Its form shows that it is admirably fitted for a life in stagnant water; and being the least carnivorous of fish, it is never likely (except driven by absolute starvation) to prey upon any of its smaller comrades in the tank. As it has the largest brain, in proportion, of any fresh-water fish, it is very intelligent, and soon becomes so exceedingly cunning that no fish is more difficult to catch with rod and line in a large pond than an old Carp. It will even with great success dodge the net. How well, then, is it named the "fresh-water fox"! Though it is one of the most troublesome of all fish to catch, it is one of the easiest to tame when caught.

Cyprinus carpio will live apparently quite contented where any other fish — except perhaps a tench — would very likely die. It seems to be almost indifferent to either heat or cold, for it has been proved that it will survive being placed in water heated to 109deg., or frozen up in a mass of solid ice. The Common Carp will also live for several hours out of water; and fishermen sometimes tell us how that after a long and successful day's Carp fishing, they have found their spoil still alive on their return home. On the Continent Carp are even fattened by being suspended in the air in a net containing damp moss, and in that position they are fed upon bread and milk, put into their mouths with a wooden spoon. At first, however, until they get accustomed to this extraordinary treatment, the net, moss, and fish are occasionally dipped in water. Carp are said to live 150 or even 200 years, but this is not proved. However, at any rate it is certain that they are capable of attaining a great age. Fontainebleau, in France, is among other things noted for its very old Carp, some of them being described as "white with age"; but it is not unreasonable to suppose that this whiteness is not so much an indication of great age as of disease, for fish, especially the Carp, are subject to a vegetable parasite (*Saprolegnia ferox*) which gives to its victims a hoary appearance. This mould or fungus is chiefly caused by the presence of decaying animal matter in the pond or tank. The disease is contagious. Whenever, therefore, the least appearance of this growth is noticed, the suffering fish should be at once removed from its fellows and be kept quite alone until a cure has been effected. The best manner of accomplishing this end is to keep the fish in running water, and this may be done in one of the following ways :

(1) Put the fish in a box having perforated sides and lid, and sink it all but 3in. or 4in. in a running stream. (2) Or place the patient in a shallow vessel covered with wire netting or the like, under a gently running tap. (3) Should no tap be conveniently at hand, a contrivance may be made (out of doors for preference) by the help of a siphon, a tub, and a

large flower-pot saucer. It will save trouble if this arrangement is carried out close to a pump. If the siphon is small, and the tub large, the water will run for a long time without attention. The saucer should have a small hole bored just below the rim, to allow for the escape of water, and the top of the saucer ought to be covered with perforated zinc or wire netting to keep the fish from jumping out. The fish should be kept and fed in the running water until all traces of the fungus have disappeared. Fish may be also cured of this disease by being frequently dipped in salt water, or kept in warm water, about 75deg. Fahr. When tanks are properly looked after, there is not much danger of the appearance of this fungus, which is so often a source of great annoyance and loss to aquarium-keepers.

It is supposed that Carp were introduced into this country by German monks about the middle of the fifteenth century, and now there are very few old-established ponds in England in which they may not be found. During the greater part of the winter these fish, when at liberty, eat little or nothing, and retire as close as they can to the mud of the water in which they live, or get into some cave-like hollows in the bank, or under weeds or roots of trees. They continue this practice, to a certain extent, even in the aquarium, withdrawing themselves as much as possible from sight, and hardly touching any food. The Carp grows larger and increases more quickly in stagnant than in running water. It commences to breed when about three years old, and the number of eggs deposited by each female fish depends generally upon its size. A Carp weighing 20lb. has been known to contain more than a million eggs. The ova are affixed to water-plants and the like during the latter part of May and the three or four following months.

In a state of nature the Common Carp feeds upon water-plants, larvæ of insects, insects and worms, but in confinement it may be fed upon crushed vermicelli, and on this food it will apparently live quite contentedly. This fish grows, under favourable circumstances, to a great size, occasionally reaching more than 20lb. in weight, and more than 2½ft. in length and 2ft. in girth. The body is broad and deep, but not ungraceful; the colour is olive-brown, tinged with gold; the mouth is small and toothless, and has two barbels on each side; the lips are fleshy. The head is of a darker shade than the body, and the under-part of the body is of a yellowish-white; the fins are dark brown; there is one long dorsal fin. The tail is large and deeply forked; the scales are also large, and covered with a kind of mucus.

The Prussian Carp (*Carassius gibelio*) (Fig. 89) is if possible hardier than the Common Carp. It is a great lover of stagnant water, and is therefore well fitted for a life in the aquarium. In the country from which this fish takes its

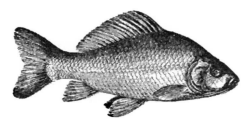

FIG. 89. PRUSSIAN CARP (CARASSIUS GIBELIO).

name, the breeding and feeding of Carp are an important and very often a profitable business. The Gibel Carp is very good to eat when properly cooked, and it does not taste, it is said, of the water in which it lives. This fish attains no great weight or size. Its habits and character are very similar to those of the Common Carp, and in confinement it should be fed on the same kind of food. It has an equal, if not a greater, power of resisting the fatal effects of an enforced absence from water. The chief difference between the Prussian Carp and the Common Carp is the absence of barbels on the sides of the mouth of the former. All fish of the genus *Carassius* are without barbels. The body is broad and deep, deeper in proportion than that of *Cyprinus carpio*. The head is blunt, and the eyes are yellow. The mouth is small.

The scales have a bronze-like tinge, and the fins are red. This fish seldom exceeds 1lb. in weight.

The Crucian Carp (*Carassius vulgaris*), sometimes called the German Carp, is very suitable for the aquarium. It has for a long time been domesticated on the Continent, and now shows several varieties. It seldom exceeds 3lb. in weight. The characters and habits of the German Carp and Common Carp are very much alike. The Crucian Carp is a much rarer fish in England than the Prussian Carp; the latter being found in nearly every part of the country, while the former has been caught, I believe, nowhere but in the Thames. The body is flat and very deep and much curved both above and below. The stiff rays of the dorsal and anal fins are finely serrated. The head is small in proportion to the size of the body. The scales are large and of a light golden tinge. The mouth is without barbels.

The Speigel or Leather Carp (*Cyprinus rex Cyprinorum*), a variety of the Common Carp, is a most interesting and handsome fish. I have kept a fine Speigel Carp in the same aquarium with a number of smaller fish of different kinds, and found it to be very gentle and tame, Its movements are generally sedate, but occasionally it indulges in a little violent exercise. It seems to be a very inquisitive fish, apparently taking notice of all that goes on in the room. This Carp is sometimes called the "mirror or looking-glass fish." It is not rare, and is certainly worthy of a place in any fairly large fresh-water aquarium. It may be fed upon vermicelli. This fish, I believe, originally came to this country from Silesia. The body in shape is very like that of the Common Carp; the greater part of it is without scales, and it is soft and leathery. On each side of the central line there is one row of scales, which are large and of a golden colour tinted with silver. There are also a few scales on each side of the fleshy part of the tail, and one or two here and there on other portions of the body. The tail is large and deeply forked. The mouth is small, and has two barbels on each side. I shall have more to say about this interesting fish later on.

Prussian, Crucian, and Speigel **Carp may** be bought of aquarium-dealers in London; the last is also known as the "Saddle Carp."

The Gudgeon (*Gobio fluviatilis*) (Fig. 90) is a general favourite. It is a favourite with the aquarium-keeper, for it is hardy, handsome, and easily tamed; it is a favourite with the fisherman, for it is a bold biter and provides excellent sport; and it is a favourite with the epicure, for when freshly caught and properly cooked it is most delicious to eat. An old writer says that this fish used to be swallowed alive as a cure for consumption. The Gudgeon is generally found in those rivers in England which possess a gravelly bottom. It may be readily taken with rod and line, or with a net. The

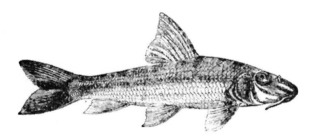

FIG. 90. GUDGEON (GOBIO FLUVIATILIS).

fish can be collected together by scraping the bottom of the river with a heavy rake: this raking disturbs and exposes the animal life upon which the Gudgeon feeds, viz., larvæ of insects, water-worms, and the like. As these fish are gregarious, it is wise and kind to keep a few of them together, but they will not die if kept in solitary confinement: they seem soon to learn how to be happy and contented in the aquarium. The bottom of the tanks in which Gudgeon live should be covered with a layer of gravel of extra depth, for without such precaution these fish, being bottom feeders, would interfere greatly with the clearness of the water. The Gudgeon generally spawns about May, and the ova, it is said, take nearly a month to hatch. This fish, while in the aquarium, should be fed upon small garden worms, water-

worms, larvæ of gnats, or pieces of raw meat. After a
time it will learn to eat Ants' eggs. The body is cylindrical
in shape, and olive-brown in colour, and spotted ; a dark line
runs along the sides. The eye is placed high up in the
head, and the mouth possesses two small barbels, one on
each side. The scales are large and the snout is somewhat
blunt. This fish sometimes grows 7in. long.

The Roach (*Leuciscus rutilus*) (Fig. 91), if young, will live
fairly well in an aquarium. He is rather a handsome fish,
and by no means the "fresh-water sheep" which some people
think him to be. He may not have the intelligence of the

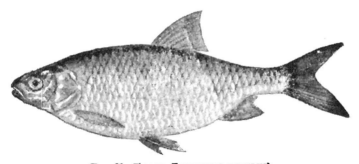

FIG. 91. ROACH (LEUCISCUS RUTILUS).

carp, but he has certainly enough common sense to profit
by experience, for he soon becomes so suspicious that it
is by no means an easy matter to catch him with rod and
line. Roach are found nearly everywhere, and in great
numbers; for though trout feed upon their eggs, and pike
and perch upon their fry; though so many men like to
catch them when mature; and though they so often fall
victims to more than one disease, they are still able, by
means of their wonderful reproductive powers, quite to
hold their own in the battle of life. When the aquarium-
keeper wishes to procure Roach of the right size for his
tank, he should, during the autumn, pass his hand-net along
the weedy edges of those streams which run into some river
where these fish are known to exist. Roach ought to be kept

in a rather large and shallow aquarium, and not crowded there; for they are subject, not only to the fish fungus or mould, but also to another disease which causes their scales to turn black. Roach while in confinement may be fed upon crushed vermicelli.

The depth of the body of this fish is a little greater than the length of the head. It is stoutly built, of a silvery colour on the sides, and of an olive-brown upon the back. In maturity the fins are red. The lateral line has a downward curve. The mouth is toothless, and rather blunt. The scales are large, and become easily detached. This fish seldom exceeds 1ft. in length and 2lb. in weight.

The Chub (*Leuciscus cephalus*) (Fig. 92) is a hardy and handsome fish, and will live for a long time in an aquarium

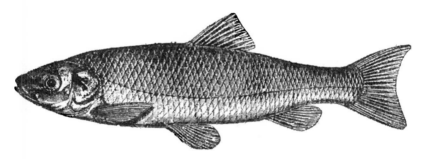

FIG. 92. CHUB (LEUCISCUS CEPHALUS).

under judicious management. He is rather a large eater for his size, and seems to prefer insect food. A small kitchen blackbeetle (so called) will soon tempt him to feed from the fingers. In a natural state he lives upon larvæ of insects, worms, and the tender shoots of water-plants, but in the aquarium he will readily learn to feed upon Ants' eggs. Chub are found in many of the rivers in England, especially in those which have a gravelly bottom. They may be caught with either a fly or a minnow as a bait or by "float fishing." They ought not to be more than 3in. or 4in. in length for the aquarium; but should they be larger than this, it will

not be wise to keep fish smaller than they are in the same
tank with them. Their great appetites would sooner or later
tempt them to devour their companions. A large dace and
a small Chub are so much alike that one is often mistaken
for the other; but this error need not be made if it be
borne in mind that the rear part of a Chub's anal fin is
convex, while that of the dace is concave (Figs. 92 and 93).
The Chub is noted for its extreme quickness of sight and
for its power of rapidly rising and sinking in the water
at will.

The depth of the body of the Chub is a little greater than
the length of the head. The scales are large and thick. The
lateral line curves slightly towards the ventral fins. The
head is blunt and the mouth toothless; the lips are very
leathery. The colour of its back is olive-brown, of its sides
silvery when the fish is young, but bronze-like when the fish
is mature. The under-part of the body is silvery-white. The
tail is large, dark in colour, and slightly forked. The pectoral
fins are olive-green, and the ventral and anal fins bright
pink. This fish does not often exceed 5lb. in weight.

The Dace (*Leuciscus vulgaris*) (Fig. 93) is a lively, graceful,
and active little fish, and a great favourite. Its glittering

FIG. 93. DACE (LEUCISCUS VULGARIS).

scales are very conspicuous in the aquarium. The Dace is
hardy and soon becomes quite tame. As an instance of the
hardiness of this fish, I may mention that a young pupil
of mine one day brought me two little Dace, not 2in. long.
I placed them in some water in a shallow vessel, which I
foolishly neglected to cover, and left the room. On returning
about an hour afterwards I found that both fish had jumped

out of the water and were on the floor, apparently quite dead. However, I replaced them in the temporary aquarium, and one of them recovered: the other died. The former I kept for three years and then I gave it, together with a gold-fish, to one of my sisters, under whose care it lived for about five years longer. The hardy gold-fish was the first to die. The Dace lived altogether about eight years in captivity, and during this time it grew from 1½in. to 6in. or 7in. in length, and became so tame that it would take a fly from the fingers. The aquarium in which Dace are kept should be covered, for they are great jumpers. They will live upon vermicelli, a fly or two being given to them now and then as a treat. Dace are generally found in clear, deep water, and may be caught with a hand-net or fly or by "bottom-fishing."

The general appearance of the Dace is very graceful. The depth of its body equals the length of its head. Its colour on the back is brownish-green, on the sides silvery, and on the under-part of the body nearly white. The dorsal and tail fins are brownish-green; the ventral and the pectoral are slightly pink, and the anal fin is white, tinged with green. The tail fin is rather deeply forked. The Dace does not often exceed 9in. in length or ¾lb. in weight.

The Rudd (*Leuciscus erythrophthalmus*) (Fig. 94) when young will live very well in an aquarium. It is decidedly a handsome fish, handsomer than the roach, with which it is often confounded. I do not know whether Rudd sleep more than other fish, but whenever I took a light into my study at night they were the fish which seemed more certain to be asleep than any of the others. It is rather a curious and interesting sight to see a large and well-stocked tank which has for some time been in a state of darkness suddenly lighted up. Many of the fish will be seen resting on the sand at the bottom of the water. They appear perfectly motionless, but gradually rise under the influence of the light and begin to swim slowly and seemingly sleepily about. Rudd are found in great numbers in Norfolk. When kept in an aquarium they may be fed upon vermicelli, worms, or Ants' eggs.

The body of the Rudd is shaped very like that of the roach.

Its back is brown, and its sides are silvery, tinted sometimes with gold. The scales are rather rough. The eyes and the fins are red, the lower fins being darker than the upper. The dorsal fin is behind the ventral. This fish does not often exceed 1¾lb. in weight. The late Mr. Frank Buckland has given the following rule for distinguishing the Rudd from the roach: "In the dorsal fin of the roach it will be found that

FIG. 94. RUDD (LEUCISCUS ERYTHROPHTHALMUS).

the front ray stands almost even with the front ray of the central fin, but in the Rudd the dorsal fin stands evenly between the anal and the ventral fins. The eye in the Rudd is of a much brighter red than the roach."

The Minnow (*Leuciscus phoxinus*) (Fig. 95) is a beautiful, hardy, and, as a schoolboy would say, "cheeky" little fish. Though Minnows are generally found in clear and running water, yet there are no fish which are more ready to take kindly to a life in confinement than they. They will live,

FIG. 95. MINNOW (LEUCISCUS PHOXINUS).

apparently happily, where one would never expect a fish to exist at all. I have known two Minnows to live for six weeks or two months in a small bottle, containing less than half-a-pint of water, and the surface of the water exposed to the air not being more than could be covered with half-a-crown. The Minnows did not die even under these circumstances, but were killed by a Water-boatman (*Notonecta furcata*), which lived in the bottle with them. These fish will live almost equally well in the smallest vessel worthy of the name of an aquarium, or in the largest tank. They can be caught in nearly every pond, river, or stream. They may be taken in a small hand-net, which should be sunk a little way in the water where these fish are seen swimming about in shoals. In the centre of the net a piece of bright red braid or cloth should have been tied. When the Minnows, urged by their curiosity, have come in some numbers to examine the gay colour, the net ought to be suddenly raised in the air, and if adroitly done, it will be found to contain not a few captives. Another way to catch the Minnow in the hand-net, is to run it along under the overhanging banks of the stream or pond, or among the weeds (especially if the weather be cold). A glass fly-catching bottle is very useful for taking these fish, if a piece of red flannel be fastened to the inner end of the cork, and the opening of the vessel be placed facing down stream. The Minnows seldom find their way out again when once they have entered the bottle.

Minnows very soon become tame enough to feed from the fingers. They will live upon vermicelli. It is pleasant to see a small shoal of these active little fish busily picking up their food as it is thrown to them in the aquarium. They will also eat flies, small worms, and pieces of meat. Sometimes their boldness and impudence cause them to be quite a nuisance in the tank, for when a portion of food has been carefully dropped in front of some shy-feeding fish, a " cheeky " little Minnow will very likely dash suddenly forward and greedily devour that which was meant for his more retiring companion. Minnows are longer-lived than most people imagine them to be. Mr. Jones, of Woolwich, put a few of these fish in the same aquarium with the silver carp before mentioned (p. 112), and thirteen years elapsed before the last of them died.

In the spring-time the male Minnow becomes tinged with green and red, and when thus coloured it is difficult to find a more beautiful little fish. Minnows spawn where the stream or river has a gravelly bottom. The ova hatch in about ten days. It seems very wonderful that Minnows should be as numerous as they are, when one considers how many enemies they have. Almost every fish will, at times, devour them. Man has also found that they make delicious food when properly cooked. The body of the Minnow is a little less in depth than the length of its head The colour

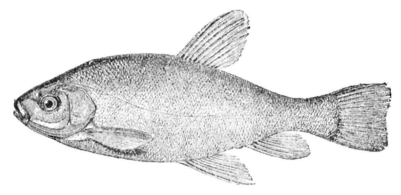

FIG. 96. TENCH (TINCA VULGARIS).

of the back is olive-brown, the sides being lighter in shade and spotted. The colouring, however, of these fish varies a good deal according to the localities in which they are found. The dorsal fin is just over the space between the ventral and anal fins. The tail is somewhat deeply forked, and there are dark spots at its base. This fish does not often exceed 3in. in length.

Though the carp and the minnow are so extremely hardy, I believe the Tench (*Tinca vulgaris*) (Fig. 96) is hardier than either. It will live for a very long time out of water; in fact, it is said that when this fish has been brought to the market, and has failed there to obtain a purchaser, it has been taken back again and returned to the water whence it came. Tench are sometimes found in rivers, but more frequently in weedy and muddy ponds, and often in the pits of disused brickfields. The muddier the water, the better the flavour of the fish. The habits of the Tench are very like those of the carp—both fish growing larger and increasing more quickly in stagnant water than in running, and both getting, during some portion of the winter, as far into the mud at the bottom of the water in which they live as possible. The Tench has been often called the " physician fish," from the idea that it has the power, by means of the sliminess of its skin, of curing the diseases of all other fish. And it has been said that the pike, out of gratitude to the Tench for his skill in healing, will refrain from devouring him. Gratitude is so rare that one would be glad to discover it even in a fish ; but we do not really find it there, at least so far as the pike is concerned, for that "fresh-water shark," notwithstanding his reputation of being possessed of the "grace of courtesy," will not hesitate, if pressed by hunger, to make a dinner of his "kind physician." On one occasion, in an aquarium of mine, a pike took, not his medicine, but his " doctor." In the Tench's power of healing himself and other fish I do not for a moment believe. On another occasion a Gibel Carp was sent to me, and was placed in the same tank with three Tench. Now, had these fish their reputed gift of healing, I do not understand how it was that they did not prevent their new companion from showing signs of fungus, which it did shortly after its arrival. As Tench delight in stagnant water, they are very well suited to a life in the aquarium. Their natural food consists of larvæ of insects, worms, and the tender shoots of some water-plants. In confinement they will live upon vermicelli, to which should be added a little animal food occasionally.

The Golden Tench or Golden Schlei (*T. v. aurata*), a variety of the Common Tench, is a very handsome fish and a great acquisition to an aquarium. It originally came to this country, I think, from the Continent, and now it is quite acclimatised in England. It is "of a most lovely yellow colour mixed with the gleam of gold."

K

Tench, either the Golden or the Common, will increase very rapidly in suitable ponds. Two males should be allowed to each female. The males are distinguished from the females by the large size of their ventral fins. The mouth of the Tench is blunt, very leathery, toothless, and possesses a small barbel at each corner. The scales are very small, and are covered with a thick mucus. The dorsal fin is just opposite the ventral fin. The former and the anal fin are without bony rays. The tail fin varies in form according to the age of the fish, being at first concave, then truncate, and finally convex. The colour of the Tench, which is really

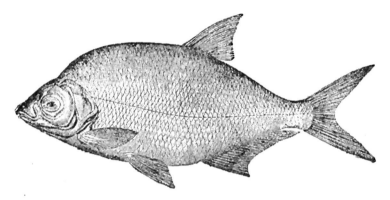

FIG. 97. CARP-BREAM (ABRAMIS BRAMA).

very beautiful when closely examined, is difficult to describe. Perhaps the most approximate description is dark green and golden. The lips are flesh coloured, and the fins darker than the body. The Tench does not often exceed 6lb. in weight, or 18in. in length.

Both the Common and the Golden Tench may be readily bought in London—the former, when small, for about 4d. each, and the latter for about 2s.

The Carp-Bream (*Abramis brama*) (Fig. 97) is rather a good-looking fish, but it is not so easy to keep in health in an aquarium as any of the fish already mentioned. It should be obtained when young, and placed in a tank which presents a large surface of water in proportion to its size, and which also possesses plenty of freely-growing plants. Worms, insects, and the tender parts of water-weeds are the natural food of the Carp-Bream. It is a hearty eater. In the aquarium it will feed upon vermicelli. Personally, I have a great regard for the Carp-Bream; not because it is a very good fish for the aquarium, for it is not, but because it used to provide me with such famous sport when I was a boy. The usual weight of this fish when full grown is from 4lb. to 7lb., but sometimes it has been taken weighing upwards of 14lb. The late Mr. Frank Buckland mentions a Carp-Bream which weighed 11¾lb., measured 2ft. 2in. in length, and which a gentleman asserted that he had placed in the pond in which it was caught fifty years before. Upon the Continent the Carp-Bream is more highly esteemed as food than in this country; but I believe that in some of our large towns great numbers of them are eaten during Lent and the Hebrew Passover. These fish are found in many of the rivers, lakes, and canals of both England and Ireland. They spawn during May, the eggs of a single fish sometimes numbering more than 120,000. The body of the Carp-Bream is deep, flat, and much curved above and below. The lateral line is rather low down. The mouth is small, toothless, and without barbels; the snout is blunt; the scales are rough and have a yellow tinge, which becomes a brown tinge with age; the pectoral and ventral fins are tinged with red, and the other fins are slightly brown; the dorsal fin is small, and the anal fin large; the tail is deeply forked.

The White Bream, or Bream-flat (*Abramis blicca*), is more difficult to keep alive in the aquarium than the carp-bream. It is a pretty fish, its silvery and glittering scales showing off well in the tank. It is very subject to fungus, but in a well-arranged and well-cared-for aquarium it will live in health, and will certainly be an ornament there. The tank in which it is placed must have been some time established, or this fish will not do well—at least, such has been my experience. There will of course be little or no difficulty in keeping the White Bream in an aquarium in which a fountain is continually playing. This fish can be distinguished from the carp-bream by its longer scales and smaller size. The habits and habitat of both fish are alike. The White Bream is rather common. It takes the bait of the fisherman in such a manner as to make the float lie flat upon the water instead of going under its surface. Young carp-bream and White Bream are not by any means difficult to catch in their native waters. If, however, they cannot be conveniently procured in this way, they may generally be purchased cheaply enough from some of the London dealers in aquarium requisites.

The Pomeranian Bream (*Abramis Buggenhagii*) is rare, and Dr. Günther regards it as a hybrid between the roach and

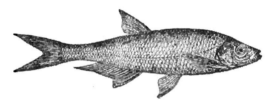

FIG. 98. BLEAK (ALBURNUS LUCIDUS).

the carp-bream. It is certainly more like the former than the latter. It should be treated according to the directions given for the keeping and feeding of the carp-bream. The Pomeranian Bream can sometimes be bought at the London dealers.

The Bleak (*Alburnus lucidus*) (Fig. 98) is a very active and beautiful little fish, with bright glittering scales, and looks exceedingly well in an aquarium; but unfortunately it is not by any means easy to keep alive in confinement. It should be placed either in a large and shallow tank which is well stocked with growing plants or in one possessing a constantly-playing fountain. As Bleak are great jumpers it is necessary to cover the aquaria in which they are confined. These little fish abound in many of the rivers of England, swimming near the surface in the swiftest part of the stream. Their natural food consists of flies, midges, and other insects, and various decaying matter; out in the aquarium they should be fed upon vermicelli, to which flies may be added when they can conveniently be obtained. Though while at liberty in the river the Bleak is said to help to purify the water by feeding upon decaying substances, the aquarium-keeper must not think that he is providing food for his fish by allowing such matter to remain in the tank. It is wise never to presume upon the presence of any scavengers in the aquarium, but constantly to attend to the cleanliness of the tank, as if there were no such animals. The scavengers will find plenty of food, notwithstanding all the owner's care. Bleak can be caught by fishing for them with a fine line and a

FIG. 99. STONE LOACH (NEMACHEILUS BARBATULA).

very small hook, baited with a fly or gentle : the hook should be quite hidden by the bait. The Bleak is the narrowest British fresh-water fish, its body being shaped very like that of a sprat. The colour of the back is a faint brownish-green, and the rest of the body is a glittering silvery-white. The dorsal fin is small and the anal fin large. The lower jaw projects beyond the upper. The Bleak is about 7in. long when full grown.

Many people who keep aquaria declare that the Stone Loach (*Nemacheilus barbatula*) (Fig. 99) is a delicate fish and will not live for any length of time in confinement; and they are right, for it will not continue very long in health in an ordinary deep tank. In such an aquarium it will be often seen, especially towards evening, rising in its curious newt-like motion to the surface of the water, and after obtaining what oxygen it can, sinking again quickly to the bottom. Sometimes, in order to remain as near to the surface of the water as possible, it will rest upon the top of the rockwork or upon the broad buoyant leaves of some aquatic plant. Such conduct as this shows that the poor fish is uncomfortable, that his surroundings are not suited to his requirements, and that sooner or latter, unless it be removed, it will die. As long as the Loach remains contentedly on the bottom of the tank, the aquarium-keeper may be sure that the water contains all the oxygen necessary for the welfare of his fish. In this way the Loach is useful as a gauger of the condition of the tank. Few deep aquaria, however, are so well balanced that Stone Loach within it will remain in perfect health. As these fish are generally found in shallow running water, it is reasonable to suppose that tanks of the least depth and the greatest area are the most suitable for them; and in an aquarium about 4in. deep, 18in. long, and 12in. wide, I have found them to live in perfect health, and apparently quite happily. I have never seen them come to the surface of the water in a tank so constructed. Such an aquarium as this can be made with hardly any expense in less than two hours, and filled with water as soon as completed; short directions for making it have already been given in Chapter II. A few rather large and flat stones should be placed upon the bottom of the aquaria in which Loach are kept, for on and under these the fish will frequently lie.

Loach are easy to catch. A short hunt among the stones of the stream in which these fish are found will soon drive a few from their lairs. When disturbed they swim only a short distance, then sink to the bottom and remain motionless there. After a fish has been "marked down," it may be snared with a horsehair tied to the end of a short stick, or filliped with the fingers, or driven by a splash, into a hand-net held just in front of it. The net should touch the bed of the stream, or the fish will very likely escape by getting under it. The natural food of the Loach is larvæ of insects, water-worms, and the like. In captivity it should be fed upon water-worms, small garden-worms, and tiny pieces of raw meat. This fish appears to discover the presence of its food by smell rather than by sight. In an aquarium made to suit its convenience, the Loach will soon become tame enough to feed from the fingers, and will as quickly prove itself to be a most interesting little fish. The flesh of the Stone Loach is highly esteemed as a great delicacy. The body of this fish is almost cylindrical in shape. The mouth is surrounded by six barbels. The colour of the back is a kind of olive-brown, which becomes lighter in shade on the sides. The whole fish is more or less covered with dark spots. The dorsal fin is placed over the ventral fin. The dorsal and tail fins are brownish and marked with little dark dots arranged in lines; the other fins are tinged with red. The tail fin is slightly concave. The Loach has the power of using its intestines as a supplementary means of respiration. The body is covered with mucus. This fish rarely exceeds 5in. in length.

The Spinous Loach (*Cobitis tœnia*) is not nearly so common as the Stone Loach, and is found where the water is muddy rather than clear. Of the two fish the former is perhaps the hardier. Both, however, should be treated in precisely the same way while kept in confinement. The colour of the Spinous Loach is a kind of orange-brown. On the sides there is a row of brown spots, somewhat similar to those often found upon the sides of the minnow. The barbels are short. There is a small spine below each eye: the fish is able to raise these spines at pleasure. This fish, in common with the Stone Loach and another loach (*Misgurnus fossilis*), has the power of using the intestines as supplementary breathing organs. The Spinous Loach does not exceed 4in. in length, and is not much esteemed as food.

The Golden Orfe (*Leuciscus orfus*) (Fig. 100) is a very beautiful and interesting little fish, and is in every way suitable for the aquarium. It originally came to this country, I think, from Austria. While in captivity it should be fed upon vermicelli and occasionally small garden-worms. A friend of mine has told me that he has more than once seen his Golden Orfe devour young minnows. My Orfe, though I never saw it take minnows, at first preferred worms to vermicelli, but it afterwards showed a decided preference for the latter. The Golden Orfe is a hardy and lively little fish, and very quick and graceful in its movements. The length of the head of this fish about equals the depth of its body. Its back and the upper part of its sides are orange in colour, which colour gradually becomes silvery as it nears the lateral line. The fins are white and slightly tinged with silver. The tail fin is rather deeply forked. The eyes are unusually full and beautiful. The head is small, and the snout blunt. This fish does not exceed 3lb. in weight. Small Golden Orfe can generally be bought in London for about 1s. 6d. each.

Fig. 106. Golden Orfe (Leuciscus orfus).

The Common Perch (*Perca fluviatilis*) (Fig. 101) is an extremely handsome fish and very suitable for the aquarium. It is hardy, and if properly cared for readily adapts itself to a life in confinement. The only drawbacks to the Perch as an inmate of the tank are its voracity and a proneness to devour its companions. These drawbacks, however, may be easily overcome in one of the following ways: (1) By only keeping very small fish of this species, considerably smaller than the rest of their comrades; (2) by keeping them in a separate aquarium; (3) by dividing off a portion of the tank for them by means of pieces of glass. This glass division is occasionally very useful if the aquarium is large. It is easily arranged and by no means unsightly. It is thus constructed: Two pieces of thin copper wire are

stretched tightly side by side across the top of that part
of the tank where the division is desired. If the aquarium
is made of slate, the wire is fastened to the iron bolts;
if of zinc, through tiny holes made in the framework; if
of wood, to four little screw-eyes placed in the cross-bars
Three or more pieces of glass about 3in. wide, the length
of which exactly equals the depth of the tank, are cut, and
one piece is placed between the cross-wires, pressed against
the side of the aquarium, and then sunk at the lower
end as deeply in the sand and gravel as possible. A short
piece of wire is now twisted tightly once round the two

FIG. 101. COMMON PERCH (PERCA FLUVIATILIS).

parallel pieces and then pushed quite close to the glass
just inserted. The remaining pieces of glass are fixed in
the same way until a partition has been made across the
tank. The twisted wires not only keep the portions of the
glass division firmly in their places, but the proper distances
apart—close enough together to prevent the passage between
them of small fish, and wide enough asunder to allow for
the free circulation of the water. A piece of perforated
zinc, cut the right size and fixed in the same manner, is
another method of making a partition; but it does not
look so neat as the glass, nor is it so good for the fish.
These divisions may be made when the tank is full of
water and stocked, care of course being taken that the

place chosen for the partition is free from plants or rockwork. None but large and rectangular aquaria should be thus divided.

The Perch is one of the most intelligent of all the fresh-water fishes, soon learning to know its owner and its feeding time. In a very little while it will become tame enough to take food from the fingers. It is, however, rather nervous and easily frightened while in captivity. Perch are found in most of the rivers, canals, and lakes of Great Britain ; it is somewhat rare in the North of Scotland. As these fish are bold biters, they are not by any means difficult to catch ; but unfortunately they are generally hooked in such a manner that it is often a very difficult matter to free them without seriously hurting them. The best way to procure Perch for the aquarium is to catch them with a hand-net, according to the directions given for taking roach ; for the young of the former as well as of the latter during the autumn ascend those streams which run into the rivers and canals where these fish are found, and retire into the weeds and under the banks. The fish thus caught will be of a suitable size and free from injury. The Thames is noted for its very beautiful Perch. Perch are able to live out of water almost as long as the tench and the carp. They can be carried a considerable distance by wrapping them up in wet grass or moss. As Perch swim in shoals, two or three should be kept together in the aquarium.

Perch deposit their eggs during the latter part of April and the beginning of May. The eggs are laid in strings or ribbons, which are sometimes 4ft. or 5ft. long. These strings of spawn are very interesting, the ova being placed closely side by side in what appears to be a kind of tube. At first sight it seems impossible that a fish the size of an ordinary Perch could contain such a string of eggs ; but a closer examination will show that what takes place in the case of the spawn of frogs and toads is repeated in that of the Perch. Each egg is surrounded by a membranous enve-lope, which absorbs a great quantity of water as soon as it is exuded from the fish. The ova are hatched in about ten days. Perch will spawn in a suitable aquarium, depositing their strings of eggs among the weeds and rock-work; and if the old fish are withdrawn from the tank, the fry can be easily reared. The little ones, of course, should be supplied with as much small aquatic animal life as possible. Perch usually begin to spawn when they are three years old. They are most prolific. Mr. Frank Buckland has said that he and his secretary counted 155,620 eggs in a fish which weighed 3lb. 2oz.; and 127,240 in another 2lb. 11oz. in weight; while Mr. Yarrell records that 280,000 ova were found in a fish weighing only half a pound.

When at liberty, Perch feed upon insects, worms, and fish; and in captivity they may be fed upon garden-worms, minnows, and pieces of meat. It is wise to get them to partake of the last as soon as possible. Perch ought not to be crowded in the aquarium, and care should be taken that the water in which they live does not rise much in tempera-ture. These fish are so handsome and interesting that it is quite worth the trouble and expense of providing a tank especially for them. A full-grown Perch does not often exceed 2lb. in weight.

The length of the head of this fish about equals the depth of its body. The back rises rather suddenly, giving a "high-shouldered" appearance, and the fleshy part of the tail as suddenly becomes very slender. There are two dorsal fins; the front one has fourteen bony rays, developed into sharp-pointed spines, and the back one (which is situ-ated almost directly over the anal fin) has soft rays. The colour of the back is greenish-brown, the sides are golden, and the under part of the body is white. Six broad dark green stripes run vertically down the sides. The lateral line is high up on the side, and follows the curve of the back. The ventral, anal, and tail fins, are bright scarlet; the posterior dorsal fin is greenish, slightly tinged with red. The tail fin is small, and slightly forked. The mouth is large, and the teeth small and pointed backwards.

Though a very handsome fish, the Pope or Ruffe (*Acerina cernua*) is not so easy to keep alive in confine-

ment as its near relative the common perch. The reason
of this may be that it is nearly always found in running
water, and hardly ever in stagnant. Ruffes are very often
caught while gudgeon are being fished for. They are bold
biters, but are seldom taken in such numbers as to make
it worth while to carry them home for food. The flesh
is, however, highly valued upon the Continent. The Ruffe
is really a very beautiful fish, and, when in good condition, his scales seem to glisten with all the colours of
the rainbow. Though he is so handsome, he has, however,
such an inexpressibly sad-looking face as almost to make
one miserable to look at him. While in captivity he
generally swims, with dorsal fin erect, close to the bottom
of the tank. He is a great eater, and must be supplied
with suitable food, or he will certainly die. When at liberty,
he feeds upon insects, worms, and the like; and in the
aquarium he ought to be fed upon the same until he can
be induced to take raw meat. All the carnivorous inhabitants of the tank should be fed, where possible, upon
meat instead of living animals; for continually feeding
one's captives upon live minnows, tadpoles, worms, and the
like, must tend to make one callous to the feelings and
fears of one's fellow-creatures; though I think the sufferings
of the minnow when seized by a pike, or the pains of a
tadpole while in the clutches of the pupa of a dragon-fly,
are extremely slight, for not only are they cold-blooded,
but it is mercifully ordained—I believe—that all animals
more or less lose all sensation when being preyed upon.
Dr. Livingstone has recorded that when under the paws
of a lion he was unconscious of either fear or pain. The
Ruffe should not be kept with fish smaller than himself,
or very likely he will devour some of his companions;
neither should he be placed in an aquarium where there is
even the slightest approach to crowding of its occupants, or
he will be one of the first to die. The chief differences
between the perch and the Ruffe are that in the case of
the former, the dorsal fin is divided into two fins, the one
with spines, the other without: while in the case of the

latter the two fins are joined into one; the Ruffe, too, is
without the vertical bands of the perch, and the perch is
without the spots on the dorsal fin of the Ruffe. The
general appearance of the Ruffe certainly seems to justify
the erroneous idea that it is a cross between the gudgeon
and the perch. It is said to have received its name from
the want of smoothness of its scales. This fish does not
often exceed 5in. in length. It spawns during March and
May among the weeds of streams and small rivers.

The Black Bass (*Grystes nigricans*) is now acclimatised
in Britain, owing to the efforts and enterprise of certain
noblemen and gentlemen, but especially of the Marquis of
Exeter. The Black Bass is common in the lakes and rivers
of Canada and the United States, where it affords excellent sport to the fisherman. It is a bold biter, full of
fight, and very good for table purposes; the flesh, it is
said, tasting very much like that of the whiting. No
fresh-water fish that we have in this country, with the
exception of the salmon, is capable of providing more
amusement for the angler than the Black Bass. It will
take minnows, flies, or worms; and as it grows sometimes
so large as to weigh 7lb. or 8lb. it generally affords no
small amount of excitement and requires not a little skill
to land it safely. The Black Bass, I find, makes an excellent fish for the aquarium; for it is handsome, hardy,
intelligent, and easily tamed. Of course, owing to its
predaceous habits, it must not be kept in a tank among
small defenceless fish, or the aquarium-keeper will find
them gradually disappear. I keep my Black Bass in a
divided part of a tank which is 2ft. wide, 2ft. 11in. long,
and 1ft. deep, his separate compartment being 11in. wide,
and running the whole breadth of the tank. The division is
of glass, and made according to directions given on page 136.
The Bass has for companions two English perch (*Perca
fluviatilis*) nearly its own size. The three perch (for the Bass
is a perch) agree very well together. I notice, however, that
the English fish do not venture to dispute with him the
possession of a minnow or worm. The Black Bass does not

make a sudden dash at its prey, like the pike, but hunts it down with persistence, as a greyhound does a hare.

Black Bass spawn about May and June, and prepare for the reception of their ova a kind of nest, which they scoop out in the gravel or mud at the bottom of the water in which they live. The parent fish protect the eggs and fry, and accompany their little ones for some time after they are able to leave the nest. I see no reason why Black Bass should not be induced to breed in a large aquarium; in fact, they may have already done so.

Like the carp and the tench, the Bass retires during winter to the bottom of the pond, lake, or river in which it lives. The Black Bass while in confinement should as soon as possible be encouraged to eat pieces of raw meat. One of these fish about 6in. long will devour several small minnows a day. A specimen of mine has taken five within a few hours.

The length of the head of the Black Bass about equals the depth of its body. It is not so "hog-backed" as the English perch. The mouth is rather large and cruel-looking, and the under-jaw projects a little beyond the upper. The front dorsal fin has nine spines, the tallest of which is in the middle, the others gradually decreasing in height towards each end. The back dorsal fin, which is the taller of the two, is joined to the front one in a way which is somewhat similar to the junction of those of the ruffe (*Acerina cernua*). The spines are very sharp, and blackened near their points. They are not so often carried erect as are those of the common perch (*Perca fluviatilis*). The back dorsal fin is nearly always erect and vibrating. All the fins are large in proportion to the size of the fish, and are continually in motion, especially the pectoral fins. The tail fin is large, powerful, slightly forked, and black along its edges. All the fins are dusky at their bases, becoming of a light greenish tinge towards their extremities. The anal fin has a sharp spine. The general colour of the fish is a dark olive-green. Sometimes the body is marked with black spots or blotches. The sides of the head are a dusky

kind of white, on which are two broad reddish stripes
running parallel with the mouth. The scales are small.

The River Bullhead, or Miller's Thumb (*Cottus gobio*)
(Fig. 102), is a very interesting little fish, and will live well
in an aquarium. It may be caught in the same places and in
the same way as the loach. After turning over a few of the
rather large and flat stones of those streams in which Miller's
Thumbs are known to exist, one or two will be almost certainly

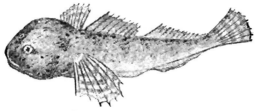

FIG. 102. BULLHEAD (COTTUS GOBIO).

discovered. Upon the removal of the stone, the cunning little
fish will remain perfectly motionless, trusting, no doubt, to
its chameleon-like power of assuming the shade of the gravel
upon which it is resting. Now is the opportunity of the
aquarium-keeper, for, if he be quick, he can either catch the
Bullhead in both of his hands, or he can throw it with one
hand into a net held in front of the fish with the other. If
the Bullhead is allowed to escape it will dart away with such
quickness to some other retreat that it will be almost impossible to follow it with the eye, especially when the water has
been disturbed by the ineffectual attempt to throw it into the
net. It is wiser, therefore, to hunt for another fish rather
than waste time in looking for the one that has just evaded
capture.

The Bullhead will live more happily in a shallow aquarium
than in a deep one. It is a great eater, and when at liberty
feeds upon the larvæ of insects, worms, and the fry of fish.
In confinement it will be satisfied with small garden-worms
or pieces of meat, and will soon learn to take its food
from its owner's fingers. The Bullhead is a plucky little
fish. I once witnessed an interesting struggle between

one and a young axolotl. I had given the latter its morning
worm, which it immediately began to swallow, beginning
at one end, when a Bullhead darted from its retreat under
a stone, and seized the other end of the worm. This action
on the part of the fish commenced a furious struggle between
it and the axolotl. As the reptile was the stronger of the
two, the fish was literally tossed about in all directions, sometimes to the right side of its opponent, sometimes to the left,
and sometimes it was turned completely upside down; nevertheless, the plucky little fish continued to hold on until the
worm of contention parted in the middle, and each combatant
got a portion of the prey. The fight between the batrachian
and the fish seemed to last for quite half a minute.

Miller's Thumbs are said to guard their ova and their little
ones, but I have never been able to witness this evidence of
parental care on the part of these fish. Perhaps they might
be induced to breed in a suitable aquarium, since they so soon
become quite tame.

The Bullhead has a flat and broad head and a wide mouth.
The body (seen from above) is very wedge-like in shape.
There are two dorsal fins: the front one is short and something like the front dorsal fin of the perch; the back one
is very long, and extends quite close to the base of the
caudal fin. The pectoral fins are large and powerful in
proportion to the size of the fish. The anal fin is also very
long, and is just under the long dorsal fin. The ventral fins
are rather small in comparison to the other fins, and upon
them the fish often raises itself from the bed of the stream
or aquarium. The tail fin is slightly convex. The eyes are
rather close together on the top of the head, have golden
irides, and are very bright. The colour of the fish varies,
but it is generally of a yellowish-brown, blotched and spotted
with black. The under-part of the body is nearly white.
There is a small spine on each side of the head.

The Three-spined Stickleback (*Gasterosteus aculeatus*) (Fig.
103), though very beautiful and interesting, ought never to
be confined in the same aquarium with any other fish: even
in a very large tank it will be a great nuisance. But if it

be placed in a suitable and separate vessel during early spring, it will afford much amusement, interest, and instruction. The male fish will have then put on his strikingly beautiful courting dress, the colours of which almost equal in variety and brilliancy those of the rainbow. He is, especially when excited during a fight with a rival, or elated over a victory, a most lovely little fellow—his colouring under such circumstances becoming brighter and more iridescent than ever. Sticklebacks may be caught in most of the ponds, ditches, and slow-running streams of this country; and they can be readily taken according to the directions already given for capturing newts (p. 100).

If it be wished that the Sticklebacks should build their nests in confinement, they should be caught during the latter part

FIG. 103. THREE-SPINED STICKLEBACK (GASTEROSTEUS ACULEATUS).

of April, and placed in an aquarium which is well stocked with growing plants and which contains a great quantity of minute animal life, such as water-fleas and cyclops. These insects will serve as food for the young Sticklebacks. Of course, no other fish but Sticklebacks should be placed in the tank. Should there, however, be other piscine occupants of the aquarium, they would be almost certain to lead a short and unmerry life. If the tank which is to be set apart for these nest-building little fish be of a fair size, two males and about eight females may be introduced. The former during the courting season are distinguished by their crimson breasts and emerald-green eyes. Almost immediately after entering their new home, each little male will choose for himself a corner or some other part of the aquarium. They will then, though at the same time guarding the chosen spots with the greatest courage

L

and alacrity, hunt for suitable materials for the construction of their nests. These materials consist of small vegetable fibres and other substances of the like kind. The nests, when completed, vary somewhat in shape, but they may be described as rather like a hedge-sparrow's nest, having a top and a hole in the side for a door. They have also been occasionally likened to a flattened hay-cock, a tiny barrel, or a lady's muff. They are generally about 1¼in. in length. The building materials are kept together by a kind of mucus or cement, which comes from the fish as they draw their bodies over and about the nest. Sometimes if the fibres and other substances are not heavy enough to keep in their proper positions until the cementing operation is completed, the clever little nest-builders will weight them down with sand or minute particles of gravel, which they will collect in and discharge from their mouths. Such are the energy and skill of the little fish that the nests are frequently finished within a few hours. Immediately they are completed, the fish set out in search of wives. And should these gaily-coloured courtiers meet one another while on this errand there is sure to be a fight, especially if they happen to make up their minds to pay their respects to the same lady Stickleback. As they quickly make preparations for the encounter their colours grow more brilliant than ever, while the coveted little female retires demurely to one side and becomes a silent, though not an uninterested, witness of the battle. The fish charge furiously at one another, and then, if no great harm has been done, continue to swim round and round, trying to bite with their strong mouths or to pierce each other with their sharp lateral or dorsal spines. So the fight goes on until one is obliged to give in. The poor defeated fish—one feels so sorry for him—loses at once his gallant bearing, and swims away with quickly-fading colours, while the conqueror becomes, if possible, more gorgeous than ever as he claims the gentle spectator of the fray as his lawful prize. With all the address of which he is capable he persuades her to inspect the little nest which he has built. He then pressingly invites her to enter the door, in order that she may lay her eggs within. In a few minutes the eggs are laid, and the fish, instead of backing out by the way she entered, makes for herself a door in the opposite side of the nest. The eggs just deposited, only a few in number, are of a yellowish-pink colour and about the size of a German rape-seed. A slight current of water now sets in between the two doors of the nest, which is of great benefit to the ova inside. The fickle little male, after entering the nest himself, at once discards his bride, and in a few hours sets out to find and win another. In this way the nest is visited by several female Sticklebacks until the necessary number of eggs has been laid. The male now becomes more vigilant than ever, and jealously guards the nest and spawn, furiously attacking any other inhabitant of the tank that may venture too near. The little fish spends the greater portion of his time in re-arranging the eggs, and in fanning them with his fins as he balances himself obliquely before a door of the nest. After a short time the young fish may be seen moving slightly within the eggs—that is, supposing they are closely examined—and in about a month (according to the temperature of the water) from the day they are deposited the fry are hatched. At first they are so small and transparent that it is not an easy matter to see them. With the appearance of his offspring the male Stickleback's cares seem to increase, and though he worked so hard during the incubation of the ova, he has to work much harder now; for not only has he to guard his little ones from the attacks of his discarded wives and other fish, but he has carefully to confine them entirely to the nest. Should they, however, elude his vigilance for a moment and escape from the nursery they are either quickly driven back or are seized in their protector's mouth and forcibly returned. Old Sticklebacks are exceedingly fond of Stickleback fry, and should the father of the little ones die or be taken away, every other Stickleback in the aquarium will immediately act the part of cannibals, and much enjoy the acting.

The eggs of Sticklebacks are very large in proportion to the size of the fish which lay them; and in comparison with the quantities of eggs deposited by many other fish they are very few in number. As the eggs are so large, so plainly seen, and such tempting food to fish generally and even to

the Sticklebacks themselves, they must be protected in some
way or other. For this purpose therefore the male Sticklebacks are instinctively taught to build nests and to guard
their eggs and little ones to the utmost of their powers.
Indeed so great is the strain of the building, the necessary
fighting, the incubation of the ova, and the nursing of the
fry, that the plucky little fellows often leave off living at the
end of their labours. In no circumstances can the Stickleback be described as a long-lived fish: he rarely attains a
greater age than three years—oftener it is much less, especially
in an aquarium.

In a state of nature these fish are exceedingly destructive
to the fry of other fish. For instance, it has been recorded
(I believe, by Dr. Günther) that one of these Sticklebacks,
while in a tank, devoured seventy-four young dace, each about
¼in. long, in five hours. Two days afterwards the same
little glutton ate sixty-two more, and then seemed quite ready
to continue his feast. During this huge gastronomic feat this
Stickleback was under close observation.

The Stickleback in a natural state feeds upon small aquatic
insects, water-worms, eggs and fry of fish. In captivity he may be
fed upon tiny portions of worm and pieces of meat. (Before
worms are cut up they should be killed by dashing them down
upon the ground or pavement. Their death then must be
quite painless.) Sticklebacks soon become very tame, and are
nearly always bold enough to charge one's finger or one's
pencil if placed too near the jealously-guarded nest. They
are intelligent and amusing little fish, but I venture to repeat
they should not be kept in confinement unless they can be
provided with an aquarium entirely to themselves. In any
other circumstances they will be a source of annoyance and loss
to their owner and of great discomfort and even misery to
their companions.

The Stickleback has three strong and sharp spines on the
middle of his back in place of the usual dorsal fin. There is
a fin behind the spines. The body is rather long and compressed; it is without scales, but is more or less protected on
the sides by small plates. The ventral fins have one strong

spine each, but no other rays. The anal fin is opposite the dorsal fin, and is about the same shape and size. The caudal fin is slightly convex. The male fish lose their brilliant colours when the breeding season is over. The general colour of Sticklebacks varies greatly according to the condition of the water in which they live. I have found specimens of them almost black. The Three-spined Stickleback is from 2in. to 3in. long.

The Ten-spined Stickleback, or Nine-spined Stickleback (*Gasterosteus pungitius*) (Fig. 104) is one of the smallest of British fishes, hardly ever exceeding 2in. in length. It is often found in brackish water, and will live in either a fresh or a salt-water aquarium. This fish also builds a nest, but affixes it to aquatic plants rather than building it upon the gravel

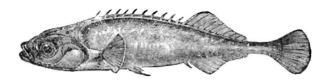

FIG. 104. TEN-SPINED STICKLEBACK (GASTEROSTEUS PUNGITIUS).

at the bottom of the water. The nest in shape is very like a barrel, and is about 1in. long. The male fish during the breeding season, instead of becoming crimson, golden, and green, assumes a "velvety-black." The habits and character of the Nine-spined Stickleback are very like those of the Three-spined. The fish has nine spines in front of the dorsal fin: I have never found one with ten spines. The spines are small and fine. It is not so stoutly built as the Three-spined Stickleback, nor is its body protected by plates, but is quite smooth. The fleshy part of the tail is very slender. The ventral fins each consist of one bony spine and no other rays. The caudal fin is slightly convex.

The Common or Yellow Trout (*Salmo fario*) is a very beautiful and popular fish, and one that will live in an aquarium. The tank in which it is kept should be of rather large dimensions, and ought to present a great surface of water in proportion to its size; it must also contain a quantity of growing aquatic plants. But Trout, however well they may be cared for, and however suitably the aquarium in which they are confined may be constructed, will lose a great deal of the beauty and brilliancy of their colouring. There are, perhaps, no fish whose colouring and form are influenced so much by food and locality as Trout. For instance, it has been said that "the Trout of Lynn Ogwin, almost the whole bottom of which is formed of grass, have, when first caught, a brilliant emerald gloss over their golden and yellow tints." And if the bottom of the water in which Trout live is black, the fish will be very dark. Sometimes, when the same lake or river varies in character as to the bottom soil, the Trout taken from the same water, but from different parts of it, will also vary in colour. That it does not take long for a Trout to change the shading of his colouring, may be easily proved by placing a captured fish for a few minutes only in a large white basin of water, and he will be seen to grow pale under the influence of the colour with which he is surrounded. However, I believe that any fish will alter the shading of its colours under similar circumstances. I can remember my astonishment when I first saw an instance of this chameleon-like power on the part of fish. A good many years ago I had asked a Thames professional fisherman to net me some gudgeon for an aquarium. A day or two after I had made the request he brought me the gudgeon, but more than my tank could conveniently hold. However, not wishing to send them back, in case some of those which I had retained for the aquarium should die, I placed the surplus fish (for the time being) in a large sponge bath. There they remained for more than a week, and at the end of that time they had become almost white. Since then I have often had occasion to keep fish temporarily in a bath (not half a bad receptacle for them), and have not failed to notice the great influence which the white interior has had upon the colouring of the different species of fish—a black bass, for instance, becoming in a day or two anything but a black bass in appearance.

Though a Trout will live fairly well in the stagnant water of a well-formed, well-arranged, and well-cared-for aquarium, it will of course live better in a tank which has the advantage of a continually-flowing fountain. Care must be taken, however, that the water which comes from the fountain is of a suitable character: otherwise it would be wiser to have no fountain at all.

The natural food of the Trout is larvæ of insects, aquatic insects, flies, fresh-water shrimps, young snails, worms, minnows, ova and fry of fish. It has been often seen to eat its own ova soon after it has deposited them. In confinement it may be fed upon minnows, worms, many kinds of aquatic insects, flies, and especially fresh-water shrimps. These last form one of the very best foods, making the flesh of the fish of the much-desired pink colour; they may be bred for it according to directions which will be given in another chapter. The quantity of minnows which a tame Trout (about 7in. long) of mine ate was surprising.

Trout 3in. to 5in. in length are of a suitable size for the aquarium. Fish of such dimensions may be readily obtained from dealers.

Trout fed upon suitable food will grow from 1lb. to 10lb. in weight within four or five years. As the Trout is so subject, owing to locality and food, to considerable variety of both form and colour, it is somewhat difficult to describe. However, as a rule, it may be said that its body is rather long and compressed at the sides, its head thick, its muzzle wide and blunt, and its eyes large. The upper part of its body is of an olive-green colour, the sides are lighter in shade. The under-part is often of a yellowish-white. Its back and sides are nearly always (more or less) beautifully spotted with red. There are two dorsal fins, which are far apart; the first has soft rays, and the second, which is much smaller, is without rays, and adipose. The front dorsal and caudal fins are spotted with black. The other fins are yellowish and edged with black.

Charr (*Salmo alpinus*) are nearly always found in the deepest part of large lakes, excepting during the breeding

season, when they ascend the rivers and streams to spawn.
Some of the Charr spawn during February, others during
autumn.   Many years ago, while going down one of the
London streets, I saw in an aquarium-dealer's shop some very
beautiful little fish in a large tank. On stopping and asking
what they were I was told that they were Charr. As the
fish were new to me I bought two of them. When I got
home I put them in a large and rather deep tank, which was
well stocked with growing weeds, and there they lived quite
healthily, and apparently perfectly happily, for nearly two
years. At the end of this time I changed my house, and
during the trouble and inconvenience of moving, the Charr
and other fish were placed, rather early on the day of
" flitting," in a large disused aquarium which had been carried
into the garden of the new house. Late in the evening I
went with a lantern to catch the fish and put them in a tank
inside, but in my hurry and in the darkness I caught all the
fish but the Charr. When next I saw them they were frozen
up in a mass of ice. These were the only Charr I ever kept
in confinement, and they might, I think, have lived for years
but for my carelessness. During the time I had them they
fed upon the eggs and fry of water-snails, small aquatic
insects, and occasionally vermicelli. They were always very
lively and active.

Charr, like trout, vary in form and colour with the locality.
It has been said that in some lakes they are nearly as round
as eels, while in others they are as flat as herrings. The chief
difference between the Charr and the trout is that the under-
part of the body of the former, during the breeding season,
acquires an orange or bright red tinge; and that on the
central bone in the roof of the mouth of the Charr, called the
vomer or vomerine bone, there are only a few teeth, while
the trout has two complete rows. The Charr has reached
2lb. in weight, but generally it is not more than from ¼lb.
to ½lb.

There have been more extraordinary stories told concerning
the Pike (*Esox lucius*) (Fig. 105) than any other fish; and anyone who would believe them all must possess a power of

"taking in," as the schoolboy would say, equal to that of the fresh-water shark himself.

Small Pike or Pickerel can easily be kept in an aquarium, but of course it is almost unnecessary to say that they should have no companions. Even two Pike, especially if one were much bigger than the other, would not be safe together. I have seen it seriously stated that Pike will not touch tench, perch. or gold-fish. And the reasons given for the Pike's very unusual reluctance to dine upon his fellow-fish are, that he is never ungrateful enough to forget that the tench is the curer of all the ills the piscine tribe is heir to; that he dare not attempt to swallow the perch and his formidable "fixed bayonets"; and that the gold-fish is quite safe because of his colour. But I

FIG. 105. PIKE (ESOX LUCIUS).

am quite sure that if a hungry Pike had these three fish for his companions in an aquarium, it would not be very long before he and his friends became so closely acquainted as to arrive at a state of perfect unity. Most fishermen know quite well that the Pike is often ready to take both perch and tench; and as for the gold-fish, there can be for Pike no more deadly bait. There are, however, circumstances in which, with care, Pike may be allowed companions while in confinement. The circumstances are these: If when a young Pike is first caught he is placed in an aquarium with other small fish also just caught, he seems to look upon them as companions of his misfortune, and will not touch them, at any rate for some days. Directly he begins to get very hungry a strange fish should be placed in the tank, and he will, if the owner will stand far back, most likely immediately pick this one out from the rest and devour it. If this manner of feeding is carefully continued, never allowing the Pike to become very hungry, his companions will be safe. I have thus kept a Pike among several young roach and perch. A friend of mine tells me that he has seen in the aquarium at Kensington a Pike living peaceably among young roach, and only feeding upon those small fish which are specially introduced for his food.

The Pike soon becomes very tame, and will learn to know the tank in which his food is kept and the net with which it is caught. Directly the net is taken in his owner's hands a curious hungry gleam is seen in his eye, but he himself remains almost motionless. It is very interesting to watch this gleam appear as the fish's master takes the net, and to see it as quickly disappear if he should put it down unused. The Pike will not be very long in confinement before he will allow himself to be touched with a pencil or even a finger.

Pike, as everyone knows, are tremendous eaters. They are well described as omnivorous, for they will—some of them—take anything, e.g., the hand of a boy when bathing, a mule's nose, or a swan's head. Mr. Jesse is reported to have said that eight Pike, about 5lb. each, in three weeks consumed 800 gudgeon. A clerical friend of mine told me that on one occasion when he arrived at some water where he was going to fish for Pike, he found one jumping about upon the bank. He immediately secured it, and when he examined it he found that it weighed 17lb., and that it contained within its stomach a water-vole and a moorhen. The fish is supposed to have jumped upon the bank while capturing the bird, and had not time to get back again to the water before he was caught.

The growth of Pike, of course, greatly depends upon the amount and quality of the food they are able to obtain. Mr. Cholmondeley Pennell, in the "Badminton Library," quotes a letter, published in the *Field*, in which it is said that "Mr. Kinsey, of Melbourne (Derbyshire), put a Pike into a well when a few inches long. Food was given to it for several years, but it grew very slowly, and at last reached 3lb. It lived fourteen years, and latterly became very tame—so much so as to take food from the hand." Another Pike kept in confinement in the Zoological Gardens, Regent's Park, is said to have only increased 1½lb. in ten years. On the other hand, where Pike have been better fed, they have been known to increase in weight as much as 4lb. every year until they arrive at maturity, when they generally begin to get lighter.

Pike commence to spawn when about three years old, and deposit their ova during March and May among the aquatic plants growing in those streams and ditches which they are able to ascend. During the breeding season these fish are generally seen in pairs. The young are hatched in about a month. The late Mr. Frank Buckland found in a fish which weighed 32lb., and which measured 3ft. 8in. in length, no less than 595,200 eggs.

When at liberty Pike will feed upon almost anything which they find alive in the water, providing that it is not altogether too big. They will not, however, swallow a toad. Sometimes they will take fish nearly as large as themselves, devouring as much of their prey at one meal as they can, and trusting to their great powers of digestion to be able to finish it at another; their mouths, for the time, being turned into larders. The principal food of Pike, however, is frogs and fish of all kinds. In captivity these fish may be fed upon minnows and lob-worms. I have never been able to induce any of my tame Pike to eat dead fish or raw meat.

Pike, small enough for the aquarium, may be caught either in a net, or by fishing for them with a large worm placed upon a single hook. Pike can be separated from other fish in the same aquarium by means of the glass division already recommended for perch (pp. 136-7) and black bass.

The "Water-wolf," as this fish is well called, is really very handsome. It has a long and rather compressed body, uniform in depth from just behind the eyes to the commencement of the dorsal fin, when it suddenly becomes much narrower. The scales are small, and the lateral line is not very distinct. The dorsal fin is placed very far back. and just over the anal fin. The caudal fin is broad, strong, and rather deeply forked; the pectoral and the ventral fins are small. The head is broad, long, and depressed. The jaws are capable of great distension; the upper one being "duck-billed," and the lower projecting. The mouth contains numerous strong and very sharp teeth, all pointing backwards. The colour of the head and back is olive-brown. The sides are lighter in shade, and are beautifully mottled with green and yellow. The under-part of the body is silvery-white. The dorsal, caudal, and anal fins are dark brown, the pectoral and ventral fins being of a lighter brown. The former three fins are blotched and spotted with dark green. Trout and Pike are subject to a parasite (*Argulus foliaceus*).

There are few fish, with the exception, perhaps, of the lampern, which will give less trouble in an aquarium than the Sharp-nosed or Common Eel (*Anguilla vulgaris*) (Fig. 106). Its movements when swimming are exceedingly graceful, and its wants are few and supplied without difficulty. The only drawbacks to its presence in an ordinarily-arranged tank are its readiness to devour, if it

FIG. 106. SHARP-NOSED EEL (ANGUILLA VULGARIS).

be of any size, very small fish, and a disposition to disarrange a little of the sand and gravel at the bottom of the water.

The Eel should be procured when very small—about 5in. long is a suitable size for an aquarium. Eels of so short a length, however, are not often taken with a hook, and, besides, an Eel caught in this way is likely to be more or less injured. I have often caught Elvers (as young Eels are called) by passing, during autumn, a hand-net along the weedy edges of slowly-running streams. Not seldom at the same haul have I secured along with Elvers, fry of perch and roach.

In the autumn, adult Eels migrate towards the mouths of those rivers in which they live. During this migration they are supposed to spawn: very little, however, is known of their spawning. Not only do Eels migrate towards the mouths of rivers, but also from one piece of water to another. They are able to take these overland journeys by reason of their well-known power of living, without ill-effect to themselves, for a long time out of water, and because, owing to their snake-like form, they can travel at a considerable pace along dew-covered grass. Some time ago I saw an Eel, about 18in. long, which had been dug up by a man who was making a surface-drain across a field. It was not found in water, but in moist clay. It was very lively. The nearest stream was about 50yds. away from the spot where it was discovered.

Eels are very fond of burying all their bodies, with the exception of their heads, in the soft mud at the bottom of the water. They have been known to live twenty or thirty years in an aquarium, and they soon become tame enough to take food from the fingers. During winter, especially if their tank is in a cold room, they are very likely to pass a great portion of their time in a state of torpidity—at any rate, they will take hardly any food; but when the weather becomes warm they will make up for lost time by becoming rather greedy, readily devouring worms, and if the Eels are of any size, small minnows, roach, and the like. If well fed they grow quickly.

An Eel is exceedingly interesting in many ways. For instance, there is the remarkable contrivance by which it is enabled to keep its gills moist during the time it is out of water. Each gill is inclosed in a kind of pouch or bag, and within these bags or pouches the fish can retain water for the purpose of moistening its gills during its overland journeyings. Then, again, as the fish often live under stones, mud, and sand, its eyes must be protected in some way, so it is provided with an arrangement which may be likened to a pair of spectacles; and again, some people are said to carry their hearts in their pockets, but an Eel carries one in its tail, called a lymphatic heart, the pulsation of which may be seen under a microscope. Eels can be killed by striking them upon their tails. As they are able to ascend perpendicular surfaces, the aquarium in which they are confined should be securely covered.

The Eel in shape is very like a snake. The scales are small
and embedded in the skin. It has no ventral fins, but it
possesses pectorals. The dorsal, caudal, and anal fins are
joined together, the dorsal one commencing some distance
behind the pectorals. The eyes are beautiful. The body is
very slimy, and beneath
varies in colour from
silvery-white to golden.

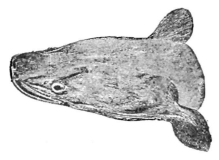

FIG. 107. BROAD-NOSED EEL
(ANGUILLA LATIROSTRIS).

The Broad-nosed Eel
(*Anguilla latirostris*)
(Fig. 107) is almost as
common as his Sharp-
nosed relative. It is distinguished from the
latter by its broad head,
blunt nose, thick skin,
and its proportionately
thicker and slimier body.

The Snig Eel (*Anguilla mediorostris*) (Fig. 108) is said to
be common in Hampshire. Its nose is neither blunt nor
sharp. It does not grow so heavy as the common Eel, but
it is described as being very
delicious eating. Unlike its
relatives, it feeds during
the day. All Eels, however,
are occasionally day-feeders,
but the Snig Eel is espe-
cially so. The three dif-
ferent species of Eel should
be treated alike in the
aquarium.

FIG. 108. SNIG EEL
(ANGUILLA MEDIOROSTRIS).

The Lampern, or River Lamprey (*Petromyzon fluviatilis*)
(Fig. 109), is a curious little fish, though by no means
beautiful, and has much attraction for the aquarium-keeper,
for it has a very remarkable structure, it gives no trouble,
and is very graceful while in motion. The Lampern is found
in many of the rivers and streams of England, especially in
the Severn, Trent, and Thames. When the water is quite clear

these fish can often be seen clinging in masses with their leech-like mouths to stones, while the rest of their bodies waves up and down with the current. The Lamprey is shaped somewhat similar to an eel, being round for about two-thirds the length of its body, when it gradually flattens towards the tail.

The mouth of this fish is very curious, and something like that of a leech; when open it has been well described as "circular and terminal, so that the fish appears as if the head had been cut off." The lips are fleshy. This mouth, and these lips, and a piston-like tongue, form a kind of powerful sucker, by which the fish is able to cling firmly to stones, rocks, and the like. On each side of the head there are seven openings in a horizontal line which lead to an equal number of bronchial cells or gills. When the fish is not

FIG. 109. LAMPERN, OR RIVER LAMPREY (PETROMYZON FLUVIATILIS).

clinging to anything with its mouth, water passes through the mouth to the gills; but when the Lampern is adhering to a stone, the water, being unable to enter by the mouth, passes to the gills through these openings in each side of the head. There is a small aperture or hole in the middle of the back of the head just in front of the eyes: this is a nostril, and water does not pass through it (as some writers say) to the gills when the mouth is fixed to any foreign body. Such a passage of water is impossible, as there is no direct communication between the nostril and the gills. The mouth is well provided with teeth. There are neither pectoral nor ventral fins: there are caudal and dorsal fins of a certain kind, but as they have no rays proper they can hardly be called true fins. The Lampern swims with a lateral undulatory motion. Where the streams are very rapid, it frequently rests by anchoring itself with its mouth to a stone. When

wishing to spawn, this fish scoops a shallow hole at the
bottom of the water, about 15in. or 16in. in diameter, for
the reception of its eggs. The Lamprey removes the stones
by fixing itself to them by the help of its suctorial mouth,
and then swimming backwards down the stream, drops them
at some distance from the spot that has been chosen for
the ova.

It has been said that the Lampern feeds not only upon
dead fish, but also upon living ones : the latter, it is recorded,
have frequently been caught showing the marking of the
rasping of the Lampern's teeth. However, none of the
Lampreys which I have from time to time kept in aquaria
have attacked any of the fish which were confined with them—
at least, so far as I know. Indeed, I have found that "Seven
Eyes," as he is sometimes called, is very peaceful, spending
most of his time under the sand and gravel. He generally
chooses the same spot as his lair, and when he is wanted
he can be roused by a gentle probing with a stick. He
often attaches his suctorial mouth to the glass sides of the
aquarium, thus forming a very interesting object. As he
can easily climb by the help of his mouth, the tank in
which he is confined must be covered. The natural food of
the Lampern is said to be aquatic insects, worms, and dead
and live fish.

The fresh-water Lamprey is from 6in. to 10in. in length,
and is of a dark olive-brown on the upper part of its body
and silvery beneath. This fish can be caught in a hand-net
when seen in masses, as already described, or when making
its way alone up the stream. I have also taken it by passing
the hand-net along the overhanging sides of the stream or
river.

There are some very beautiful little fish called Paradise Fish
(*Polyacanthus viridi-auratus*) (Fig. 110), which are in every way
suitable for the aquarium. They were taken from a brook near
Canton, China, and brought to France by M. Simon, who was
French consul at Ningpo. These fish, up to the time of their
introduction into Europe in 1869, were said to be unknown to
naturalists. M. Simon placed them in charge of M. Carbonnier.

under whose care they soon began to spawn. After the spawning, the male fish ejected bubbles from his mouth which did not break when on the surface of the water. He then, much to M. Carbonnier's astonishment, began to swallow the eggs, which he afterwards discharged under the shelter of the bubbles. The female fish was then driven by the male from the neighbourhood of the bubbles and ova, over which the latter fish kept a vigilant watch. In about three days the young fish were hatched, and soon began to feed upon

FIG. 110. MALE AND FEMALE PARADISE FISH (POLYACANTHUS VIRIDI-AURATUS),
(*From a Photograph by the Author.*)

cyclops, water-fleas, and the like. The Paradise Fish will breed more than once in the year if the water is kept of a suitable temperature. Mr. Frank Buckland, who had a pair of these fish given to him, declared that they were certainly the most beautiful little fish he ever saw. The scales glisten with all the colours of the rainbow. Their fins are most extraordinary: the dorsal fin extends from near the back of the head quite to the caudal fin (Fig. 110); the anal fin is as long as the dorsal. Both fins have bony rays, which gradually increase in height from the commencement of the fin, the last

M

ray in each fin extending to the extremities of the caudal fin. The caudal fin is large and forked, and also consists of bony rays; these rays have sharp points. The ventral fins each have a few short bony rays and one exceedingly long and apparently strong ray. The pectoral fins have soft rays; the male fish, when making love to the female, spreads out his extraordinary fins, often in doing so bending himself almost into a circle. While in confinement these fish should be kept rather warm and fed upon small aquatic insects. Their aquarium ought to be well stocked with water-plants.

Since the above remarks in regard to the Paradise Fish were written, this beautiful little creature has become much more plentiful. Of all fish it is, perhaps, most suited to a life in confinement. It is a domesticated variety of the genus *Polyacanthus,* and came originally from China and Cochin-China. When properly and regularly fed and kept in water of a suitable temperature it will live for a long time, and prove itself to be a very hardy little fish. The temperature of the water in which it lives should never be allowed to fall below 50deg. Fahr., and during the breeding season it must be higher than 80deg. and lower than 90deg. It is wise, therefore, to keep it as nearly as possible 85deg. This is an important matter.

Fig. 111 shows a simple and inexpensive contrivance for keeping Paradise Fish in water of the right temperature. A represents an ordinary all-glass aquarium (a common propagating glass). Though it is generally prudent to avoid an aquarium of this kind, it nevertheless forms a very suitable abode for the Paradise Fish, for not only does this fish assume its most beautiful colours under the influence of light, but in such a receptacle its great beauty can be more easily seen. B is an ordinary metal beetle-trap filled with water, and always kept full. C is a strong tin canister in which a small paraffin lamp is kept constantly burning. D is a sixpenny lamp which will burn for twenty-four hours at least; it needs neither chimney nor globe. B and C can be hidden by means of plants or in some other simple way.

I have sometimes kept these fish in a large enamelled bowl placed directly on the top of the canister. The fish in such circumstances do **excellently**; but they cannot so well be seen as in the inverted propagating glass.

Of course, there are many other ways by which the water in which these fish live can be kept warm: *e.g.*, a metal receptacle capable of containing water might be made to receive the propagating glass as far as that part where the sides begin to become **vertical, and** raised sufficiently high to receive a small lamp

FIG. 111. AN INEXPENSIVE CONTRIVANCE FOR KEEPING PARADISE FISH IN WATER OF A SUITABLE TEMPERATURE.

beneath; or a metal tank could be made, having either one or two glass sides, and this could be placed directly on the canister (Fig. 111). However, the least costly contrivance with suitability is represented by Fig. 111.

As the Paradise Fish is a great jumper—indeed, it might almost be called a flying fish—the tank in which it is confined should always be carefully covered—of course, arranging that the air has free access to the water.

It has already been mentioned that this fish builds a nest, which it constructs of bubbles or froth. The bubbles are strengthened and made elastic by the help of buccal secretion. They are filled with air, which he—for it is the male fish that is the nest builder—has obtained by means of his gills or sucked from the surface of the water. The bubble-nest is generally placed among some weed about an inch below the surface of the water. It is sometimes as much as 6in. across and nearly $\frac{1}{2}$in. in depth.

When the nest is completed, the builder tempts the female to deposit her eggs either in the nest or as near to it as possible. Those eggs which are not laid in the nest are blown there by the male. His method of doing this is very interesting. When he wishes to put an egg into the nest he first ascends to the surface of the water, and having sucked in as much air as he needs he descends below the egg and forcibly exhales the air, which raises the egg into the desired position.

Like the male Stickleback, the male Paradise Fish guards the eggs lest his wife should eat them. The eggs number, generally, more than 200, and they hatch in about thirty-six hours. When the young ones arrive, the father is most attentive, keeping them in the nest and protecting them from the mother, who would very likely devour them. If they should stray from the nest he will take them in his mouth and gently return them. When they are about a fortnight old he will cease to tend them, considering, apparently, that they are quite able to take care of themselves. However, it is wise to remove the parent fish from the aquarium when the young ones are four or five days old. The former will probably soon recommence to nest again, and the latter will run no more risks from their mother's appetite.

Entomostraca, obtained as described later on, will serve the young fish until they are capable of taking the food that is usually supplied to the mature fish. This food should consist of water-worms (*Tubifex rivulorum*), pieces of small garden-worms, shreds of raw beef, ants' eggs, and flies. The food ought to be given every day, and only so much as to satisfy the immediate wants of the fish.

Paradise Fish should always be kept in pairs. They will commence to breed when they are a year old—sometimes sooner. The female loses her bright colours just before spawning. She is always less beautiful than the male, and much smaller.

Paradise Fish, now, can generally be bought for from 3s. 6d. to 7s. 6d. each, according to the season, their age, and condition. They live perfectly well in comparatively small vessels, and the owner ought not to think that the vessel is too small because they come frequently to the surface of the water for air. This is their habit, and because of it they are able to thrive in such an

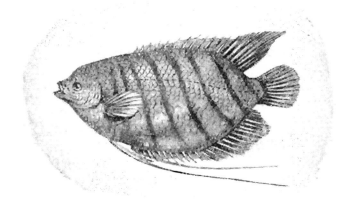

FIG. 112.—GURAMI (OSPHROMENUS OLFAX)

aquarium as would be altogether unsuitable for most fish. Nevertheless, they should be confined in as large a tank as can conveniently be kept at a proper temperature. Suitable aquatic weeds ought always to be growing in the water in which these little fish live.

The Gurami (*Osphromenus olfax*) belonging to the same family (*Anabantidæ*) as the Paradise Fish, is, like its relative, beautiful, interesting, hardy (under proper treatment), and well-suited to a life in an aquarium. It is also a native of China and Cochin-China; but now it is naturalised in many other countries, such as India, Australia, Mauritius, and Penang. Like all the members of the group (Labyrinth-Gilled Fishes) in which it is placed, owing to the special formation of its gills, the Gurami has the power of remaining for a considerable time out of water and of obtaining a certain amount of oxygen from the atmospheric air. This fish, therefore, need not be kept in a large aquarium; but of course the larger, in reason, the better.

The Gurami may be described as omnivorous : nevertheless, it is chiefly herbivorous, feeding generally upon aquatic plants. It will also eat pieces of cabbage, lettuce, and turnip leaves. The Gurami is noted for the goodness of its flesh as food for man, and as it is a quick grower, occasionally weighing, it is said, as much as twenty pounds, its cultivation is certainly worth the attention of those who could supply it with enough water of a temperature varying from 65deg. Fahr. to 80deg. It does best in clear water, well stocked with healthy growing weeds.

Like the Paradise Fish, the Gurami is a nest-builder. The nest is made of portions of aquatic plants, and measures about five or six inches across. The eggs deposited by the female in the nest sometimes number as many as a thousand. When the young fish appear they feed upon the materials of which the nest is formed.

Fig. 112 gives a good idea of this interesting and delicious fresh-water fish. The curiously-shaped mouth is capable of not a little protrusion. The first ray of each ventral fin consists, not like that of the Paradise Fish, of a sharp spine, but of a long slender filament which reaches beyond the tail, and which, perhaps, is chiefly used for balancing and steadying purposes. The bands down the body, which disappear with age, are blue and the ventral fins are tipped with crimson. In addition to these colours, the fish possesses a beautiful sheen.

The Gurami, when small, may be kept in a tank heated in the same manner (Fig. 111) as has been suggested in regard to the Paradise Fish. As soon as it grows too big for this receptacle it might be removed to one of those tanks which are often found in large greenhouses, and which generally contain water of a fairly high temperature. The Gurami, during the summer months, may be purchased in London.

The Siamese Fighting Fish (*Betta pugnax*) is also a member of the family *Anabantidæ*, and another of the interesting domesticated fish of the East. It is distinguished from its relatives by a short and deep spineless dorsal fin; but, like them, it possesses ventral fins, each having the first ray much prolonged, and a long anal fin. The caudal fin is large and fan-shaped. " Cantor writes that when the fish is in a state of quiet, its dull colours present nothing remarkable, but if two be brought together, or if one sees its own image in a looking-glass, the little creature becomes suddenly excited. The raised fin and the whole body shine with metallic colours of dazzling beauty, while the projected gill membrane, waving like a black frill round the throat, adds something of grotesqueness to the general appearance. In this state it makes repeated darts at its real or reflected antagonist. But both, when taken out of each other's sight, become instantly quiet. This description was drawn up by a gentleman who had been presented with several by the King of Siam. They were kept in glasses of water, fed with larvæ of mosquitoes, and had thus lived for many months. The Siamese are as infatuated with the combats of these fish as the Malays are with their cockfights, staking on the issue considerable sums, and sometimes their own persons and families. The licence to exhibit fish-fights is farmed, and brings a considerable annual revenue to the King of Siam. The species abounds in the rivulets at the foot of the hills of Perang." (The Royal Natural History, p. 413.)

These fish are also nest-builders; they should be kept in pairs. They may be confined in such a tank as has been recommended for the Paradise Fish, and the water ought to be of a like temperature.

The Climbing Perch (*Anabas scandens*) is an interesting inmate of an aquarium, where it will live for a long time if it can be provided with water of a temperature varying from 55deg. to 80deg. Fahr. It will do well in the same kind of vessel as that illustrated at Fig. 111. Of course, as this Perch is a larger animal than its relative, the Paradise Fish, it should be confined in a larger receptacle. *Anabas scandens* when fully grown is about 8in. in length, and is very Perch-like in appearance.

Though it has the reputation of climbing trees after food, it has, I believe, been seen to do so on only one occasion—by Daldorf, in the year 1791. It does indeed scramble over land by the help of its pectoral fins, which it hooks round grass and weeds.

This fish, as well as the others of the same group, is provided with a special organ for assisting in the oxygenization of the blood; consequently it is enabled to live for some time out of the water and, indeed, in hard mud, and out of the latter it is frequently dug by the natives of the countries in which it is found. It is reported that boatmen carry them alive in earthernware jars, without water, and cook them as they need them, and that even after several days the remaining fish are still lively.

The body of the Climbing Perch is oblong, and somewhat compressed. The dorsal fin is spined for by far the greater portion of its length, the smaller (the posterior part), being soft, rounded, and higher than the rest. The caudal fin is convex. The anal fin, in regard to its spined and soft parts, corresponds to the dorsal, except that the spines on the former are less numerous. The scales of the fish are large, and its general colour is dark green, marked with dark bands. The Climbing Perch is found in India, Ceylon, Burma, the Melayan Archipelago, and the Philippine Islands.

Though I have kept this fish for a long time, I have never seen it in any way exhibiting its climbing or crawling powers. It will eat small aquatic animals, water and garden worms. Rather large specimens of the last will be found its most convenient food. The Climbing Perch is sometimes offered for sale, during the summer months, by the London dealers in aquarian requisites.

The Black or Small-mouthed Bass (*Grystes nigricans* or *Micropterus dolomieu*, Fig. 113) has already been described at some length on p. 141. Since the remarks here referred to were written this interesting and useful American game fish has been established in this country as well as on the Continent.

Black Bass fishing is perhaps more popular in America than even that of Salmon or Trout; not because it is more attractive, but by reason of its being generally more easily obtained. particularly during the chief holiday time of the year, and supplying nearly, if not quite, as good sport and heavier baskets.

In this country owners of fishing waters frequently hesitate to introduce Black Bass into their rivers, lakes, and ponds, chiefly because they fear for their Trout. Indeed, their fears are not unfounded, for the Black Bass is extremely pugnacious, and is able to do fatal damage to an opponent by means of its formidable dorsal fin. It is also a great feeder on fish smaller than itself.

FIG. 113. BLACK BASS (MICROPTERUS DOLOMIEU)
(*From a Photograph by the Author.*)

As already mentioned, Black Bass weigh occasionally 8lb.— and I have read of one fish scaling as much as 12lb., and measuring 27in. in length and 9in. across the body. It was said to have been caught in Lake Minnetonka, in the State of Minnesota. A fish which weighs 2½lb. is about 15in. long, and one which scales 8lb. is about 2ft. in length and possesses girth of a little more than 17in.

The baits generally used for these fish are Minnows (Fig. 114), frogs, spoon-baits, Crayfish, worms, crickets, grass-hoppers, and artificial flies as big as those made for Salmon. The use of the fly supplies, as a rule, by far the best sport.

Black Bass vary in colour and marking not a little. They may possess any shade of green from light to almost black, either spotted or barred. The Black Bass is a member of the family *Centrarchidæ* which contains ten genera of Perch-like fishes, but it and its relatives are distinguished from the true Perches (*Percidæ*) by the possession of at least three spines on the anal fin. All *Centrarchidæ* are more or less suited for a life in the aquarium, and while in confinement quickly become very tame.

In an American magazine devoted to sport, I found an article headed "How to Make and Care for an Aquarium,"

FIG. 114. A SMALL SHOAL OF MINNOWS (LEUCISCUS PHOXINUS).
(*From a Photograph by the Author.*)

which is taken almost word for word without any acknowledgment from the former edition of this book, with the exception of the last few words some of which I now quote as an endorsement of my remark in regard to the tameness of the Black Bass. "I have had a Black Bass as tame as a dog. When the time came for me to feed him he would swim near the surface, watching my movements. I could hold the food 2 or 3 inches above the water, and he would jump at it, and tear it out of my hand."

Those who possess rather large ponds would not be likely to regret stocking them with a few of these interesting and useful fish, which supply both sport and, if the cooking be not at fault, most delicious food. Besides, there is always a ready market for healthy young Bass.

The Large-mouthed Bass (*Micropterus salmoides*, Fig. 115), also known as the Trout Bass, differs in appearance, as may be easily seen from the photographs, from the Black Bass. Both fish, indeed, are commonly known as Black Bass, but are distinguished from each other by the epithets "Large-mouthed" and "Small-mouthed."

The mouth of *M. salmoides* extends to some distance behind

FIG. 115. LARGE-MOUTHED BASS (MICROPTERUS SALMOIDES).
(*From a Photograph by the Author.*)

the eye, while that of *M. dolomieu* ends just beneath the eye. The scales on the cheeks of the latter are small, while those on the cheeks of the former are larger. As a game fish for food and sport the Small-mouthed Bass is far superior to his larger-mouthed relative.

The Trout Bass, however, is a good inmate of an aquarium, and is very hardy and easily obtained; but care must be taken that it is not associated with fish smaller, or even as small as itself. It may be fed upon garden worms, Minnows, and flies.

The Calico Bass (*Pomoxys sparoides*, Fig. 116) can be easily distinguished by means of his photograph from the two

Basses just mentioned. It is a lively and beautiful little fisn, and well adapted for a life in an aquarium. This Bass is also useful for table purposes, being a fish of an excellent flavour. Like the Small-mouthed Black Bass, it is a very suitable species for stocking ponds. It is, however, small in comparison to its somewhat distant relative just mentioned. It can be bought in this country for about half-a-crown, and may be fed while in confinement upon garden worms and pieces of raw meat.

In a state of nature " it is found from New Jersey to

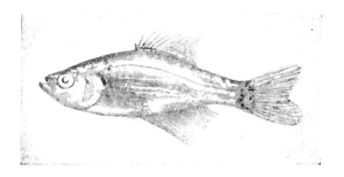

FIG. 116. CALICO BASS (POMOXYS SPAROIDES).
(From a Photograph by the Author.)

Georgia, in the Great Lake region, and through the Mississippi and Ohio Valleys."

The Rock Bass, or Red-eye (*Ambliopsis rupestris*), is another species of Bass occasionally imported into this country and sold for aquarium purposes. It is a useful food fish, and grows to a length of from 10in. to 12in. It is found in the Canadian Lakes, and as far South as Louisiana. It is some. times advertised for sale, and costs about 1s. 6d. While in captivity it should be treated as suggested for the other Basses.

The Common Sun-fish (*Eupomotis gibossus*, Fig. 117) belongs to the same family (*Centrarchidæ*) as the fresh-water Basses, and is a very beautiful, though common (in America) little fish. It is also known as "Pumpkin-seed" and "Sunny." It should not of course be confused with its huge namesake of the salt-water.

The Sun-fish is very suitable for the aquarium because of its docility and great beauty. The illustration gives a good idea of both the shape and the markings of this interesting fish. The late Mr. Frank Buckland described it as of most lovely colours—green, brown, and pale blue. It can be easily distinguished from other American Sun-fishes, by the bright scarlet spot or blotch on the gill-covers.

FIG. 117. THE COMMON SUN-FISH (EUPOMOTIS GIBOSSUS).
(*From a Photograph by the Author.*)

It is extremely hardy while in captivity, if kept out of the reach of frost, which proves fatal to it. Its food should consist chiefly of small worms. It may be bought generally for about 9d.

The Common Sun-fish will breed in this country in ponds, provided that they are deep enough to allow it to get well out of the reach of frost.

The Cat-fish (*Amiurus nebulosus*, Fig. 118) is a member of the *Siluridæ*, a large family of fresh-water fishes which includes the "Wels" (*Silurus glanis*), the largest fresh-water fish of Europe, with the exception of the Sturgeon.

The chief characteristic of the Siluroid fishes is that the
" skin is either naked or armoured with bony scutes, but
scales are not developed."

The family of the *Siluridæ* (which numbers about 120
genera, natives of both the Old and the New World) has been
divided by Dr. Günther into eight sub-families, and of these
the *Proteropodes* is that to which the genus *Amiurus*, con-

FIG. 118. CAT-FISH (AMIURUS NEBULOSUS).
(From a Photograph by the Author.)

taining some twenty species, belongs. All the members of
this genus possess eight barbels.

The Cat-fish (*A. nebulosus*) is known locally as the "Bullhead" and the "Horned Pout." It is a very hardy little
fish, and lives well in an aquarium. It is of a sluggish and
retiring nature, hiding itself during the daytime and
becoming lively towards night.

This Cat-fish grows usually to a length of about 10in.
When fishing in North America, I found that this was the

easiest of all fish to catch. It gives fair sport, and is considered by many to be very good eating.

This Cat-fish has a dorsal fin, which is short and placed a little behind the pectoral fins; an adipose fin; small ventral fins situated near the middle of the body; a large and rounded anal fin, shorter than the tail, which is only very slightly concave. The colour and skin of the fish are like those of the Eel.

A. nebulosus would do very well in the ponds of this country, and would also provide good sport for children and others and supply wholesome food.

In captivity it may be fed on worms, and it can be bought for about 1s. 3d., or £5 a hundred.

FIG. 119. THE BOWFIN (AMIA CALVA).
(*From a Photograph by the Author.*)

The Bowfin (*Amia calva*, Fig. 119) is a member of an order (*Ganoidei*) of fishes which is gradually becoming extinct, and is indeed the only living representative of the sub-order (*Amioidei*). The *Amia calva* is also known as the "Mud-fish," the "Dog-fish," and the "Marsh-fish."

It is exceedingly tenacious of life, and is able to exist for more than an hour out of water. It frequently, especially when living in foul water, comes to the surface to breathe, occasionally making as it does so a bell-like sound. The Bowfin is a native of the fresh waters of the United States, and has been imported into this country in considerable numbers. It breeds during the month of May, and deposits its numerous small eggs among the water-plants, to which they adhere. The eggs and the young fry are guarded by the male fish.   The *Amia calva* feeds upon crustaceans, aquatic insects, frogs and other batrachians, as well as small fish.   Owing to its great liking for the last named it has been placed among the "fresh-water sharks."   **Fig.** 119 gives a good idea of the general appearance of this fish, whose body is long and compressed behind.   Its head is broad and its snout short.   Its cycloid scales are rather large and covered with a thick mucus.   The animal's colour is a dark green, generally marked as in the illustration.   It possesses a

FIG. 120.   THE CHAMELEON FISH (HEROS FACETUS).
(From a Photograph by the Author.)

very long dorsal and a rounded caudal fin.   While in captivity the Bowfin may be fed upon large garden worms and small frogs and fish.   It can occasionally be bought in London at prices ranging from 7s. 6d. to 12s. 6d.   It is an interesting fish to possess.

I must confess that I know very little about this beautiful little fish (*Heros facetus*) (Fig. 120), having only possessed one specimen for a short time.

For some seven or eight years it has been bred in warm water tanks in this country and on the Continent.   It is a native of South America, and by some it is called the Chameleon Fish. It is very hardy in water of a temperature of about 75deg. Fahr., and should be fed upon worms.

This fish may be kept in such a vessel as that recommended for the Paradise Fish and others, and it can be bought in London for from 5s. to 7s. 6d. It will breed in a large tank containing water of about 80deg. Fahr.

A correspondent, who is supposed to possess the best collection of fresh-water fishes in Europe, has kindly written to me that Chameleon Fish "require plenty of room, but are very quarrelsome, and will soon kill any fish weaker than themselves

FIG. 121.   LEATHER, SPEIGEL, OR MIRROR CARP (CYPRINUS CARPIO VAR.).
(*From a Photograph by the Author.*)

Mine spawned in 1897. They cleared all the shingle away from a corner of the tank and rubbed the slate bottom quite clean, where the spawn was laid on the 17th June, both parents taking charge of this at first, and keeping it quite clean and free from dirt by constantly fanning it with their fins. It hatched on the 22nd, when the male would not let the female go near, and kept the young ones by him all day, and at night put them in a hole in the shingle and sat on the top of them ; but I don't remember for how long he continued to look after them."

The **Speigel**, or Mirror Carp (*Cyprinus carpio var.*) (Fig. 121; see also page 120), an interesting form of the

Common Carp, is now much more plentiful in England than
it was when the first edition of this book was published.
This fish is not only suitable and interesting as an inmate
of the aquarium, but it is also useful for stocking ponds,
canals, and small lakes, and so it will add weight and variety
to the ground-fisherman's basket.

It grows quickly and attains, in this country, a weight of
7lb. or 8lb. and a length of about 2ft. On the
Continent, however, some of these fish have been known to
weigh 20lb. and to grow as long as 3ft.

By some it is recorded that, in order to make the flesh of
this fish and that of the Common Carp more tender, it has
been customary to remove the roe from the living animal,
supply its place with a roll of felt, sew up the opening with
a few stitches, and return the poor thing to the water to
recover and grow fat and heavy.

This fish is also known as the " King-Carp "—the " Carp-
King," the "Saddle Carp"—and the "Leather Carp." The
scales are often many times the normal size, being at least as
large as a florin. They are sometimes arranged in two or
three horizontal rows, having the bare skin between. The
scales occasionally, instead of being in rows, are placed in
a batch in the middle of the back, and reach down to
about the lateral line. When this is the case the fish is
known as the "Saddle Carp," and when, owing to age or
accident, the scales, or most of them, fall off, it is called
the "Leather Carp."

This fish can be bought tor from 6d. to 1s. each, or
from 30s. to 70s. a hundred.

The Golden Tench (*Tinca aurata var.*) (Fig. 122 ; see
page 129). This variety of the Tench is one of the most beautiful of European fresh-water fishes. The male is known from
the female not only by the larger ventral fins, but also by the
larger head and the steeper arching of the fore part of the
back. The eye is large and of a red, brown, or nearly
black colour. The body is frequently spotted or blotched
with black.

These fish breed readily in ponds, particularly those which

contain muddy bottoms and plenty of weeds such as *Potamo-geton natans* and *P. densum.* The spawn either sinks to the bottom or attaches itself to the plants. It is, as a rule, deposited near to the banks of the pond. The spawning time lasts from May to August. The young, according to the temperature of the water, take about seven or eight days to hatch.

Directions as to feeding these fish have already been given. They may be bought at prices ranging from 9d. to 2s. each, or from £2 to £5 a hundred.

The Bitterling, or Bitter Carp (*Rhodeus amarus*) (Fig. 123),

FIG. 122. THE GOLDEN TENCH (TINCA AURATA VAR.).
(*From a Photograph by the Author.*)

is one of the smallest of European fresh-water fishes, the male being, when fully grown, about 3in. long, while the female is only 2in., or even less. Its appearance suggests a cross between the Common and the Prussian Carp. The dorsal fin commences at the middle of the back and ends a little beyond the centre of the anal fin. The pectoral and ventrals are of equal size; the anal fin being nearly as large as the dorsal. The caudal fin is moderately concave. The vent, which is surrounded by a kind of scaly sheath, is mid-way between the anal and ventral fins.

The male, during spawning times, assumes very beautiful colours, for which it has received the name of "Rainbow-

coloured Fish." The gill-covers, back, and sides are of a
beautiful violet colour, while on each side of the body,
beginning at the centre of the caudal fin, is a bright green
stripe reaching nearly to the middle of the body. Behind
the gill-covers there is a silvery patch spotted with violet.
The anal fin is a bright red edged with black. Altogether,
the Bitterling during summer is one of the most beautiful
of European fishes, as well as one of the most hardy.

The female, though not nearly so beautiful as the male, is,
nevertheless, a handsome little fish. Her back is greenish-
brown and her sides silvery. The line running from the

Fig. 123. The Bitterling Carp (Rhodeus amarus).
(*From a Photograph by the Author.*)

centre of the caudal fin towards the middle of the body is of
a blackish colour, and sometimes is absent.

She has a curious possession in the shape of a long
reddish oviduct, which sometimes hangs down from the body
as much as 1in., or even more. After the spawning is ended
it gradually disappears.

It is not known, I think, whether this tube, which is said
to possess its own nerves and blood vessels, is used as an
ovipositor or not.

The size of the Bitterling and its bitter flavour debar it
from being useful as food for man. As a bait for other fish
it rarely has any attraction, except for Eels, and sometimes
Perch.

It is widely distributed throughout the centre of Europe. It is not found as a native in Great Britain.

The Bitterling may be bought in England at prices ranging from 6d. to 1s.

As food it will take, while in captivity, vermicelli, small worms, and ants' eggs.

The Thunder, or Mud-fish (*Misgurnus fossilis*) (Fig. 124), is also known as the Pond Loach or Weather Fish. It is a very large Loach, which for some reason is so sensitive that it becomes highly excited during the approach of a storm, evincing its excitement by leaving the mud at the bottom of the water, in which it prefers to live, and

FIG. 124. THE THUNDER OR MUD-FISH (MISGURNUS FOSSILIS).
(*From a Photograph by the Author.*)

swimming about most energetically near the surface. The people of the country of which it is a native look upon it as a kind of barometer, and for this reason keep it in a glass vessel indoors. Hence it has obtained the names of "Thunder Fish" and "Weather Fish."

It often discharges air with a kind of "popping" noise. When I first obtained specimens of this fish and placed them in an aquarium, I could not understand for some time whence this curious sound came. This, no doubt, has been the experience of many others.

This fish, like all Loach, has a very elongated body, a small head and eye, ten barbels around the not large

mouth—four of which are attached to the lower jaw. All
the fins are rounded. The dorsal fin is placed in the
middle of the back, and directly opposite the ventral fins. The
pectoral fins are larger than the latter; and the anal fin is
of the same size and shape as the dorsal. The caudal fin is
as deep as the deepest part of the body, and is convex.

The scales are small—the largest being on the sides. The
appearance and the feel of the fish remind one of an eel.

The head is covered with blackish streaks. A broad dark-
brown band runs along the lateral line, and above and below
this band the sides are yellow, which is bounded at the
abdomen by a blackish line. The lower parts are orange
spotted with black. A white line, on the under surface,
extends from the throat to the vent, which is rather prominent
and which is placed a short distance in front of the anal
fin. The fins are dark brown spotted with black. The iris
is a rich yellow.

This fish, though found in rivers and lakes, seems to
prefer ponds and slow-running streams which have muddy
bottoms. It is essentially a mud-fish. This hardy Loach
should be fed on aquatic insects, water-worms, garden-
worms, and the like. It sometimes exceeds a foot in length.
It may be bought in London at prices ranging from 6d.
to 1s. each. This Loach is found in France, Holland,
Germany, Belgium, and in Russia. It is not found in
Great Britain nor out of Europe.

The Dog-fish (*Umbra krameri*, Fig. 125), related to both
the Garfish and the Pike, is a beautiful and interesting
little fish. It has received the name of "Dog-fish" from its
manner of swimming, the ventral and pectoral fins moving
alternately like the feet of a running dog.

The genus *Umbra* contains two species, one a native of the
Old World, the other of the New. The former is found only
in Southern Europe.

The Dog-fish generally lives in stagnant water, and consequently does well in an aquarium. When fully grown it is
about 3in. in length.

The rather long dorsal fin commences at the middle of the

back, and contains fifteen or sixteen rays. The caudal fin is rounded and nearly as long as the head. The anal fin has a short base, and terminates just opposite to the end of the dorsal fin. The pectoral and ventral fins are equal in length, the latter reaching as far back as the vent.

The head, which gives the fish its distinctive character, is covered with scales except on the nose and jaws. For the size of the fish the scales are large, they are circular in shape, and over-lap each other. The lateral line is marked by a light yellow or reddish streak which is placed rather high

FIG. 125. THE DOG-FISH (UMBRA KRAMERI).
(From a Photograph by the Author.)

up on the side. The colour of the body is a pretty reddish-brown, growing darker in the back and lighter towards the abdomen. The head and body are covered with dark-brown spots. The caudal and dorsal fins are brown, while the other fins are of lighter colour. The eye is large and beautiful.

The males are said to be much rarer than the females, and may be distinguished by their smaller size and "projecting papilla" near the anal fin.

These fish will deposit their large eggs while in confinement. Some superstitious fishermen regard the fish as poisonous, and consider that to catch a Dog-fish means ill luck.

This fish, in confinement, will eat tiny worms, aquatic
insects, water-worms, and small pieces of raw meat. It is
exceedingly hardy.

There are many other interesting fresh-water fishes occasionally imported into this country from various parts of
the world which are suitable for confinement in a tank, but
their cost, as a rule, places them out of the reach of the
ordinary aquarium keeper.   But I hope that enough has
already been said in regard to fish to enable anyone to keep
successfully any fresh-water fish which is likely to come into
his possession.

CHAPTER IX

THE DIFFERENT VARIETIES OF GOLDFISH AND HOW TO BREED THEM.

IT is more than half-a-century since the English people began to take an interest in matters of the aquarium, and such naturalists as Mr. P. H. Gosse, Mr. Saville Kent, Dr. Ward, Mr. R. Warrington, Dr. Lankester, and others helped to make them very popular; so much so, that in many of our chief towns, large and well-appointed aquaria were established for the interest and instruction of the public. Now, however, when a visit is paid to some of these places, one cannot but conclude that the public interest in them is on the wane, though, at the same time, it ought to be acknowledged that the love for Natural History is increasing very quickly. It may be that people prefer to keep and tend animals of their own, rather than have them kept for them.

Though our interest, and really the beginning of our knowledge, in aquarium matters is little more than fifty years old the Chinese and Japanese, in their own clever way, have carried on the keeping and breeding of fish in confinement for many centuries.

It is said that in China at the present day there is some sort of an aquarium, containing two or more goldfish, in nearly every house. These fish, however, are not as a rule the common kinds with which we are so familiar here; but animals of good or extraordinary shape and of most beautiful colours. It is only comparatively recently that the good fish of China and Japan have found their way into our country.

In the breeding and selection of these creatures the Chinese seem to devote their attention chiefly to the production of fish of beautiful and various colours; while the Japanese, though giving some thought to the colouring, give more to the shape of the body and the delicacy and size of the fins (see Fig. 126).

FIG. 126.   FAN-TAILED JAPANESE CARP (CARASSIUS JAPONICUS VAR.).
(From a Photograph by the Author.)

The following are a few of the varieties which the Chinese in their enthusiasm and perseverance have produced:

The Mottled Beauty is a gorgeously-coloured fish, having the back, especially the posterior part, of a deep velvety black; the sides brightly mottled with yellow, blue, rose, and black; while the under parts are silvery.

The Blue is comparatively a small fish, having its back and sides coloured a rich blue possessing a beautiful metallic sheen. Its under parts are silvery.

The Superb is generally a large fish, growing sometimes to more than a foot in length. The colour of its back is black and scarlet, the scales being edged with gold. The lower parts are silvery.

The Red-fin, as its name implies, has fins of a bright scarlet, the head also being of this colour. The rest of the body is blue.

The Tumbler is a fish of curious shape as well as of remarkable colour. It is described as having the head and tail bent upwards, giving to the creature a crescent-like shape. When swimming, it tumbles in the water as the pigeons of

FIG. 127. THE TELESCOPE FISH (CARASSIUS JAPONICUS VAR.).

the same name do in the air. The colour is a beautiful blue tinged with orange.

In addition to the varieties briefly described above there are several others more or less beautiful.

As already mentioned, the Japanese pay more attention to the shape and fins of the fish than to its colour, though the last is not by any means neglected.

Fig. 126 is a good representation of the Japanese Fan-tailed variety. It is a lovely fish. The tail is longer than the body, and of delicate and beautiful structure. The ventral and dorsal fins are also of unusual size and delicacy. The colours are vermilion and white; sometimes the body is of one colour and all the fins are of the other. In the case of the fish figured on page 186 the body is white, glittering like mother-of-pearl, while certain portions of the fins are vermilion. The iris of the eye is a brilliant red. The tail of this variety is frequently double, having the appearance from behind of an inverted capital Y; when it is single, as in Fig. 126, the fish is sometimes called the Comet Fish.

The Telescope Fish (Fig. 127) is more of a curiosity than a beauty. It has obtained its name from the curious formation of its eyes, which project forward in a kind of telescopic fashion. The colours are generally a rich orange and white, though sometimes they are blue and black. The fins in size are often out of all proportion to the body; the tail being much longer than the body and of most delicate construction.

Of all the Japanese fish the Fringed-tailed variety is supposed to be the most beautiful, perfect specimens having been sold for five guineas each, and even twenty times their weight in gold. All the beautiful colours of the other varieties may be found in this one, e.g., sometimes the body is white and the fins are red; but more often the latter are white while the former is red. All the fins are very large, and may be said to have the appearance of most delicate lace; the tail being either double, triple, or quadruple. The body of the fish is short and egg-shaped.

There are other varieties besides these just described.

General directions have already been given on page 115 for the breeding of these fish, both in the aquarium and in ponds, by which a few young fish may be reared every year. These few are simply those which, by good fortune, have escaped the many dangers to which the spawn and fry of the Goldfish, in the circumstances, were exposed. Therefore, to rear many fish in the place of only a few, special precautions must be taken to protect the spawn and the fry from these dangers. The following are some of the dangers : The parent fish are generally eager to devour the spawn

almost as soon as it has been deposited, and any eggs which
have been unnoticed by the fish run the risk of being eaten
by the Freshwater Shrimp (*Gammarus pulex*), the Freshwater
Louse (*Asellus aquaticus*), the Common Pond Snail (*Limnea
peregra*), and other such animals.   The fry as soon as they
leave the egg are in danger from their parents, their bigger
brothers and sisters, from the larvæ and pupæ of the Dragon
Fly, the larvæ of the Great Black Water Beetle (*Hydrophilus piceus*),
the Big Diving Water Beetle and its larvæ (*Dyticus marginalis*),
the Water Boatman (*Notonecta glauca*), the *Corixæ*, and
the like.

If care be prudently taken, most of these dangers can be
removed, and a good proportion of the spawn deposited may,
in course of time, produce mature fish.   It is possible to

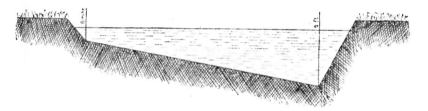

FIG. 128. SECTION OF SPAWNING OR REARING POND.

attain this end by means of indoor aquaria or by small ponds
without.   In either case the following rules should be observed:
(1) The parent fish ought to be of good shape, perfectly healthy,
and if possible of that kind which comes into colour at an
early age. It is also important that they should have been
born and reared in cold water. (2) The spawn or the parent
fish must be removed as soon as the former has been deposited.
(3) The young fish ought to be kept by themselves, sorted
according to size. (4) The young fish should be guarded from
every kind of danger as far as may be.

To breed Goldfish successfully in ponds, three at least should
be prepared.   They need not be large, but they must be
(*a*) of a suitable depth, so that (*b*) they can be filled and
emptied at will, the outlet being well guarded; (*c*) the

amount of water they contain can always be under control; (d)
they cannot overflow; (e) and there can be no chance of escape
of fish from them.

Those ponds allotted to spawning and rearing purposes
should be constructed so that they gradually slope down to
a depth of 2ft., as suggested by Fig. 128 or by Fig. 129.
They need not be longer than 10ft. nor wider than 5ft.
They should be kept empty and well-cleaned during the
winter. This will lessen the chance of the many enemies to
the spawn and fry being present in the spring.

The third pond is provided for those fish which have
grown so big that there is no danger of their being eaten
by their larger relatives, and for the wintering of all the fish.
This pond should be a little larger than the other two—varying

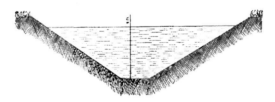

FIG. 129. SECTION OF SPAWNING OR REARING POND.

from 2ft. in depth to at least 4ft. The ice in winter
time, of course, must be broken as soon as possible after it
has formed.

The ponds should be supplied with water from a reliable
spring, from a neighbouring river or stream, or from any other
source from which water of good quality can be obtained
without fail throughout the year.

Goldfish will breed when they are a year old, and sometimes when they are only nine months; but it is wise to
choose as parent fish those which are between two and four
years old. If of the latter age, there should be four males to
three females; or if of the former, four males to six
females, but if the females are much bigger than the males,
then there should be six males to three females. It is wiser,
however, to choose fish of a like size.

It is only during the breeding season that the sexes can for certain be distinguished from each other. The males at this time develop on their gill covers tiny protuberances, which give a rasp-like feeling to the finger when rubbed over them. These little excrescences are, it is supposed, used by the male for assisting the female in the expulsion of her eggs. When the breeding season is over they disappear.

The female, near her spawning time, has an extended appearance about the neighbourhood of her ovary, which is situated immediately below her spinal column and on either side of her air-bladder.

If the spawning-pond be of the size suggested above, it may with advantage be divided down the centre by a wooden frame, carefully made to fit, and covered with fine-meshed wire netting. This must stand so high out of the water that the fish cannot jump over it. In each division a set of breeding fish can be placed.

As soon as the difference between the sexes can be distinguished the chosen fish should be placed in the spawning-pond. And in the same pond there ought to be several rather large bunches of the Canadian Water-weed (*Anacharis alsinastrum*), loosely and securely tied, floating about. If this plant cannot be obtained, any other plant which will grow while floating, and which has something of the same character, will do. But should no aquatic weed be at hand bunches of long grass, or even of soft hay, might answer the purpose. The bunches must float—and if possible near the deep end of the pond; indeed, it will be more convenient if they are fastened by a piece of string to the bank.

When the fish are about to spawn they become very excited, dashing about among the weeds, the male or males closely following the female; and as the latter deposits her eggs the former discharge their milt, which can easily be seen in the water because of its milk-like appearance, portions of which are absorbed by the ova, and so they are fertilized. As the eggs are covered with some mucus-like substance they are capable of adhering to almost anything with which they come in contact, thus they stick to the weeds or their substitutes.

The eggs are about the size of a pin's-head and of a yellowish colour. The usual spawning time is from about four o'clock in the morning to about nine, and in this country generally extends from April to August. Whenever it is thought that the fish have spawned, the bunches of floating weed should be drawn to the land and carefully examined.

If eggs are observed on the weed, a bucket ought to be half-filled with water from the pond, and with a pair of scissors the portions of Anacharis or other weed to which the ova are adhering should be cut off and gently placed in the bucket.

After returning the bunches of plants to the pond, the bucket should be taken to the house and the eggs put where they are intended to hatch.

Small aquaria, inverted propagating glasses, fish globes, or very large, wide-mouthed glass bottles—each capable of holding at least a gallon of water—should have been prepared and placed in some fairly sunny window. Either the water taken from the pond, or quite clear, soft water of *exactly* the same temperature as that in the pond, must be put in the vessels prepared for the hatching of the eggs. About one hundred eggs should be placed in each gallon of water. The eggs must not be separated from the weed when deposited in their quarters. The fry will appear in from three to seven days, according to the temperature of the water and the condition of the eggs.

Every day any unfertile eggs should be gently removed, or their presence in the water may tend to the development of fungus, particularly if its temperature be not high.

For twenty-four hours after they leave the egg the fry need no food. They exist on the yolk which is still in a bag attached to their bodies. After this time they commence to feed on the tiny animal life which will be sure to be present in the water in which they were hatched.

When they are three days old they should be removed to a large, shallow aquarium containing water of the same temperature as that from which they have just been removed, to the depth of 4in. This aquarium need not contain any aquatic plants, as it is wise to keep the little fish under observation as much as possible.

Entomostraca, obtained as suggested on pp. 37-8, should be given to the young fish as food, taking care, however, that all larvæ of beetles and the like capable of killing the young fish are excluded. When a fortnight old, the larger of the fry, which will be chiefly those hatched first, should be caught with a net and placed in the rearing-pond at such a time as the temperature of the two waters is the same.

The rearing-pond, having been filled with water the day previously, should only contain such water-plants as the Lily (*Nymphœa alba*), or others of a similar kind. These are wanted, not so much for oxygenising the water as for supplying shade and protection for the small fish. If these plants cannot well be procured, a few pieces of board floating on the water will answer the purpose nearly as well. The plants or the boards should be placed at the deepest part of the pond.

The pond being free of other weed will allow the fish to be the more readily under observation; and the presence of any of their many enemies then can be the more easily detected.

As these fish grow they should be removed to the winter pond if no large fish are kept there. This pond may be well stocked with aquatic plants, such as Lilies and the Water Lobelia (*Lobelia Dortmannii*).

In time the young fish may be persuaded to eat ants' eggs, small garden-worms, water-worms (*Tubifex rivulorum*), crushed vermicelli, stale bread dried in an oven and powdered, and the like.

Great care must be taken not to crowd the fish, nor, until they are fairly well-grown, to associate those of very different sizes. As "the garment must be cut according to the cloth" so fish must be hatched according to the size and number of the ponds.

When Goldfish are to be bred and reared in aquaria indoors. the tank which contains the parent fish should be

o

under fairly close observation, and when a female seems (judging from appearances) to be near the time of her spawning, her companions of her own sex ought to be removed, and so lessen the chance of the eggs on their arrival being devoured.

The aquarium in which the breeding-fish are kept should contain plenty of growing weed, *e.g.*, *Anacharis*, *Potamogeton densum*, and the Water Ranunculus.

As soon as the fish have spawned they must be removed to another and properly-arranged aquarium, where they will presently again deposit their eggs. The eggs left behind will hatch in due time, and the young fish will find plenty of food present in the water. As this is consumed, other food must be introduced, according to directions already given.

As the young fish grow, and if the number of aquaria is limited, they may be kept in wooden tubs, pans, baths, or any other fairly large and shallow vessel ; of course care being taken that they are fitted and managed in the same way as ordinary aquaria. There must be no crowding, no neglect, and no ill assortment of sizes if success is to be attained. The surplus fish should be disposed of at the first opportunity.

It is, perhaps, wiser to breed the better kind of Goldfish, such as the Fan-tails and Fringe-tails indoors in aquaria, than out of doors in the ponds. These fish have a little more difficulty in spawning and are slightly more difficult to rear than the commoner varieties, but they are certainly well worth the extra trouble.

The colour of the young Goldfish at first is a silvery-grey; but generally before it assumes its permanent colour it grows much darker. Some fish are "coloured" when only a few weeks old, while others have entered their second year before this happens. As before remarked, those fish which colour early should be chosen to breed from.

Goldfish will spawn several times during the season.

CHAPTER X.

SNAILS AND LIMPETS.

ANYONE who kept an aquarium or aquaria just simply for the sake of the fresh-water molluscs would be amply rewarded for his trouble by the pleasure and instruction with which they would provide him.

The Mollusca (*mollis,* "soft") form one of the sub-divisions of the Animal Kingdom whose members are characterised by

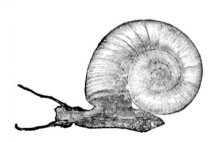

FIG. 130. PLANORBIS CORNEUS.

having soft skins and fleshy bodies, but are without bones or joints. Molluscs are either naked or are covered with a shell of one or two valves, but with some of the latter only we have to do in this chapter. The shell is composed of carbonate of lime and animal matter, which is secreted by the skin or mantle of the creature.

The Mollusca are divided into the *Encephalous* (possessing a head) and the *Acephalous* (without a head). In the former division are placed the *Gasteropoda* (belly-footed), or Univalves, &c., and in the latter the *Conchifera* (shell-bearing), or Bivalves. The fresh-water Univalves are commonly called Snails, and the fresh-water Bivalves, Mussels. Both the snails and mussels are exceedingly interesting in the aquarium. The forms, structures, and habits of the Univalves especially are very various. For example :

1. The shells of some snails are flat-coiled, like the *Planorbis corneus* (Fig. 130), while those of others are oval-oblong, like

FIG. 131. LIMNÆA STAGNALIS.

the *Limnæa stagnalis* (Fig. 131), or ear-shaped at the opening, like *Limnæa auricularia* (Fig. 132).

2. Some snails' shells are as much as 1¾in. in length, while those of others are as small as a big pin's head.

FIG. 132. LIMNÆA AURICULARIA.

3. Some snails are able to close the aperture of their shells with an operculum, and others, during an enforced absence from water, with an epiphragm.

4. Some snails are either male or female; others are both male and female; others again, when young, have the sexes

distinct, but as they grow older, each individual becomes both male and female.

5. Some snails are *oviparous*, and others *ovoviviparous* (the eggs being hatched within the oviduct of the parent).

6. Some snails are *pulmobranchiate* (possessors of lung-like branchiæ for breathing the atmospheric air), and others are *pectini-branchiate* (possessors of comb-like branchiæ, adapted for respiration beneath the water).

7. Some snails have their eyes placed upon short footstalks at the base of their tentacles, while others have theirs sessile there. The tentacles of all the species are situated above the mouth, and are used for touching, and perhaps also for smelling.

The oviparous animals, according to their different species, deposit their ova in masses, which are in shape either cylindrical or elliptical, or orbicular or round. The eggs in some of the capsules are as few as from three to six; while in others they are as many as from 80 to 130. They are affixed either to stones, or to leaves or stalks of water plants, or sometimes to the shells of one another. The eggs are hatched, according to the different species, in from ten to about twenty-six days.

Many water-snails, perhaps nearly all, have the power of "spinning" a kind of gelatinous thread by means of which they are able to ascend or descend in the water. Mr. G. Sherriff Tye, the writer of an interesting article on "Molluscan Threads," which was published in *Science Gossip* for March, 1874, in speaking of the habit of the *Physa hypnorum* as a "thread-spinner" says: "One of the most beautiful sights in molluscan economy is to see these little 'golden pippins' gliding through the water by no visible means; and when they fight, to see them twist and twirl, performing such quick and curious evolutions, while seemingly floating in mid-water, is astonishing, even to the patient student of Nature's wonders." These threads are anchored to the surface of the water in a curious way, viz., "a minute concavity at the upper end acts like a small boat of air, and thus sustains the thread."

As the tastes of the various species of Mollusca differ, some species preferring to eat the healthy growing plants, others the decaying, others confervoid growth, and a few delighting to partake of a little animal food as a relish to their vegetable, it will readily be seen that while some water-snails are useful in the tank, others are injurious there, inasmuch as they will be likely to destroy or hurt the weeds which are so necessary to the welfare of the aquarium. Those snails which prefer to feed either upon decaying vegetation or upon confervæ are, of course, the most suitable for the ordinary tank. The Univalve Molluscs are valuable in the aquarium not only from their readiness to act as scavengers and to clear away the confervoid growth which both checks the growth of the plants and interferes with the transparency of the glass, but also because their eggs and fry provide the fish with about the best of foods. However, it must not be supposed that they will mow away the algæ from the sides of the aquarium with the precision with which labourers cut down hay in the fields. Their work must occasionally be supplemented with the gentle rubbing of a bit of sponge tied to a short cane, or, what perhaps is better, a piece of coarse brown paper so fastened. Snails can keep the glass perfectly clean, but it is not wise, for the sake of the plants, to have so many in the aquarium as to force them to do this. I once placed a few half-grown snails (*Limnœa stagnalis*) in a very small aquarium, the sides of which were so covered with confervæ that nothing could be seen through them, and by the end of five or six days the glass was as clear as if it had been polished with a cloth. The snails had nothing else but the confervæ to eat.

It is an interesting sight to see a snail at work upon the transparent sides of an aquarium. The flat portion of the mollusc, which is pressed against the glass, is called the foot or disc, and the animal progresses by alternately expanding and contracting this foot or disc. The mouth of the snail will be continually opening and shutting, and from the lower part of it a curious yellowish-grey band will be seen, between each opening and shutting, to come forward and scrape the glass.

This band is known as the lingual ribbon or toothed tongue. The lingual ribbon is not only very interesting, especially under the microscope, but it is also useful in helping to determine the genera of various individuals. Some snails have a great number of teeth. The teeth are arranged on the lingual ribbon in rows, which vary in number and order according to different genera.

Snails, when kept in confinement, frequently deposit their eggs upon the transparent sides of the tank, thus giving the aquarium-keeper an opportunity, by the help of a magnifying glass, of watching the development of the fry. Soon after the eggs are laid, a small speck may be seen close to the side of each egg; as this speck grows it will gradually work its way into the middle of the egg, and then it continues to increase in size and in power of movement, until it breaks the egg-sac, and becomes free. When the young snails are hatched in an ordinary aquarium they generally fall victims to some of the watchful fish. Should it be wished, however, to rear the snails, it will be necessary to transfer the eggs to a small and shallow aquarium well stocked with growing weeds and confervæ, and where there are no fish or any other visible animals. This may easily be done by removing those portions of weed or pieces of stone upon which the ova have been deposited. The flat floating leaves and long stalks of the Cape Fragrant Water Lily seem to have great attractions for the snail which is desirous of depositing eggs.

When the ova are hatched and the fry have grown sufficiently —say so large that they can be easily picked off the plants with the finger and thumb—they may be returned to the aquarium. Snails grow slowly, and it is sometimes about two years before they arrive at màturity. As the young snail grows it enlarges its shell according to its wants. This is done by adding a small portion of mucous secretion to the edge of the shell, and when the secretion is dry it is followed by some more, but this time it is mixed with carbonate of lime. The first secretion makes what is called the epidermis of the shell, while the second forms the shell itself. These additions go on from time to time until the animal is full-

grown. Should any portion of the shell be injured by a
blow or the like, the animal, if not too much hurt, will repair
the broken part in the same way that it formed the rest of
the shell. These repairs can be plainly seen, for they are
lacking in colour and in uniformity of execution. The colouring of the shell is caused by the secretion of particular
glands in the mantle or skin. The snails obtain the chalky
matter for the formation of their shells from the food they
eat, and as aquatic plants are not rich in lime, fresh-water
Mollusca have therefore thin shells.

Certain snails are
very irritable, and
when touched or
startled in any way
some will let go their
hold and fall to the
bottom of the water,
while others will dis-
charge a coloured
liquid. For instance,
in these special circum-
stances the *Planorbis
corneus* (Fig. 130) will
frequently emit red
liquid, and the *Limnæa
stagnalis* (Fig. 131)
occasionally violet.

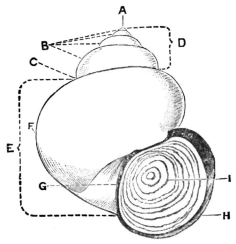

FIG. 133. ENLARGED OUTLINE OF A FRESH-
WATER SNAIL. A, Apex; B, Whorls;
C, Suture; D, Spire; E, Body-Whorl;
F, Periphery; G, Inner Lip; H, Outer
Lip; I, Operculum.

Snails are sometimes
found with the apices
of their shells eaten
away. The erosion is apparently caused by the action of
carbonic-acid gas, which is frequently present in considerable quantities in stagnant water owing to the presence of
decaying vegetable and animal matter. This gas is destructive to lime. The rest of the shell is protected by the
epidermis; but on the apex, which was formed when the
animal was very young, the epidermis is so thin that it is
frequently hardly any protection at all.

It is necessary to take care that no dead snails remain in the aquarium, or they will quickly corrupt the water.

Fig. 133 will perhaps be useful to some readers in helping them to understand the descriptions of the various snails suitable for the fresh-water aquarium which will be given.

The pectinibranchiate (possessors of comb-like gills, adapted for breathing beneath the surface of the water) fresh-water snails of Britain are divided into three families, viz.: (1) *Neritidœ*, (2) *Paludinidœ*, (3) *Valvatidœ*.

Neritina fluviatilis is the only representative we have of the family *Neritidœ*. It inhabits running streams. It will not live long in confinement, and it is only mentioned here in the hope that the assertion of its unsuitability for the aquarium will save some individuals of this species much unhappiness, and their captors not a little disappointment.

The following short description of this mollusc may help those who do not know it to identify it: The body of the animal is of a dirty-white colour, spotted with black; head almost black; tentacles long, slightly transparent, and streaked with black; eyes large and black, and placed on short pedicels at the base of the tentacles; shell nearly ½in. long, of a yellowish-brown colour, marked with spots of white, brown, purple, or pink; there are three whorls, the last very large in proportion to the rest; spire very short; sutures rather deep; operculum half-moon shaped, and yellowish, with an orange border; the shells are often covered with some chalky substance. These snails generally deposit their eggs upon the shells of one another.

All the members of the family *Paludinidœ* (dwellers in marshy places) possess an operculum, and each individual is either male or female.

Paludina contecta (whose specific name implies that it is operculate) is one of the handsomest of the British fresh-water snails. It is found in ponds, canals, lakes, and slow-running rivers in many parts of England, but especially in the South. It is an irritable animal, falling from the stones and plants to which it may be adhering as soon as it is touched or startled. The snail is ovoviviparous, the eggs being hatched within the oviduct of the mother, and the fry are retained there, sometimes for at least two months, until they are able to take some care of themselves. The young are not excluded from the parental shell all at once, but gradually. Sometimes only two or three are sent out into the watery world around them in the course of a day or longer. These fry, frequently numbering as many as thirty, have at first rows of bristles or cilia upon their shells, which after a time disappear and are replaced by the brown bands which mark the full-grown snail. *P. contecta* has long and elegant tentacles, which diverge somewhat. The eyes, which are round and black, and rather large, are situated upon short pedicels on the outer bases of the tentacles. The colour of the body varies from dark grey to dark brown, and is spotted with yellow. The foot is ovate, and has a yellowish margin; the head is small. The brownish-green shell is sometimes 1¾in. long, and more than 1in. broad. There are six whorls: the first is not much more than a mere point, but the last is very large, exceeding in length half of the entire shell. The last whorl has three, and the two whorls next to it two, rather broad brown spiral bands. The sutures of the shell are very deep, and the aperture is pear-shaped. The operculum is thin, and the lines of growth are plainly seen. This snail is very useful in the aquarium. The male has the right tentacle shorter and thicker than the left.

Paludina vivipara (Fig. 134) very much resembles the last species in habits, habitat, and structure. The body, in colour, is almost black and spotted with yellow; the tentacles are bluish-black and are thinly sprinkled with yellow or orange spots; the shell is much like that of the *P. contecta*, but it is more oblong in shape and less glossy in colour, and the whorls are not so swollen, nor consequently are the sutures so deep. The body-whorl of this snail has three bands, which are clearly shown in the accompanying illustration. The shells of both species are marked with broad brown bands, almost exactly in the same way. The apex of the shell of *P. vivipara* is blunter than that of the *P. contecta*, and the operculum thicker. This snail, which is sometimes called the

"Fresh-water Winkle," is a favourite with aquarium-keepers, and as it seems to prefer to feed upon decaying vegetation it is very useful in the tank. It is much more prolific and more active than its near relative *P. contecta*, and it also, as its specific name implies, brings forth its young alive. More than eighty fry in different stages of growth are said to have been counted in the ovary of a female of this species. The "Fresh-water Winkle," unlike *P. contecta*, clings most tenaciously to that substance to which it may be adhering when touched. Sometimes, indeed, it seems as though the animal would be injured in the attempt to detach it from the

FIG. 134. PALUDINA VIVIPARA.

side of an aquarium. In such circumstances it should be gently slid up the glass or side until it is above the surface of the water, when, as a rule, it will immediately let go its hold. The right tentacle, when it is shorter and thicker than the left, distinguishes the male.

Bythinia tentaculata (Fig. 135) is an interesting little snail, found more or less abundantly in the slow-running rivers, ponds, canals, and ditches of nearly every part of Britain except Scotland, where it is rather local. It is oviparous, and deposits its eggs, arranged in two or three rows, in an oblong mass upon stones, the stalks and leaves of aquatic plants, and, in addition to these, while in confine-

ment, upon the sides of the aquarium. The labour of
laying the eggs, sometimes numbering as many as seventy,
occupies several days. The little animal carefully cleans
every spot upon which she deposits an egg. The fry are
hatched, according to the temperature of the water, in from
twenty to twenty-five days, and do not reach maturity until
they are about two years old. The body of the animal is
almost black, and spotted with yellow. The tentacles are
filiform (thread-like), and diverge considerably; both tentacles
of the male, unlike those of the genus just described, are of the
same size. The eyes are black, large, and sessile. The shell
is conical and of a yellowish horn-colour and glossy.
There are five whorls, the last taking up more than half
of the shell. The sutures are
rather deep, and the apex is
pointed. The operculum is thick
and oval. This is a useful little
snail in the aquarium, often
feeding upon decaying vegetation, and not unwilling at times
to partake of a little animal
food. From the name Bythinia
one would imagine that the

FIG. 135. BYTHINIA TENTACULATA.

members of this genus always dwell in deep water; but this
is not the case by any means, for they are frequently found
in shallow streams, small ponds, canals, and ditches.

Valvata piscinalis is a little mollusc whose name signifies
that it possesses an operculum and lives in fish-ponds: it
should not be introduced into an aquarium which is rather
wanting in growing plants, for it will feed chiefly upon
them. It is an interesting animal and well worthy of a
place in a tank which is rich enough in vegetation to
supply it with food without suffering in consequence. The
respiratory organs of this snail are curious: it possesses a
branchial plume and a branchial thread. The former
consists of gills which somewhat resemble feathers, and
which extend beyond the edge of the mantle when the
animal is in motion. The latter is a tentacle-like appendage

on the right side of the mantle. When this snail is young
it is either male or female, but when it is old it becomes both
male and female. It is found in ponds, ditches, canals,
and slowly-running streams nearly everywhere. The body of
the animal is rather transparent, of a yellowish-grey colour,
and spotted with white. The tentacles are rather thick and
placed near together. The eyes are large and black, and
situated upon very short pedicels at the base of the tentacles.
The shell is about ¼in. long and of a yellowish horn-colour;
its shape is conical, and there are five whorls, the largest
of which more than equals in length all the rest together.
The sutures are deep; the aperture is circular and the
operculum round and horny. The shell is found attached to
the cases of certain caddis-worms. The *V. piscinalis* lays
from sixteen to twenty eggs, which are hatched in about
the same number of days. The shells of the fry are so
transparent that the young animals within can be very
plainly seen.

Valvata cristata though not large enough for the ordinary
aquarium is interesting in those small tanks in which fish
are not kept. It is found upon weeds growing in slow-
running or stagnant water. Like the last species, and as its
specific name denotes, it possesses a branchial plume and a
branchial thread. Its body is dark brown, slightly spotted
with black. The tentacles are close together and thread-like.
The shell is so much compressed that it somewhat resembles
that of the genus *Planorbis*. It is about ⅛in. in diameter,
and of a light horn-colour. The operculum has been likened
to an "inverted pot-lid."

Of the six families of British molluscs belonging to the
order *Pulmobranchiata*, only one of them is aquatic—*Limnæidæ;* and as all the members of this family are pulmobranchiate, it is necessary that they should occasionally
come to the surface of the water for atmospheric air.
Some of them, by ascending the stalks of the water-plants
and the like, even leave the water altogether for a time.
The *Limnæidæ* are divided into the following four genera:
(1) *Planorbis;* (2) *Physa;* (3) *Limnæa;* (4) *Ancylus.* All the

members of the genus *Planorbis* are more or less suitable
for the aquarium, for they seem, as a rule, to feed upon
the confervoid growth in preference to any other. They all
live in slow-running or stagnant water. There are eleven
species of the genus in this country, and most of them
are fairly common. The chief characteristic of the Planorbes
is a long body contained, with plenty of room to spare,
in a flat-coiled shell. The disc or foot of the animal is
short, and is attached to the body by a kind of stalk.
The tentacles are long and slender. Both sexes are united
in the same individual. They have no operculum. Some of
them, when out of reach of water, have the power of
closing the apertures of their shell with an epiphragm.
They are, as a rule, herbivorous, though they have occasionally been seen to partake of animal food. The snails
of this genus, when irritated, sometimes emit a red liquid;
and some of them, if not all, are at times thread-spinners.

There are few, if any, snails more suitable for a tank than
Planorbis corneus (Fig. 130). It has long been a great
favourite with aquarium-keepers. It is handsome, hardy,
large, and not given to destroying useful vegetation. It is
prolific, and ready to breed while in confinement at almost
any period of the year. *P. corneus* is found in slow-running
or stagnant water, but it is rather local. However, it can
nearly always be bought very cheaply of most dealers in
necessaries for the aquarium. It deposits its eggs upon
stones, leaves, and stalks of plants, and, while in confinement,
upon the sides of the tank as well. The eggs are contained
in an orbicular capsule, and vary in number from twenty to
forty-five. The fry are hatched, according to the temperature
of the water, in from sixteen to thirty days. The epidermis
of the young shell is covered with a kind of down, which has
been likened to velvet pile. The body of the animal is black
above and slightly greyish underneath. The mouth is
brownish-red. The tentacles are long and elegant. The
shell is flat-coiled in shape, and of a dark reddish-brown
colour, sometimes appearing almost quite black. There are
five or six whorls, and the sutures are rather deep. The shell

is sometimes **an** inch in diameter; the periphery is round. This snail has a curious habit of fixing itself by its side to perpendicular surfaces, such as the glass of the aquarium.

Planorbis carinatus is also a very useful snail in a tank, and very popular with aquarium-keepers. The periphery of the shell, instead of being round as in the last species, is distinctly keeled near the centre. Like *P. corneus*, it feeds upon confervæ in preference to growing plants. It is not a very active animal. *P. carinatus* is unfortunately by no means

FIG. 136. PLANORBIS MARGINATUS.

common, except perhaps in the ponds, ditches, **and** slow-running streams of the Eastern Counties. It is taken in other parts of England, but not in any numbers; nevertheless, it can generally be bought of aquarium dealers. This species incloses its eggs (six to twelve in number) in capsules shaped like those of *P. corneus*, and affixes them to stones, leaves, &c., and in addition to these, while in confinement, to the sides of the aquarium. The fry are hatched, according to the temperature of the water, in about fourteen days. The body of the animal is a reddish dark brown. The tentacles are slender and yellowish, with a pinkish tinge; they are also rather blunt at their extremities. The shell is about ½in. in diameter, compressed, concave above, and almost flat below. The whorls are five or six in number, and rapidly enlarge. The sutures are deep; the aperture is angular.

Planorbis marginatus (Fig. 136) is very like *P. carinatus* in structure and habits; but it is commoner, though quite as useful in the aquarium as its near relative. Great numbers of *P. marginatus* are said to be bred in those reservoirs in Yorkshire which are used for cooling the water from the condensers of the steam-engines of the factories. The tentacles of *P. marginatus* are rather more pointed than those of *P. carinatus*. In other respects the bodies of the two animals are much alike. The shell of *P. marginatus* is thicker, and a little greater in diameter than that of *P. carinatus*, and the keel is placed nearer to the lower side of the periphery than to the middle; hence the

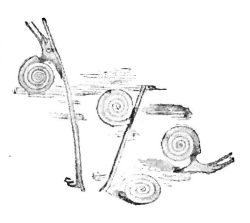

FIG. 137. PLANORBIS VORTEX.

specific name *marginatus*. The keel itself is not so prominent as that of *P. carinatus*. The eggs of this species are from six to fourteen in number, and are contained in an orbicular capsule; they are hatched, according to the temperature of the water, in about a fortnight.

Planorbis vortex (Fig. 137) is a very pretty little snail found in the slow-running and stagnant water of nearly every part of Britain. It is one of the molluscs which are in the habit of closing the aperture of their shell with an epiphragm should the pond, ditch, or stream in which they live become dry during summer; and thus protected, it will remain in a state of torpidity until the return of rain

The colour of the animal is a kind of violet-brown, the lower part of the body being of a lighter shade. The body itself is slender and the head large. The shell is thin and compressed, not quite ½in. in diameter, a little concave above and flat below, so flattened indeed as to cause the periphery to be prominently keeled at the lower side. The colour of the shell is a glossy brown, and there are from six to eight whorls. The aperture is slightly angular. This snail lays about fourteen eggs, and incloses them in an orbicular capsule. They are hatched in from ten to fourteen days.

Planorbis spirorbis is smaller and thicker than the last species: it is found in the sluggish or stagnant water of almost every part of Britain. The animal is of a purplish-grey; the tentacles are long, thread-like, and pointed at the tips; the disc is spotted with black. The shell is glossy brown and slightly concave on both sides, or sometimes rather flat below: it very much resembles that of *P. vortex*, but it is less in diameter, rather thicker, and possesses fewer whorls. The periphery is very slightly keeled below; the aperture is almost round. This species also, when out of water, closes the mouth of its shell with an epiphragm.

Planorbis albus is a beautiful snail, found in the slow-running and stagnant water of many parts of Britain. The body of the animal is greyish, and faintly spotted with black; the head is rather large, and the tentacles are slender. The shell, which is marked with raised spiral striæ (thread-like lines), is thin, brittle, about ¼in. in diameter, and of a very light horn-colour. The epidermis of the shell is thick, and is more or less covered with fine bristles. There are five whorls, and the sutures are rather deep. *P. albus* lays from ten to fourteen eggs, and incloses them in an orbicular capsule. The fry are hatched in from twelve to fourteen days.

Planorbis lineatus is not a very common snail, and is found only, as a rule, it is said, in the Home and Eastern Counties, and occasionally in Yorkshire and Nottinghamshire. The body of the animal is of a purplish-brown colour. The tentacles are long, thread-like, and yellowish-brown. The disc is small, broad, and tapers to a point behind. The shell is usually

P

described as quoit-shaped, and the upper side is more convex
than the lower: it is of a glossy reddish-brown colour, and
not quite ¼in. in diameter. There are four whorls: the body-
whorl, which is larger than all the rest, contains partitions
plainly visible through the shell. The spire is much depressed.
This snail lays about five eggs, and incloses them in an
orbicular capsule. The fry are hatched in from ten to fourteen days.

Planorbis nitidus is found in the sluggish and stagnant
water of nearly every part of Britain. It is very like the
P. lineatus, but is smaller, is without the internal partitions or
plates, and the spire of the shell is not so much depressed.
The animal is almost black, and is spotted with dark grey.
The tentacles are very slender and pointed at their tips.
The shell varies in both size and colour, but it is never, I
think, as much as ¼in. in diameter. Its colour varies from
dark to light horn-colour, and is slightly prismatic. The
largest shells are generally the darkest. There are three or
four whorls. The body-whorl, which is very large in proportion to the rest, partly covers the preceding whorl and
turns outward. The periphery is rather prominently keeled
near the centre. The sutures are fairly deep; the aperture
is angular. The eggs of this snail, which are about four in
number, are inclosed in an orbicular capsule, and are hatched
in from ten to fourteen days. It is a very sluggish
mollusc, its shell sometimes being found covered with insect
egg-cases or with confervæ.

The following Planorbes are, as a rule, too small for the
ordinary aquarium, but they will be interesting, harmless,
and useful in those tanks in which fish are not kept:

Planorbis contortus is a little snail found on plants in
clear, stagnant water throughout Britain, but it is rather local.
It is inactive. Its body is almost black and is tinged with
red. Its tentacles are unusually slender and of a brownish
colour. The shell is about ⅕in. in diameter, and of a brownish
horn-colour; it is flat above with a concavity in the middle,
and very concave below. There are eight very compact
whorls. The sutures are deep, and the aperture is narrow and

crescent-shaped. This snail lays about seven eggs and incloses them in an orbicular capsule. The fry are hatched in from ten to fourteen days.

Planorbis glaber is found in widely different parts of Britain, but it is very local. It is much like *P. albus*, but is smaller, more glossy, and without the raised spiral striæ. The animal is described as having "a yellowish-grey body; tentacles rather short, cylindrical, and ending in a blunt point; foot rather broad, especially in front, with a yellowish edge." The shell is convex above, with a slight depression in the middle, and concave below. It is of a brownish horn-colour, and slightly transparent. There are about four compact whorls, and the periphery is round. The aperture is nearly round, and the sutures are rather deep. This snail has been likened, when young, to the *Valvata cristata*.

Planorbis nautileus is a very beautiful little snail, taken on water-plants in the lakes, ponds, and ditches of many parts of Britain. It is generally found upon the under-side of broad, floating leaves, such as those of the Pond Weeds (*Potamogeton*) and the Water-Lilies, but especially upon the former. The body of the animal is greyish and is spotted minutely with black. The shell is about $\frac{1}{10}$in. in diameter, and is quoit-shaped. There are three whorls, the body-whorl being larger than the rest of the shell. The periphery is bluntly keeled. This small snail lays from three to six eggs, and incloses them in an orbicular capsule. The fry are hatched in about twelve days.

The Physæ connect the Planorbes with the Limnæidæ. There are only two species of the genus *Physa* in Great Britain, but both are suitable for the aquarium. The Physæ can be easily recognised by their sinistral shells. Sinistral shells are those whose coils instead of winding from left to right—*i.e.*, following the course of the sun—wind from right to left, the way an ordinary screw is withdrawn.

Physa hypnorum is found on water-plants in slow-running streams and ponds throughout Britain. It is an active snail, and very interesting in the aquarium, especially as a "thread-spinner." The body of the animal is generally dark grey.

thickly covered with small black spots. The tentacles are pointed and blackish in colour. The disc is narrow, and ends behind in a slightly pointed tail. The shell is about ½in. long, and is spindle-shaped; it is of a dark or yellowish horn-colour, glossy, and semi-transparent. There are five or six whorls, and the spire is produced: the body-whorl occupies more than half of the entire shell. The aperture may be described as pear-shaped. *P. hypnorum* deposits its eggs, which number from three to twenty, in a roundish capsule. The fry are hatched in from sixteen to twenty days.

Physa fontinalis is much commoner than the last species. It is found in sluggish or stagnant clear water in nearly every part of Britain. It is frequently taken upon watercress. This mollusc is also, like the *P. hypnorum,* a very busy "thread-spinner." The body of the animal is dark grey. The tentacles are of a lighter colour than the body. The disc is light grey, and ends behind in a rather pointed tail. The shell, which is about ½in. long, is very thin, and of a glossy light horn-colour. There are four or five whorls, the body-whorl more than equalling half of the shell. The spire is very short, and the apex is blunt. The sutures are rather deep; the aperture is large and pear-shaped. This snail lays from three to twenty eggs, and incloses them in a roundish capsule. The fry are hatched in from sixteen to twenty days.

Limnææ are more active, greater eaters, and fonder of feeding upon healthy growing water-plants than any of the molluscs already described; and consequently are not, on the whole, so suitable for the aquarium. However, some of the *Limnææ* are useful in the tank, and all of them are interesting there. A few are carnivorous as well as herbivorous. I have several times seen snails of this genus, especially *L. peregra,* sharing a worm or a dead fish with the beetles, Corixæ, and the like. Although *Limnææ* will eat no small quantity of necessary vegetation, they are at the same time exceedingly useful in clearing away confervæ, and in acting as scavengers generally.

I dare say I shall be laughed at by some people when I say that I believe that a taste for confervoid growth can be cultivated in a snail. But I certainly have noticed that the longer some of the *Limnæx* are kept in confinement, the less they eat of growing plants and the more of confervæ. These snails are gregarious for the most part, and extremely prolific. They are generally found in sluggish or stagnant water, crawling upon the mud or adhering to and feeding upon aquatic plants, or floating on the surface of the water. Each individual is both male and female.

Limnæa stagnalis (Fig. 138) is a very elegant snail, found in slow-running and stagnant water nearly all over Britain, and is sometimes called the "Fresh-water Whelk." It is very

FIG. 138. LIMNÆA STAGNALIS.

useful in the aquarium as a consumer of confervæ, but it is not always willing to confine itself to this food. It should therefore be watched, and removed directly it is seen destroying the aquatic plants. I have had some snails of this species which lived almost entirely upon confervoid growth, but they were those which I had had in confinement for a long time. This snail, when irritated, sometimes discharges a violet-coloured liquid. It is also occasionally carnivorous. *L. stagnalis* is not by any means difficult to recognise, on account of its large size and elegant shape. Its body is yellowish-grey with a bluish-green tinge and mottled with brown and white. The tentacles are flat and triangular. The disc is broad and has a yellowish margin. The shell is about 1½in. long, of a greyish-white or yellowish horn-colour, and is sometimes covered with some extraneous substance. There are from six to eight whorls, the body-whorl being much larger and more swollen than the others. The spire is elongated, and tapers gracefully to a fine point. The sutures are rather deep, and the aperture is almost oval. This snail incloses its eggs, sometimes numbering as many as 130, in an orbicular capsule. The fry are hatched, according to the temperature of the water, in from fifteen to twenty days.

Limnæa auricularia (Fig. 139) has a greater liking for confervæ than *L. stagnalis*, and is therefore more suitable for the aquarium. It is found in the sluggish streams, lakes, and ponds of different parts of Britain, but it is not a very

FIG. 139. LIMNÆA AURICULARIA.

common species. Even where it does abound, it frequently escapes capture, unless properly searched for, from the habit it has of remaining at or near the bottom of the water. When taken it is easily recognised. The body of the animal is a greenish dark grey, spotted with small black spots and larger white ones. The tentacles are flat, triangular, and spotted with yellowish-grey on the margins. The disc has also a yellow margin. The shell is about 1in. long, ¾in. wide, and of a light yellowish horn-colour. There are four or five whorls, the body-whorl being much larger than all the rest of the shell. The spire is short and the apex is much pointed. The aperture is very large and ear-shaped: hence the specific name. The outer lip is bent backward or reflected. *L. auricularia* lays about eighty eggs, and incloses them in a somewhat elliptical capsule: they are hatched in from sixteen to twenty days.

Limnœa palustris (Fig. 140) is rather an elegant snail, but it is too great an eater of useful growing plants to be safely trusted for long in an ordinary aquarium. There are occasions, however, upon which it may be of use, such as when there is an excess of vegetation. It is always, I think, interesting.

The tank in which it is kept should be covered, or it will be very likely to escape and die. It is found in the lakes, ponds, ditches, and sluggish streams of nearly every part of Britain. The animal is of a dark grey colour, tinged with violet, and spotted with black or yellow. The tentacles are conical. The disc is slightly notched. The shell is about ¾in. in length, conical in shape, and of a light or darkish horn-colour. There are six or seven whorls: the body-whorl more than equals half the shell. The sutures are rather deep, and the aperture is oval or almost so. This snail lays from sixty to eighty eggs, and incloses them in a somewhat cylindrical capsule. The fry are hatched in from sixteen to twenty days.

FIG. 140.   LIMNÆA PALUSTRIS.

Limnœa peregra (Fig. 141) is a rather handsome snail, and is perhaps commoner than any other aquatic mollusc. Some people do not give it a very good character as an inmate of the aquarium, but I am never without it, and find that it does more good than harm. I once examined seven aquaria, large and small, in which snails of this species were kept, and found only one solitary individual, out of the many, upon any of the plants. All the others seemed to be busy at work upon the sides of the tanks. These molluscs are good scavengers, as they are not at all unready, as I have said, to become occasionally carnivorous. They will eat a dead worm, a defunct fish, or even a deceased relative. They are most prolific, and thus provide a great quantity of

useful food for the fish. A drawback in keeping these snails
in the aquarium is their habit of escaping from it, and
dying outside of it for want of water. The tanks, therefore,
in which they are confined should be covered. The body of
the animal is a pale brown, tinged with green. The tentacles
are flat, triangular, and placed almost at right angles with
the sides of the animal. The eyes are black, and plainly
seen. The shell is obliquely-ovate, and of a glossy dark

FIG. 141   LIMNÆA PEREGRA.

yellowish horn-colour. There are five whorls, the body-whorl
taking up more than three parts of the length of the shell.
The spire, which is more or less produced in different individuals, occupies about a quarter the length of the shell. The
aperture is large and oval, and the outer lip is a little
reflected. This snail is found in the slow-running and
stagnant water of nearly every, if not every, part of Britain
It lays from sixty to eighty eggs, and incloses them in an
elliptical capsule. It produces many such capsules in the

course of a year. Dr. Jeffreys is reported to have stated that *L. peregra* deposits about 13,000 eggs. The eggs are hatched in from sixteen to twenty days.

Limnæa glabra is an elegant little snail, found in many parts of England, but more rarely in Scotland and Ireland. It lives at the bottom of rather shallow stagnant water, only coming, as a rule, to the surface of the water for the purpose of taking a fresh supply of air. The body of the animal is of a dull grey colour, spotted minutely with black. The tentacles are triangular and of a lighter colour than the body. The eyes are placed upon tubercles. The shell is cylindrical, and not quite an inch long. There are seven or eight whorls; the body-whorl does not equal half the shell. The spire is produced, and tapers to a rather fine point. The aperture is narrowly oval. This mollusc lays from twenty to thirty eggs, and incloses them in an oblong capsule. The fry are hatched in, I believe, from sixteen to twenty days.

Limnæa truncatula is found in rather muddy water in every part of Britain. It is fairly useful in the aquarium, and is not likely to do much harm. The body of the animal is almost black and spotted with black: it is of a lighter shade underneath. The tentacles are light grey, and also spotted with black. The shell is about ½in. in length, and oblong-conical in shape. There are five or six turreted whorls. The spire has the appearance of being slightly truncated; hence the specific name of the mollusc. The apex is sharp, the sutures are very deep, and the aperture is almost oval. This snail generally deposits its capsules, containing from twelve to twenty eggs, upon the mud. The eggs are hatched, I believe, in from sixteen to twenty days.

Limnæa glutinosa is said to be "locally and periodically abundant;" that is, in some localities it is common for a time, then it disappears apparently altogether, only to re-appear after an interval of longer or shorter duration as numerous as ever. It has been suggested as a reason for this strange habit on the part of the mollusc that it buries itself for some considerable time in the mud at the bottom of the water in which it dwells, and thus escapes notice and capture. The *L. glutinosa* lives in ponds and ditches in different parts of Britain. It is frequently recommended as an inmate of the aquarium, but those who introduce it among their water-plants should remember that it has a very great liking for their tender roots and rootlets, especially those of the duckweeds. With the exception of this weakness, the snail may be considered as useful and harmless. The body of the animal is plentifully covered with slime; hence its specific name of *glutinosa*. It is of a dark grey colour, tinged with yellow and spotted with orange. The tentacles are short, very broad at the base, flat, blunt at the tips, and spotted with white. The shell is about ½in. in length, "globosely-ovate" in shape, and of a glossy yellowish horn-colour. There are three or four globose whorls : the body-whorl is considerably larger than the rest of the shell. The spire is produced very little, and the sutures are rather deep. The aperture is almost oval, and the inner lip is much expanded. This snail lays from twenty-five to thirty eggs, and incloses them in a rounded and transparent capsule. They are hatched in from sixteen to twenty days.

The little molluscs called Ancyli are interesting, useful, and harmless in the aquarium. They are very sluggish in their movements, taking a long time to travel even a short distance. They do not swim, nor have I ever seen them float, though I seldom let a day go by without having noticed them and their habits. Their principal food seems to be confervæ and decaying vegetable matter. The stomachs of these "fresh-water limpets," as they are sometimes called, have been compared to the gizzard of a fowl, on account of their muscular bands and the minute particles of sand which they are found to contain. The shell is hooked like a hawk's beak; hence the generic name. There are two species of this genus in Britain : though pulmobranchiate, they are rarely seen to come to the surface of the water for a fresh supply of atmospheric air.

Ancylus fluviatilis (Fig. 142) inhabits rivers, streams, and other clear water in every part of Britain. It is generally found adhering to stones at the bottom, but occasionally it is taken upon aquatic plants or out of water altogether, though within reach of the spray of waterfalls and the like.

Mr. Darwin, in his " Origin of Species," speaks of an Ancylus as having been taken adhering to a water-beetle—a Dyticus.

A good way to obtain these interesting little molluscs is to take up and examine the flat stones at the bottom of clear and shallow streams, to which they will be found adhering. It is necessary to exercise a little care in removing Ancyli, or they may be hurt. They give no trouble in the aquarium, where they spend nearly all their time upon the sides, feeding upon confervæ. The body of the animal is greyish, and the tentacles are greyish-white and broad at their base. The shell, which is described as cowl-shaped, covers all the animal when it is moving, except the tips of the tentacles and sometimes perhaps a portion of the muzzle. It is a dark horn-colour, and about ¼in. in diameter. The spire is curved towards the right. The apex is rather blunt, and the aperture is oval. This mollusc lays about eight eggs, and incloses them in a roundish capsule. The eggs are hatched in about twenty-six days.

FIG. 142. ANCYLUS FLUVIATILIS.

Ancylus oblongus lives in slow-running or stagnant clear water throughout Britain, but it is rather local. It is found adhering to the under-side of aquatic plants, and not, like *A. fluviatilis*, to stones and wood. When it moves, which is seldom, it travels more quickly than the last species. It has a yellowish-grey body, with a greenish tinge. The tentacles are light grey, and widely separate from each other. The shell is more oblong than the last species; hence the specific name. It is about ¼in. in diameter and of a glossy yellowish-green horn-colour. The spire is bent towards the left, and not, as in the *A. fluviatilis*, towards the right. The apex is rather sharp, and the aperture is oval. The eggs are from four to twelve, and are inclosed in an orbicular capsule. They are hatched in about twenty-six days.

CHAPTER XI.

MUSSELS.

THE *Conchifera* (shell-bearers), or *Bivalves*, form one of the sub-divisions of the Molluscs. They never live (as so many of the gasteropods, or univalves, do) upon land, but always in either fresh or salt water, most of them, however, being inhabitants of the latter. The fresh-water bivalves are not only useful in the aquarium, but they are in themselves full of interest, and anyone who will watch and study them a little will certainly be rewarded for his trouble.

Those who begin keeping aquaria are sometimes advised to have nothing to do with the *Conchifera*, as they are so likely to die and corrupt the water. I cannot say that such has been my experience, for I have rarely known them die, and my tanks have never suffered any bad effects to my know-ledge through their death. Nor are they likely, as far as I know, to do any harm by their slowly ploughing through the sand and gravel at the bottom of the aquarium. As a rule, they are useful as scavengers, for they extract from the water particles of animal and vegetable matter. They are exceedingly prolific, and, breeding readily in confinement, their eggs and fry supply the fish with suitable food. Some bivalves of course are more active than others. For example, some of the *Sphæriidæ* will frequently ascend the sides of the aquarium or float along the under-surface of the water apparently with the same ease that the *Planorbis corneus* performs the like feat, or they will suspend themselves in the water by means of a "molluscan thread," while some of the *Unionidæ* will seem to remain for days in the same place without moving.

The soft parts of a "shell-bearing" mollusc consist chiefly of a mantle having two lobes or divisions, leaf-like gills, siphons, or a siphon or orifices, and a tongue-shaped foot which can be considerably elongated and sometimes possesses a tuft of muscular threads called a "byssus," by means of which the animal can attach itself to foreign bodies. There are also various muscles, a heart, a liver, a stomach, and intestines. There is no distinct head.

The two valves or shells of these molluscs are drawn together by means of muscles called the "adductor muscles." Some of the *Conchifera* have only one adductor muscle, which is situated near the centre of the body, while others possess two, one of which is placed towards the anterior extremity of the animal, and the other towards the posterior. The former molluscs are called *Monomyarian* (having one muscle), the latter *Dimyarian* (having two muscles). The places inside the shells to which these muscles are attached are marked by an impression, more or less distinct, called the "muscular scar." Another scar, the "pallial," runs from the anterior muscular scar, following at a short distance from the edge the course of the ventral margin of the shell, and then joins the posterior muscular scar. This pallial scar shows where the mantle of the animal was attached to the shell. The two valves are joined together by a hinge, which often possesses teeth. The ligament, as the hinge is sometimes called, is either external or internal. The male and female of these molluscs are united in the same individual. Figs. 143 and 144 will perhaps help to make plain the following description of some of the bivalves suitable for the fresh-water aquarium.

The *Lamellibranchiata* (possessors of leaf-like gills), as the *Conchifera* are often called, are now divided into three families, viz: (1) *Sphæriidæ*, (2) *Unionidæ*, (3) *Dreissenidæ*.

The members of the *Sphæriidæ* family have the shell either oblong or oval, and its hinge possesses teeth. They are provided with one or two siphons, which can be extended or contracted. Their foot is long, beardless, and capable of great extension. The *Sphæriidæ* are ovoviparous, and are divided into two genera: (1) *Sphærium* (a sphere), (2) *Pisidium* (pea-shaped).

The Sphæria possess two siphons, one longer than the other. The former is called the incurrent siphor, and is used for respiration and nutrition, and the latter is known as the excurrent siphon, and serves to carry away that for which the animal has no further use. The valves of the shell are of equal size, but of slightly different shape. The hinge possesses what are called cardinal or anterior teeth and lateral or posterior teeth. The Sphæria are active in their habits, and many of them, if not all, are more or less "thread-spinners." They breed readily in confinement, and sometimes before they reach maturity. They feed principally upon animalcula, and when winter comes on they bury themselves in the mud at the bottom of the water, and remain there in a state of torpidity until the spring.

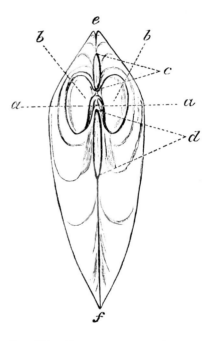

FIG. 143. OUTLINE OF THE DORSAL PART OF BOTH VALVES OF UNIO TUMIDUS. *aa*, Thickness; *bb*, Umbo; *c*, Lunule; *d*, Ligament; *e*, Anterior Extremity; *f*, Posterior Extremity.

They seem to be irritable or timid little molluscs, for when they have ascended the sides of the aquarium, the slightest touch or startling will frequently cause them to quit their hold and sink to the bottom.

Sphærium rivicolum is found in the slow-running and sometimes in the stagnant water of various parts of England, and rarely in Ireland, but it is local. It is the largest of the *Sphæriidæ*, having a shell about ¾in. long, ½in. high, and ⅜in. thick. The body of the animal is grey, with a yellowish tinge; the foot is a greyish-white; the siphons are short, nearly of the same length, and whitish. The shell is globosely-ovate, solid, and of a greenish-brown colour, marked with two or three darkish bands. The umbones are central

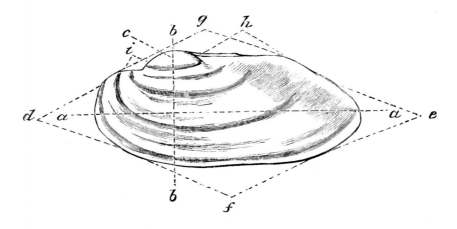

Fig. 144. Outline of Left Valve of Unio tumidus. *aa*, Length; *bb*, Height; *c*, Umbo; *d*, Anterior Extremity; *e*, Posterior Extremity; *f*, Ventral Margin; *g*, Dorsal Margin; *h*, Ligament; *i*, Lunule.

(*i.e.*, in the middle), close to the dorsal margin. The hinge is strong, and there are two cardinal and four lateral teeth. The ligament is short and external, and the muscular scars are distinct.

Sphærium ovale is a small scarce mollusc, but it is of interest in the aquarium. It is found in canals and ponds. The body is white, and the siphons are long and united nearly as far as their tips. The foot is large and tongue-shaped. The shell is oblong, one extremity being rather round and the other truncate. The umbones are a little in front of the middle of the shell. The teeth are like those of the last species, but are very small. The muscular scars are indistinct. The shell is about ½in. long, ¼in. high, and ⅜in. thick.

Sphærium corneum is very much commoner than the last species, being found in the rivers, streams, canals, ditches, and ponds of nearly every part of Britain. The body is greyish, and the foot is rather pointed and whitish. The siphons are long, and of a pale flesh-colour. The shell is rather orbicular, and of a light horn-colour. The umbones are central, and the ligament is inconspicuous and short. The teeth are like those of the last species, and the muscular scars are indistinct. The shell is about $\frac{7}{16}$in. long, $\frac{5}{16}$in. high, and $\frac{3}{16}$in. thick.

Sphærium lacustre (Fig. 145) is an interesting little bivalve, and will live very well in confinement. It is rather a busy "thread-spinner," and is found in the running and stagnant water of many parts of Britain, but it is rare in Scotland. The body is almost white, and sometimes of a

FIG. 145. SPHÆRIUM LACUSTRE.

pale flesh-colour. The siphons are white and long, and the foot is very large for the size of the animal. The shell is nearly round, and of a pale horn-colour. The umbones are prominent, central, and show the first growth of the shell. The teeth are like those of the last species, but are very small. The ligament is inconspicuous, and the scars are indistinct.

In many respects the Pisidia are very like the Sphæria, but they differ principally in having one siphon instead of two; they are also more abundant, and are divided into five species: it is rather difficult, unfortunately, to tell one species from another. Dr. Gwynn Jeffreys says, concerning them, that "size, substance, sculpture, and lustre, are not of much account, as they mainly depend on the chemical ingredients of the water inhabited by these molluscs as well as on their supply of food." He arranged the five species in the following order:

1. *Pisidium amnicum*
2. *P. fontinale* $\bigg\}$ have triangular shells.
3. *P. pusillum* has an oval shell.
4. *P. nitidum* has a round shell.
5. *P. roseum* has an oblong shell.

The bodies of all the species of *Pisidium* are very much alike; their colour is whitish or whitish-grey.

Pisidium amnicum (Fig. 146), by far the largest of the genus, is found in the slow-running and stagnant water of

FIG 146. PISIDIUM AMNICUM.

nearly every part of Britain. The shell is glossy, solid, of a greyish horn-colour, and is a little over ¼in. in length. This mollusc is said to spend the greater part of its time partly buried in the mud at the bottom of the water.

Pisidium fontinale is much smaller than the last species, being only about ⅛in. in length. The umbones of the shell are prominent. This mollusc lives in the slow-running and stagnant water of nearly every part of Britain, and is described as being the most active species of the genus to which it belongs. It is said to be fond of small splashy ponds; hence, I suppose, its specific name.

Pisidium pusillum lives in weedy water throughout Britain. The shell is more oval in shape than that of the last species, and even tinier in size; hence the specific name.

Pisidium nitidum has an almost round shell, the umbones of which are marked with rather deep grooves. It is found in clear, stagnant water in many parts of Britain, but it is not so common as some of the other species. Its funnel-shaped siphon is generally considered as a help to distinguish it from its other relatives, all of which have such a confusing family likeness. The shell is iridescent and very glossy; hence the specific name.

Pisidium roseum is also found in weedy ponds and ditches. The shell is oblong, and is about $\frac{1}{16}$in. in length, but in other respects it is very like that of the last species. It receives its specific name from the rose-colour of the upper part of its body.

The *Unionidæ* are more commonly called Mussels than any of the other fresh-water bivalves. Some of them are ovoviparous, while others are oviparous. They live in rivers, lakes, and ponds throughout Britain, and they feed upon the vegetable and animal matter which they extract from the water, as well as upon Entomostraca and other minute animals. Each individual of this family is both male and female. In winter they bury themselves in the mud. These animals, instead of having one or two siphons, like the *Sphæriidæ*, have two orifices. The lower orifice, which is bearded, is used for respiration, and the upper orifice, which is beardless or simple, serves for getting rid of that from which the animal has extracted all nutriment. The foot is large and tongue-shaped.

The *Unionidæ* are divided into two genera, viz.: (1) *Unio*; (2) *Anodonta*. The former genus possesses two species, and the latter only one.

The *Uniones* are oviparous, and some of them contain pearls; hence the generic name of *Unio*.

Unio tumidus (Fig. 147) is a handsome bivalve, found in the sluggish and stagnant water of nearly every part of Britain. It is occasionally sold by dealers in aquarium necessaries, as the "Duck Mussel." It is useful and interesting in the tank, where at times it is rather active in its movements, leaving long grooves behind it in the sand and gravel, as it travels from spot to spot. The upper orifice is a short brownish tube, and the lower or branchial orifice is somewhat lighter in colour. The shell has a swollen appearance (hence the specific name) in comparison with some other shells of this family. It is about $2\frac{1}{4}$in. long, 1in. high, and $\frac{3}{4}$in. thick, and of a yellowish-brown colour, the lines of growth being well marked. The umbones are towards the anterior extremity, and turn a little inwards. The anterior side slopes away towards the ventral

margin, and the posterior side or end tapers to a wedge-like
point. The lunule is narrow, and the ligament short and
prominent. There are four strong teeth attached to the
hinge—two cardinal and two lateral. The muscular scars
are quite distinct. M. Moquin Tandon is reported to have said

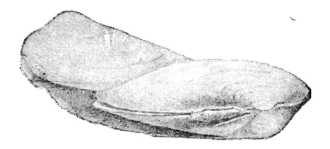

FIG. 147. UNIO TUMIDUS.

that this animal, in July and August, emits small elongated
pointed masses, each containing about 100 eggs, and a single
mollusc of this species has been known to lay about 150 of
such masses in a few days.

Unio pictorum is a species found in the sluggish and
stagnant water of England, but not, it is said, farther north
than Yorkshire. The foot of the animal is reddish. The
orifices are very like those of *U. tumidus.* The shell is about
2½in. long and more than 1in. high : it is not so thick as that of
the last species, and altogether has a slimmer appearance. The
colour is yellowish-brown, marked with darker brown bands.
The anterior side slopes away towards the ventral margin,
which is almost straight. The posterior side gradually tapers
each way, but principally from the dorsal margin, until it
comes to a round point. The umbones are towards the anterior
extremity, and turn a little in. Both the lunule and the
ligament are rather long : the former is narrow. There are
four teeth, but they are not so strong as those of *U. tumidus.*
The muscular scars are distinct, and the pallial scar is not.
One individual of this species has been said to lay the extra-

ordinary number of 220,000 eggs during the months of May, June, and July. The shells of this bivalve in former days were used for the purpose of holding the painter's colours; hence its specific name. At the present time they may be purchased containing gold and silver leaf.

Unio margaritifer is especially the "pearl-bearing" mussel, as its specific name implies. It is chiefly found in the rivers of the mountainous districts of Britain. Beautiful and valuable pearls have at various times been found in this and other species of the *Unionidæ.* Mr. Cholmondeley Pennell, in his book on "Pike and other Coarse Fish," mentions a boy who, while fishing for trout in the Chapel Brook, near Tweed Mill, Coldstream, caught a large Mussel (the species is not given) which contained no less than "forty fine pearls of different sizes, some of which were thought to be worth ten shillings each."

The body of *U. margaritifer* is a dirty grey, and its foot is large, tongue-shaped, and reddish-brown. The shell is about 4in. long and 2in. high, oblong, compressed, and of a darker colour than the rest of the *Unionidæ.* The umbones, which are more often eroded in this species than in any other of the genus, are placed towards the anterior extremity, which is fairly evenly rounded. The posterior side slopes away from the dorsal margin. The ventral margin is almost straight, the ligament is very long, and the lunule is inconspicuous. The muscular and pallial scars are very distinct.

The *Anodontæ* are the largest of our fresh-water bivalves, sometimes measuring as much as 5in. in length and 3in. in height, and they should not, therefore, be introduced into a tank unless it is very large and the sand and gravel at its bottom are deep in proportion.

Anodonta cygnea (Fig. 148) is the only species of the genus which is found in Britain. Various varieties have often been taken for different species, but I think now it is generally considered that there is only this solitary species. The body of the animal is greyish, slightly tinged with yellow or red. The foot is broad, and of a dirty yellow colour. The shell is oblong, thin, yellowish-green, or sometimes rusty brown, and the valves are rather swollen. The umbones are placed towards the anterior end, which slopes away rather suddenly in the direction of the ventral margin. The upper part of the posterior side has a "cut-away" or flattened

FIG. 148. ANODONTA CYGNEA.

appearance. There are no teeth attached to the hinge; hence the generic name. The muscular scars are indistinct. This species is commonly called the "Swan Mussel," I suppose because the swans are fond of feeding upon it.

Dreissena polymorpha is a curious and beautiful little mussel, first described as a native of this country by Mr. J. de Carle Sowerby in the year 1824. It is supposed to have been introduced here by clinging to the timber brought from the Volga. It has the power of living for a long time out of water. It also possesses a *byssus* by means of which it is able to attach itself firmly to shells of the larger *Conchifera*, wood, stones, &c. The shell is described by the author of the excellent little book, "Lakes and Rivers," as "oblong, rising in a sharp keel in the middle of each valve and flattened below, pointed at the end or beak, and gradually but obliquely widening towards the front, solid but not glossy. Beneath the epidermis it is purplish-brown. The beaks (umbones) are terminal." This bivalve is now found in slow-running water in many parts of England. It is said that it has even been discovered clinging to the inside of some of the London iron water-pipes.

CHAPTER XII

WATER-BEETLES.

IT will be wise before introducing any beetles into an ordinary aquarium to accustom them to feed upon that food with which in the future they will be provided—*e.g.*, pieces of raw meat or garden-worms. All worms should be killed by dashing them suddenly to the ground; their death is then painless. It is not a pleasant sight to see a poor worm struggling and writhing while in the clutches of several beetles. Most beetles, however, though they may do, if carefully treated, little or no harm to the usual inhabitants of a tank, are more interesting, satisfactory, and ornamental in an aquarium which is entirely given up to their use.

Aquatic beetles are not only ornamental and very interesting in an aquarium, but not a few of them are useful there· All of them, however, are not suitable for the ordinary tank, as some are too small and others too predaceous, but they—both the small and the predaceous ones—are quite deserving of a place in portable and separate aquaria, where their forms and habits will afford much pleasure and instruction. Many of these coleoptera which must not be trusted among defence-less inhabitants of the water, will look well and thrive in those vessels which are kept for beautiful and interesting aquatic plants—plants, I mean, which are too choice or too delicate to be trusted near hungry snails or strong and active fish. Under such circumstances care should be taken to give the beetles just enough food to satisfy them, but not enough to run the risk of corrupting the water, which ought always to be, and will always be if the little necessary attention is regularly given, perfectly clear.

Coleoptera are generally classified in four sections, according to the number of the joints in their tarsi or feet: *Trimera, Tetramera, Heteromera,* and *Pentamera.* Those possessing feet having five joints are placed in the *Pentamera,* which contains most of the aquatic beetles. And to two families of this section are confined nearly all the coleoptera with which we have to do in this chapter, viz., the *Dyticidæ* and the *Hydrophilidæ.* The former family belongs to the sub-division *Hydradephaga* (aquatic carnivorous beetles) of the tribe *Adephaga* (predaceous beetles), and the species are therefore carnivorous. The *Hydrophilidæ* are herbivorous, and are members of the only family of the tribe *Palpicornia* (possessing long and slender palpi).

The *Dyticidæ* differ from the *Hydrophilidæ* chiefly in the formation of their antennæ and palpi (Fig. 149). In the former the antennæ are slim and elongated, and in the latter they are short and clubbed. But in the *Hydrophilidæ* the maxillary palpi are long and slender, and are much more conspicuous than their antennæ, which are often placed close to the body, out of sight; while the palpi of the *Dyticidæ* are quite small when compared with the length and prominence of their antennæ. There is a difference also in the formation of the legs of the two families. In the *Dyticidæ* the legs are especially adapted for swimming, the fore and middle pairs of legs being placed closely together, while the hind-legs are placed at some little distance from them to allow of plenty of room for the swimming movement. But in the *Hydrophilidæ* the three pairs of legs are almost equal distances apart. When swimming, the hind-legs of the *Dyticidæ* move together, while those of the *Hydrophilidæ* move alternately. The former may be said to swim somewhat similar to a frog and the latter like a dog. This difference in the manner of swimming is more or less apparent in most of the species of the two families. But some of the *Hydro-philidæ* seem to have legs fitted for crawling over aquatic plants rather than for swimming, while not a few of the *Dyticidæ* progress in the water like members of the *Hydro-philidæ*. In distinguishing the different genera and species of aquatic beetles it is necessary to pay attention to colour, size, structure, and sculpture, but especially to the latter two.

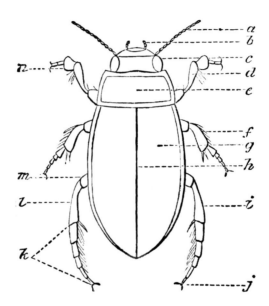

FIG. 149. ENLARGED OUTLINE OF MALE WATER-BEETLE (DYTICUS MARGINALIS).
a, Antennæ; *b*, Maxillary Palpi; *c*, Eye; *d*, Fore-Leg; *e*, Thorax; *f*, Middle Leg; *g*, Elytron; *h*, Suture; *i*, Hind-Leg; *j*, Claw; *k*, Tarsus or Foot; *l*, Tibia or Shank; *m*, Femur or Thigh; *n*, First three Joints of Foot, widened into a Plate possessing Suckers underneath.

Certain *Dyticidæ*, such as *Dyticus marginalis*, must not, as every keeper of an aquarium knows, be placed among fish and other defenceless inhabitants of the water, but in separate vessels, where they will be interesting and instructive. But some of these beetles, if properly managed, can be with advantage placed in the ordinary aquarium, for they will act the part of scavengers. The herbivorous beetles, *e.g.*, *Hydro-philus piceus*, are especially suitable for the tank, and are also perhaps more interesting in it than any of the others, particularly in regard to their egg-laying arrangements. The eggs of aquatic beetles are oval or oblong, and are placed usually either in cocoons or upon or in slits of aquatic plants. The larvæ of both the carnivorous and the herbivorous beetles are far too predaceous to be trusted in the general tank. They are, however, full of interest and quite worthy of separate aquaria easily prepared for the purpose. If it is wished that the larvæ should change to the perfect beetles while in confinement, it will be necessary to make for them an especially arranged tank, for most of them pass their pupal state not in the water but in the damp earth at its side. Some larvæ are a long time before they become pupæ, while others are only a few weeks.

The carnivorous beetles are much more likely to be a source of danger to their defenceless comrades during summer than during winter. The keeper should therefore guard against jumping to the conclusion that since he has been able to keep certain of the *Dyticidæ* among fish without the latter suffering any hurt during winter, he can always do so.

The *Hydradephaga* are divided into two families: (1) The *Dyticidæ;* (2) The *Gyrinidæ*.

The *Dyticidæ* family numbers in Britain about 114 different species; but many of them are very locally distributed. These beetles, which prefer stagnant to running water, are extremely predaceous, and devour small fish, tadpoles, insects, larvæ of insects and beetles of their own and other species. They have good powers of flight, and frequently travel, chiefly during the evening, from one piece of water to another. No pond or puddle seems to be too small for them. They have often been found in the latter which had been formed by recent rains. An instance indeed is recorded of a Dyticus being discovered in a tumbler of water after a shower. They have also been known to dart at and kill themselves against the roofs of greenhouses and the like, under the idea that they were flying into water. They are said to be influenced by atmospheric disturbances, and during storms to descend to the bottom of the water, only rising towards the surface as the weather becomes calmer.

The bodies of the *Dyticidœ* are generally smooth and ovate, and the different parts of the body, as a rule, fit into each other. The eyes do not project. The hind-legs are long and fringed, and the feet are broad and also fringed. The antennæ, as before mentioned, are long and slender. The anterior tarsi of the fore-legs of the males are frequently more or less widened, and the elytra of the female are sometimes furrowed or sulcated.

When these beetles hibernate or are at rest, they retire into the masses of aquatic plants or into the mud at the bottom of the water. They all breathe atmospheric air and are therefore obliged to come frequently to the face of the water. Their manner of respiration is very interesting. The upper part of their abdomen is provided with breathing tubes or spiracles, which are hidden by the elytra when the insects are not flying. The back of the abdomen is nearly flat; above it the elytra when shut form a kind of arch, and thus inclose the spiracles in a chamber into which water cannot enter to wet the wings inclosed within. When the beetles wish to take a supply of air they gently protrude the extremities of their bodies above the water, and allow the air to enter the chamber upon their backs. The air so obtained can enter the spiracles as the beetles require it, and thus they are able to remain in the depths of the water until all the supply of air has been utilised, when they are again obliged to return to the surface for more. If, for some reason or other—such as their antennæ being held by the valves of a mussel, of which I have read—the insects cannot return to the surface of the water, they, though aquatic, will be drowned, and sooner, it is said, than even land-beetles in the same circumstances. As these beetles swim to and fro under the water, a small bubble of air is seen attached to their extremities.

The tanks in which the *Dyticidœ* are confined should be kept covered. Carnivorous beetles while in the aquarium may be fed upon small garden-worms, a tiny dead fish, or pieces of raw meat suspended in the water by a little hook. The meat should always be removed before there is a chance of its corrupting the water.

The larvæ of these beetles, which are hatched from cylindrical eggs during the autumn and early spring, are carnivorous in habit and elongated in shape, gradually tapering towards the tail. Their heads are usually provided with sickle-like jaws, through which they are able to suck the juices of their prey. They are very great eaters, and as they grow quickly they frequently change their skins, which are interesting under the microscope. The food of the larvæ, according to their size, consists of small fish, tadpoles, aquatic molluscs, insects, and larvæ of insects, even occasionally of their own species. When it is time for them to enter the pupal state, they leave the water and make small caves or hollows in the damp soil at its edge, from which hiding-places they emerge in about a fortnight, or more or less according to circumstances and species, perfect beetles. Though these larvæ are so rapacious and fierce, they are not very tenacious of life, for a small hurt will be quite sufficient to cause their death. It will be frequently found, while examining the spoils of a hunt, that they have been among the first to succumb.

The *Dyticidæ* are divided into four sub-families, viz., *Dyticides, Pelobiides, Haliplides,* and *Hydroporides.*

The sub-family of the Dyticides comprises at least eight genera, which are indigenous to Britain, and are (1) *Dyticus,* (2) *Acilius,* (3) *Colymbetes,* (4) *Ilybius,* (5) *Hydaticus,* (6) *Agabus,* (7) *Laccophilus,* (8) *Noterus.*

As there are about 220 or 230 different species of British aquatic beetles, it will be quite impossible to refer in this handbook to anything like the greater portion of them. I will only attempt, therefore, to describe a few of the most suitable for, and interesting in, the aquarium.

In writing of the carnivorous aquatic beetles, one naturally thinks first (though, perhaps, scientifically it is not quite right so to do) of the handsome, bold, popular, and greedy *Dyticus marginalis* as worthy of heading the list of those which may be readily kept in confinement. It is common, hardy, and interesting; but, as already mentioned, it should not be allowed companions during its captivity. It is well described as the "ogre" among insects; for it is indeed as much a source of fear and danger to the small aquatic animals among which it lives as is the pike—the fresh-water shark—to its fellow fish.

The generic name of *Dyticus* implies that it and its near relatives are great divers. *D. marginalis* is nearly the largest of the British aquatic coleoptera, and it is certainly by far the most rapacious. The strength of this beetle is amazing, as anyone may prove for himself, either by taking it up in his fingers and feeling how strongly it struggles with its posterior legs to escape from the fingers which are pressing each side of its elytra, or by endeavouring to remove the insect while it is clinging with its fore-legs to a water-plant or to the edges of the aquarium. One has read of the Stag Beetle (*Lucanus cervus*) pushing along the tumbler under which it was confined; but the water-beetle (*D. marginalis*) is not far behind its distant relative in physical powers. No wonder that this fresh-water "ogre" is such a source of terror to its fellows in the pond when its huge strength and great appetite are taken into consideration.

These Dytici are very abundant, and may be obtained in most weedy ponds and ditches; but one must acquire a little adroitness with the water-net before one can be sure of catching them, for they are very wary and quick, diving to the bottom on the first sign of danger, and remaining there clinging to some weed or stone. They are obliged thus to anchor themselves, for otherwise, while remaining motionless—as they are specifically lighter than water—they would rise to the surface. A good plan of capturing these and other aquatic beetles is to go quietly to the side of a pond, stand there with the net in readiness, and, as these air-breathing insects make their necessary journeys to the surface, place it gently under them as they dive down with their fresh supply of air. This method of capture does not disturb either the water of the pond or its inmates. These beetles will be often seen, especially if the weather be fine, floating, close to the surface,

head downwards, and with their posterior legs at right angles
to their bodies. Another way to catch them is to sweep with
the net, backwards and forwards, the weedy edges of the
pond or around the masses of aquatic plants. If the first
attempt is unsuccessful, another should be made in an undisturbed part of the water. These beetles will generally be
found in pairs, male and fema'e (Fig. 150). They should not
be placed, when caught, in the same vessel with other insects
of different kinds, or, notwithstanding the terrors of new
captivity, they will be found to have re-commenced their work
of destruction before they arrive at their future home. It

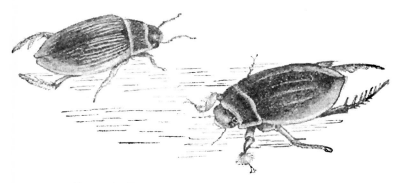

FIG. 150. DYTICUS MARGINALIS (MALE AND FEMALE).

will be frequently noticed by the hunter for aquarium specimens that pieces of water which have supplied certain species
of beetles one year will be without them the next, and *vice
versâ*. This is accounted for by the power and love of migration which aquatic beetles possess.

As before suggested, a separate tank should be prepared
for *D. marginalis*. An inverted propagating-glass, about 10in.
or 12in. in diameter, will do very well; but a small rectangular aquarium will do better, for the forms of the beetles
as they swim to and fro will then not be distorted. The
aquarium should be placed out of the rays of the sun and
not in too much light, as it will not be wise to depend upon

snails to remove any confervæ, for instead of eating the algæ the unfortunate molluscs would be eaten by the beetles. A single *D. marginalis* will live longer in confinement than a pair would. One solitary beetle will sometimes survive two or three years passed in captivity; but when a male and a female are kept together it will be generally found that after a few months, perhaps owing to some conjugal misunderstanding, the male dies. Celibacy certainly in this case conduces to longevity. The males, when both sexes are together, nearly always die first. The female, I believe, is more rapacious than her mate; she often eats him : he would eat her, no doubt, if he had the opportunity.

It is not a difficult matter to provide these beetles with food, for they will eat small fish, young newts, little frogs, tadpoles, water-snails, garden and other worms, insects and larvæ of insects, and pieces of raw meat.

Dytici are very destructive to the fry of fish, and often kill more than they can eat. In the aquarium they will feast, if no other food be given them, upon a small fish until nothing but the skeleton is left. A good way to feed these beetles is to put their food in a separate vessel (a large jam-bottle will do), and remove them to it : when they have eaten to repletion, return them to the aquarium, and throw the discarded food and the water which the bottle contains away. The beetles need only be fed thus twice a week, and their aquarium will be kept quite clear and sweet; but if they are not provided with a special vessel in which to feed they must be fed very carefully in their own tank, which should contain a good supply of healthy growing weeds. The best way to do this is to attach a piece of raw meat to a small hook and suspend it in the water, removing it as soon as the beetles have done with it.

Though *D. marginalis* is such a terror to small aquatic insects, they are avenged, for the "ogre" himself sometimes dies under the ravages of a parasite. A water-mite (generally *Hydrachna globulus*) at a certain stage of its existence is frequently found living as a parasite upon this beetle, and not seldom is the cause of its death. These parasites attach themselves to the back of the abdomen beneath the elytra, and they are, we may conclude, breathers of atmospheric air. *D. marginalis* is also subject to parasitic fungus (*Saprolegnia ferox*), which I believe is not nearly so fatal to beetles as it is to fish.

The male *D. marginalis* is so unlike the female that sometimes they have been taken by the inexperienced as members of different species. These beetles are about an inch long, oblong-ovate in shape, and olive-brown in colour. The margins of the thorax and elytra are marked with a yellow band. There is also a rather indistinct yellow crescent in the apex of the latter. The males are distinguished by having the first three joints of the fore tarsi developed into a round sucker, and by having smooth elytra; while the females have no widening of the tarsi, and possess wing cases which are furrowed or sulcated. The eggs of these beetles are laid in slits made in the aquatic plants by the help of a contrivance called an ovipositor, possessed by the female, and are hatched in about a fortnight.

The larva of *D. marginalis* (Fig. 151), when full-grown, is about 2in. long. It is such a rapacious creature that it has received the names of "Water-Devil" and "Water-Tiger," while its shape has given it the title of "Fresh-water Shrimp." The body of the animal is a dirty brown in colour and elongated in shape, and gradually tapers towards the tail. There are six legs and eleven segments, the former being affixed in pairs to the first three of the latter. At the extremity of the last segment there are two appendages fringed with hair, and close to these appendages are two spiracles, or breathing holes, by means of which the animal respires atmospheric air. The spiracles at the sides of the body, not being required at present, are unopened. The larva is furnished with some terrible-looking sickle-like jaws, which are hollow, and through them it is able to suck the juices of its captives. It also possesses undeveloped palpi and antennæ.

The Water-Tiger is a great eater, having, if possible, a larger appetite than its parents. It seizes its prey with its jaws, and, with head thrown back, extracts its food. The favourite attitude of this larva is to float, head downwards, with its caudal appendages just touching the surface of the water. It does not swim so fast as, nor are its jaws so strong as those of, the perfect insect. It changes its skin from time to time, according to its growth. The food of the animal consists of small fish, tadpoles, insects, and larvæ of insects. Two of these creatures will never live long together in the same vessel, for sooner or later one will be almost certain to eat the other. They may be fed upon garden-worms, but they do not care very much for them. They seem to prefer Corixæ to any other food, and it is rather surprising to see how cleverly the comparatively slow-moving animals are able to catch the fleet ones.

If it be wished to give these larvæ an opportunity of becoming beetles while in confinement, it will be necessary to prepare an aquarium especially for the purpose. The tank for this arrangement should be rather large, and before the water is introduced a bank of soil, sand, and gravel should be built at one end. When the water is put in it must be in such a quantity that it will not cover all of the sloping bank. A very fine siphon ought to be used

FIG. 151. LARVA OF THE WATER-BEETLE (DYTI-CUS MARGINALIS).

or the water will not be clear. The larva spends about a fortnight in its pupal state.

The aquarium-keeper will find that this beetle and its larva are very interesting. Of course the two must never be kept together, or the latter will never have the chance of becoming the perfect insect.

I have written so much concerning D. marginalis because its habits are more or less characteristic of its smaller relatives.

There are five other species of the genus Dyticus, very like in appearance and habits to the D. marginalis; but none of them are so common—except, perhaps, **D. *punctulatus***, which may be distinguished by its somewhat smaller size, and by the perfect blackness beneath its body.

We have only two species belonging to the genus *Acilius*: of these *A. sulcatus* (Fig. 152) is by far the commoner. This beetle is a favourite with aquarium-keepers, and is abundant in still water almost everywhere. It and many of its relatives, near and distant, certainly do not altogether deserve the bad character which some people give them. It is not at all likely that the *Acilius sulcatus* and other beetles nearly related to him will do any harm in the ordinary aquarium if they are properly and regularly fed. I have kept for many months several beetles of this species in a small tank with a few

FIG. 152. ACILIUS SULCATUS (MALE AND FEMALE).

little fish, and not one fish, to my knowledge, has been hurt in any way by them. These beetles, of course, had plenty of food. *Acilius sulcatus* is a handsome beetle, and well adapted by nature for an aquatic life. It is a flatter and smaller insect than *D. marginalis*: it is ¾in. in length, ovate in shape, and greyish-brown in colour. The under-part of the body is black, with the exception that the sides of the abdomen are distinctly and regularly spotted with yellow. The margins of the thorax, and a transverse band in the middle, are a brownish-yellow. In the male insect the first three joints of the anterior *tarsi* are dilated, and the elytra of the female have furrows filled with hairs, these furrows extending to the apex of the elytra. This beetle, when placed upon its back while out of the water, makes a curious noise as it springs to its feet. It also, when out of its natural element, emits, as

R

so many of its tribe do, a not very pleasant scent. The odour of some beetles, however, in these circumstances is by no means unpleasing. *Acilius sulcatus* is very adroit in escaping from the aquarium if it has the slightest opportunity. The larva of this beetle is not unlike that of a *D. marginalis*, though it may be distinguished from that species by its smaller size and by its having the first segment of the body so much elongated as to look like a neck. It catches its prey by stealth, and, after it has seized it, sometimes shakes it as a dog does a rat. This larva may be treated in the same way as its larger relatives. *A. fasciatus* is the other species which belongs to this genus.

It differs from *A. sulcatus* chiefly in having yellow abdomen and legs, and it is not quite so large or so common an insect.

Colymbetes striatus (Fig. 153) is a beetle of about the size of *A. sulcatus*, but rather more oblong in shape. It is very common, and may be found at any time during the year. This

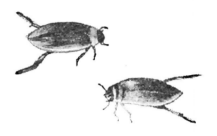

FIG. 153. COLYMBETES STRIATUS
(MALE AND FEMALE).

and other species of *Colymbetes* are strong and ready flyers, and are perhaps a little more likely to attack their piscine companions than are the members of the last genus. The shape of *C. striatus* is oblong; the elytra are brownish and the thorax is a yellowish brown, having a dark stripe in the middle; the body underneath is black and the legs are a dull red. This beetle while in the general aquarium should be watched from time to time, and if it seems likely to hurt the fish, should be removed. But as a rule it may be taken for granted that as long as it is properly fed it will do no harm to its companions, at any rate during the greater portion of the year. *C. fuscus* is rather smaller in size and more ovate in shape than the preceding. Its elytra are brown, with yellowish-brown lateral margins. Its thorax is also brown, but rather darker in the centre, and its wing-cases have the appearance of having been scratched from side to side. Its legs are brown. This insect is common, and is frequently found in the company of *C. striatus.* There are five other species belonging to this genus, the smallest of which is about ⅓in. in length. The larvæ of all these beetles are somewhat like those of Dytici, but of course smaller in proportion.

The genus *Ilybius* also possesses seven species, of which *I. ater* (Fig. 154) is one of the largest, handsomest, and most interesting. Its form is oblong-ovate and convex. Its

FIG. 154. ILYBIUS ATER (MALE AND FEMALE).

colour above is black (whence the specific name) with a bronze tinge, and there are upon the elytra two brownish-yellow streaks. The under-part of the insect's body is brownish-black. This beetle is found in many parts of Britain —e.g., around London, in Kent and Norfolk, and in Scotland. *I. fuliginosus* has somewhat the appearance of a small *Dyticus marginalis*, and is found in many parts of Britain. It is about ⅓in. in length, rather handsome, and looks well in the aquarium.

There are only two species of the genus *Hydaticus* found in Britain, both of which are oblong-ovate in shape and about ½in. in length. The males, like those of the Dytici and

Acilii, have the first three joints of the anterior tarsi dilated. The only species calling for mention here is *H. transversalis*. The upper part of the body of this beetle is black, the margins of the thorax are a dull red, and those of the elytra are yellow. The legs are also a dull red. This insect is found in the ponds of different parts of England, and is fairly common.

We have in Britain nineteen species belonging to the genus *Agabus*, of which *A. bipustulatus* is one of the largest, being nearly ½in. long. It is an active and handsome beetle, and looks exceedingly well in the aquarium as it swims to and fro, with a most conspicuous bubble of air attached to the apex of its elytra, looking like a drop of quicksilver in contrast to the blackness of the insect's body. Although *A. bipustulatus* has a rather large appetite for its size, it is not likely to do any harm in a general aquarium if it is well fed. I have observed one of this species sharing a worm with a small minnow, or rather the insect was attacking the head of the worm while the fish was trying to swallow the tail. This beetle is ovate in shape and black in colour. There are two red spots upon the crown: hence the specific name. The legs are a brownish black, and there are three rows of punctures and quite a network of scratches upon the elytra. *A. bipustulatus* is common almost everywhere, and may be found at any season of the year. *A. bipunctatus* is somewhat smaller than the last species. It is ovate and rather flat in shape. The upper part of its body is yellowish, and the under brownish-black. Upon the thorax there are two round dark spots, whence the specific name. The legs and the tip of the abdomen are a reddish colour. *A. maculatus* is an active and prettily-marked beetle; it is rather common, but looks very well in the aquarium. The shape of the insect is oval. The elytra, which are black, have pale yellowish spots, lines, and margins. The thorax is yellow, with its anterior and posterior margins black, and the legs are of a reddish colour. The beetle is about ¼in. in length.

Two of the three species belonging to the genus *Laccophilus* are very common and very small. They are only about ⅛in. in length, and are occasionally found in brackish water. These insects are noted for the great development of their hind-legs and for their excellence as swimmers. *L. minuius* is ovate and rather convex in shape and greenish-grey in colour. The head and thorax are yellow, and upon the elytra there are some rather faint spots. The legs are reddish. This little beetle is abundant. *L. hyalinus* is, if anything, rather a commoner insect than the preceding. In shape it is oblong-ovate and rather flat. The elytra are a greenish brown, with rather lighter-coloured margins. The legs are yellowish.

The beetles belonging to the genus *Noterus* are in form somewhat like those known as "Whirligigs." There are only two species, and both are rather common. *N. semipunctatus* is a small dark-red and shining beetle, a little more than $\frac{1}{6}$in. in length. The elytra are rather lighter in colour at their margins, and are covered with large punctures; the antennæ are short and thick; and the under-part of the body is not quite so dark in colour as the upper. *N. crassicornis* is very like the preceding species, but a little lighter in colour.

Pelobius hermanni (Fig. 155) is the only representative in this country of the sub-family to which it belongs. It is an

FIG. 155. PELOBIUS HERMANNI (MALE AND FEMALE).

interesting and handsome beetle, and very popular with aquarium-keepers. From a habit it has of rubbing the hard edge of the last segment of its body in a groove under its elytra, and so making a curious noise, it has received the names of the "Squeaker," the "Screech Beetle," and the "Chirping Beetle." Its body appears more fitted for moving upon the land than through the water. It is, however, very convex, and is able, with an ambulatory motion, to swim fairly well. It does not seem to be a great eater, and I have never seen it attempt to attack a fish or any other of its companions. This beetle, and many others, are fond of hiding themselves in the gravel of the aquarium, only leaving exposed the bubbles of air which are attached to the apices of their elytra. *P. hermanni* is so convex that when it is taken out of the water it can hardly move at all. It is never a very active insect. Its colour is a dull red. A patch round the eyes, the exterior and posterior margins of the thorax, and a very large spot on the elytra, are black. It is also a dull red underneath its body, except the breast and the apex of the abdomen, which are black. This insect is about ½in. long, and is fairly abundant in the weedy ditches and ponds of many parts of England, but especially in the neighbourhood of London. This species is more correctly known as *P. tardus.*

The sub-family *Haliplides* possesses two genera—*Haliplus* and *Cnemidotus.* The *Haliplides* have more the appearance of terrestrial beetles than aquatic, their legs not being very well adapted for swimming, and their heads are more prominent than those of most of their relatives. They swim with an ambulatory motion, although not very often, as they spend a considerable portion of their time in crawling upon the water-plants. They are broad and convex in shape, and are hardly ever more than ⅙in. in length, but often less. Their elytra, which are generally of a yellowish colour, have large punctures. Their antennæ are ten-jointed, while those of the rest of the *Dyticidæ* are eleven-jointed. In distinguishing one species from another, one should be guided more by the shape of the beetle and the punctures upon its wing-cases than by its size and colour.

The genus *Haliplus* contains eleven species, the commonest perhaps of which is *H. ruficollis.* This is a very small beetle, less than ⅛in. in length, and abounds almost everywhere. It is ovate in shape, and of a dark yellowish-red colour. The crown and the base of the abdomen are dark brown, and the thorax and the elytra are impressed with punctures. The suture is dark, and there is a small line or stria on each side of the base of the thorax. *H. lineatocollis* is also a very common little beetle, and somewhat larger than the last species. Its shape is ovate, its colour brownish-yellow, and it may be distinguished by a dark longitudinal line upon the thorax. Its elytra are punctured and faintly spotted with brown.

There is only one solitary species belonging to the genus *Cnemidotus*, viz., *C. cæsus*. It is $\frac{1}{6}$in. in length, ovate and convex in shape, and of a shining yellow colour. Its elytra are rather deeply punctured.

The sub-family *Hydroporides* is represented by the genera *Hyphydrus* and *Hydroporus*. The former genus possesses only two species, one of which is doubtful, as a British insect; the latter forty-seven.

The *Haliplides* and *Hydroporides* do exceedingly well in small aquaria which contain plenty of growing plants. They will not hurt tiny fish; large fish might eat them. But if a fish should die, they will feed upon it until only the skeleton is left. They are very useful scavengers. The water of the tank in which such insects as these are kept, if they are properly treated, will remain beautifully clear. These little beetles will not, as a rule, hurt snails; but if one dies they will quickly empty its shell and use it as a hiding-place. They do not require much feeding.

Hyphydrus ovatus (*a*, Fig. 156) is a most curious-looking insect, less than $\frac{1}{4}$in. in length and globose in form. Its colour is of a rusty red, and the thorax and elytra are punctured. When captured it is often found covered with mud or algæ; and when out of the water it is said to emit a rather pleasant smell similar to that of honey.

The species belonging to the genus *Hydroporus* are by no means easy to distinguish from each other, and one of the largest is *H. duodecim-pustulatus* (*b*, Fig. 156). This is about $\frac{1}{4}$in. in length, and its form is oblong-ovate. The thorax which is a light rusty red, has the anterior and posterior margins black. The elytra are black and are covered with reddish spots placed in threes. The legs and antennæ are a rusty red. This beetle is fairly common. *H. palustris* is a small insect found in great abundance almost everywhere. It is about ⅛in. in length. Its head, margins of thorax, and legs, are red, and its elytra are dark brown, spotted with yellow. This beetle, however, varies much in its colouring. *H. rivalis* (as its specific names implies) is found in streams, while most cf its relatives live in stagnant water. The colour of this very pretty little insect is brownish-yellow, and the thorax has a black line down the centre. There are two irregular black

FIG. 156. *a*, HYPHYDRUS OVATUS; *b*. HYDROPORUS DUODECIM-PUSTULATUS.

patches upon the elytra, jointed together by three or four lines of the same colour. This beetle, which is not ⅛in. in length, is not very common.

All the Hydroporides are small, and some of them are very prettily marked. The males can often be distinguished from the females by their shining appearance.

The Gyrinidæ, which includes the genera *Gyrinus* and *Orectochilus*, form the latter of the two families of the Hydradephaga.

Few water-beetles are more commonly known than the merry and active little insects which belong to the genus

Gyrinus. They may be seen keeping up their lively gyrations on the surface of almost any pond or sheltered nook of many a stream during nearly every fine and mild day throughout the year. Their habit of continually moving in either curves or circles has given them the generic name of *Gyrinus,* and the more familiar ones of "Whirligigs" and "Whirlwigs," and the sheen of their elytra has also caused them to be called, most appropriately, "Shiners." These beetles are gregarious, and are generally seen together in numbers ranging from ten to thirty, and this custom of theirs should be remembered by those who intend to keep them in confinement. The genus *Gyrinus* contains about five British species, the members of which are in shape either ovate or oblong-ovate, and in size vary from $\frac{1}{6}$in. to a little more than $\frac{1}{4}$in. Their elytra, which are very glossy and are turned a little under the body at their edges, do not reach to the apex of the abdomen, and their antennæ are short and thick. It will be noticed that the posterior legs of most other aquatic beetles are the longest; but in the case of the Gyrinidæ the anterior legs are of the greatest length, while their others are very short and strong, and at the extremities rather fin-like. The "Whirligigs" use their long fore-legs for seizing and holding their prey, and also, it is said, for directing their way upon the surface of the water. The eyes of these insects are most curious and interesting. Each eye, so to speak, is divided into two by a partition, in which an antenna is fixed. The upper of the two eyes thus formed is used for looking at objects above the surface of the water, and the lower for those beneath it. This accounts for their extraordinary quickness of sight, which anyone can prove for himself by trying to catch them in a net. These active and alert little beetles dive under the water at the slightest appearance of danger from above, often coming up again beneath some flat floating leaves. They will also thus hide below pieces of paper placed upon the surface of the water of the aquarium.

The Gyrinidæ are very good flyers, and therefore the tank in which they are confined should be carefully covered.

In captivity these beetles, which are not great eaters, may be fed upon pieces of raw meat, water- and garden-worms, or house-flies killed and placed upon the water. While watching the quick and intricate movements of the "Whirligigs" upon the water, one wonders how they are always able to avoid colliding; and they travel with such rapidity that it is difficult to follow them with the eye and see how they steer themselves. Mr. H. W. Bates, writing in Cassell's "Natural History," while speaking of their gyrations, says: "The two hinder pairs of legs are extremely short, broad, compressed—modified, in fact—to suit their extraordinary mode of locomotion—a rapid skimming in curves or circles over the surface of the water. The rapid forward motion is produced by the quick fore and aft movement of these strong and well-knit members, and the curves by the long anterior legs, which, usually kept folded under the breast, are jerked out one at a time, so as to change the straight line of progression into a curve." The Gyrinidæ lay their cylindrical eggs (which hatch in about a week) end to end upon water-plants. The larvæ look somewhat like aquatic centipedes, owing to the filamentary appendages which are fixed to the abdominal segments of their bodies. These appendages are hollow, and are used for respiration. When the larvæ are ready to assume the pupal state, they ascend the stalk of some aquatic plant, and then, above the surface of the water, spin a cocoon, from which they emerge in about a month perfect "Whirligigs." These larvæ, which seem to be rather hardier than those of other aquatic beetles, can easily be kept in confinement. Small aquatic animal life, water-worms, and the fry of molluscs, form their best food.

FIG. 157.   GYRINUS NATATOR.

Gyrinus natator (Fig. 157), which is about the commonest of the Gyrini, is ovate and convex in shape, and very glossy bluish-black in colour. The edges of its elytra, which are turned a little under the body, are red, and the whole insect measures about ¼in. in length.

FIG. 158.
GYRINUS BICOLOR
(ENLARGED).

Gyrinus bicolor (Fig. 158) is more oblong in shape than the preceding species and is of a glossier bluish-black colour. The reflected edges of the elytra, middle of the breast, and legs, are reddish. This insect, which is a little longer than *G. natator*, is generally found in rather brackish water.

Orectochilus villosus is the only species which belongs to this genus. It is so covered with short hairs that it has a much less glossy appearance than the rest of its relatives. This hirsute peculiarity has given it its specific name. The upper part of the body of this curious insect is of a dull, brassy-black colour, and the lower, red. The beetle is about ¼in. in length and oblong in shape. It is found (though not very abundantly) in different parts of England. Unlike the Gyrini, it prefers to sport upon the water in the dark, and not during sunshine. In the daytime it hides under the banks or suitable weeds.

The family *Hydrophilidæ* of aquatic *Coleoptera*, whose members are, to a great extent, herbivorous, contains thirteen genera, of which the most interesting and important is *Hydrophilus piceus* (*e*, Fig. 159). This very handsome and gentle beetle is as well suited for the aquarium as any yet described, and as it is about 1¾in. in length, it is one of the largest of the British Coleoptera.

Two of the more apparent differences between the *Hydrophilidæ* and the *Dyticidæ* have already been referred to, and they will be of much help in distinguishing the members of the two families.

This beetle and *D. marginalis*, or any of the latter's near relatives, should never be put together in the same vessel, for the larger insect would almost certainly, sooner or later, be devoured by the smaller.

H. piceus has frequently been called the "Harmless Water-Beetle," but it does not altogether deserve the name, for it will be quite as unwise to place this large herbivorous insect

among useful or choice aquatic plants as it would be to associate an unfed *D. marginalis* with fish and other defenceless
animals. Though *H. piceus* will not, as a rule, hurt any of
the inhabitants of an ordinary aquarium, it will be more
interesting in a separate tank, where it can lead the retired
life it loves among the plants it feeds upon. As *H. piceus*
has no need to pursue its food, it is only adapted for travelling
somewhat slowly through the water by the alternate movements of its legs. It spends a great portion of its time either
at rest among the weeds or crawling over them. Though this
beetle is generally described as herbivorous, it will occasionally,
at any rate while in captivity, partake of animal food. It
destroys a great deal of the plant upon which it feeds, and
therefore it is wise to provide it with Anacharis or some
other quickly-growing and easily-obtained weed. A pair of
these beetles will live, to all appearance perfectly happy, in
an inverted propagating-glass, or a small rectangular tank,
well stocked with suitable vegetation, and there the female
will very likely construct her nest or cocoon (*b* and *c*,
Fig. 159), and lay her eggs. The nest is woven by the
help of two small spinnerets, which are placed near the
apex of the abdomen of the insect; it is shaped somewhat like an ordinary retort. This egg-sac is formed of a
substance which is perfectly impervious to water, and which
has rather the appearance of paper. Inside this pouch,
which at its largest part is about ¾in. in diameter, eggs to
the number of fifty or sixty are inclosed, and are hatched,
according to the temperature of the water, in about six weeks.
The young larvæ (*d*, Fig. 159) escape through the bottom
of the sac, and seem from the first to be quite vigorous. This
sac or pouch is so constructed that it will float upon the
water with the stem or horn-like part of it uppermost, and
is attached by the beetle to some portion of an aquatic
plant which is upon the surface (*f*, Fig. 159). The spike or
horn-like part, which is hollow, rises above the water, and
thus admits air to the interior of the sac. The insect is
sometimes able to spin her cocoon and lay her eggs within
three hours.

The larvæ. although their parents are almost entirely herbivorous, are carnivorous. They are great eaters and quick growers; and they are not so long in the larval state as are the larvæ of the Dytisci, but are ready to become pupæ within a few weeks from the time they are hatched, if they have been able to obtain a sufficiency of suitable food. The

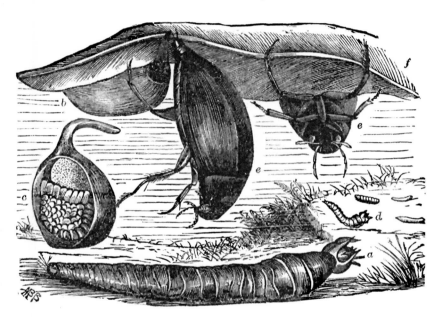

FIG. 159. HYDROPHILUS PICEUS. *a*, Full-grown Larva ; *b*, Egg-sac, affixed to Aquatic Plant; *c*, Egg-sac opened, showing Eggs; *d*, Young Larvæ; *e, e,* Mature Insects; *f*, Leaf of Aquatic Plant.

larvæ of *H. piceus* are very difficult indeed to rear from the egg while in captivity. The only chance of doing so is to provide them with a great quantity of small aquatic animal life, and especially the fry of water-snails. These larvæ, when well fed and full grown (*a*, Fig. 159), are longer and thicker than are those of *D. marginalis* under similar circumstances. They have the power of moving the head, apparently with great ease, in every direction, and as they feed upon their prey they frequently throw their heads so far back as to rest them upon their backs. These larvæ must be handled with great gentleness or they will die.

These beetles do not obtain air in the same way as the *Dyticidæ* do, by protruding the apex of their elytra above the surface of the water, but by means of their antennæ, which they raise above the water, and which conduct the air to the hair-like surface of the lower part of the thorax, and thence to the spiracles. This method of respiration gives to the breasts of these beetles a silvery appearance while they are under the water.

The male (*H. piceus*) is distinguished from the female by having the last joint but one of the tarsi of its fore-feet dilated into a kind of triangular plate. The colour of the elytra of these beetles is a beautiful olive-black. The abdomen beneath is also black, having quite distinct yellow spots upon the margin. The antennæ, which are reddish, are nine-jointed, the four terminal joints forming a club. There is upon the under-part of the body a prominent ridge ending in a sharp spine. The posterior tarsi are well adapted for swimming, being much compressed and ciliated.

These beetles may be found in the ponds, ditches, and canals of England, chiefly the southern part, but they seem to be rarer than formerly. They may be generally bought of those who deal in aquarium requisites, however, at from 1s. to 2s. 6d. a pair, according to the dealer and the season. The aquarium in which these insects are confined should be covered, or they are likely to escape, especially just about the time they lay their eggs; but anyone, I think, who keeps them will come to the conclusion that they are the most interesting and the least trouble of any of the aquatic coleoptera.

The only species belonging to the genus *Hydröus* is *H. caraboides,* an insect somewhat similar in appearance to *Hydrophilus piceus,* but smaller in size, being about ¾in. long, different in puncturation, and darker in colour; its keel is also much shorter in proportion to the length of its body. The shining blackness of its elytra occasionally has a greenish or violet tinge. This rather common beetle is very suitable for the aquarium.

Of the five species comprehended in the genus *Hydrobius*, *H. fuscipes* is, perhaps, the commonest and most suitable for the tank. This elegant insect can be found upon the weeds of ponds, ditches, and slow-running streams in many parts of England. It is sometimes useful in the aquarium as a consumer of confervæ. About June the female makes a cocoon for her eggs, and attaches it to the under-side of floating leaves. This sac is somewhat similar in substance and appearance to that constructed by the *Hydrophilus piceus*, but is without the hollow stem. *H. fuscipes*

FIG. 160. HYDROBIUS FUSCIPES.

(Fig. 160) is about ½in. in length, and is of a very glossy, brownish-black colour. Its shape is oval, and its elytra, sides of its head, and thorax, are deeply punctured. The clubbed antennæ are rather large and conspicuous for the size of the insect, and the legs are of a reddish colour.

The ten or twelve species belonging to the genus *Helophorus* are found crawling upon the weeds, bottoms, and sides of ponds and slow-running streams in many parts of Britain. They are frequently found out of the water, and often covered with mud. *H. grandis* (Fig. 161) is the largest and one of the commonest of the Helophori. It is oblong in shape, the thorax being somewhat narrowed behind. The latter and the head have a metallic appearance, and there are a few faint

FIG. 161. HELOPHORUS GRANDIS.

brown spots upon the yellowish-brown elytra. The legs, palpi, and antennæ, are of a yellowish colour. This insect, which measures about ¼in. in length, may be found in ponds and sluggish streams in almost all parts of the British Islands, and at any season of the year.

S. emarginatus is the only representative of the genus
Spercheus. It is a very rare insect—so rare, indeed, that for
some time it was thought to be extinct as a British beetle.
It was formerly found in Whittlesea Mere, Kensington Gardens,
and at Windsor; but in recent years I believe it has been
discovered near the South of London. The female is said to
inclose her eggs in a pouch, and carry them about affixed to
the under-part of her body. The eggs are hatched in about
ten days, and as soon as the young larvæ appear, the busy
and prolific mother immediately commences a new cocoon
to contain more eggs. But notwithstanding the fecundity
of this insect, it is not only rare in this country, but also on
the Continent. This interesting beetle has been described
by the author of the "Coleoptera of the British Islands"
as having the power, both in its larval and in its perfect
state, of walking upon the under-surface of the water, in the
same way that many of the aquatic snails do. *S. emarginatus*
is about ¼in. long, and is of a yellowish-brown colour. Its
head is flat and almost black. Its elytra, which are wider
than the thorax, are spotted with brown; its legs are reddish;
and its palpi and six-jointed antennæ (the last five joints of
which form a club) are yellowish. The larvæ of this beetle
are said to be so full of air that they seem to have quite a
difficulty in sinking in the water.

The seven species of small beetles which are comprehended
in the genus *Philhydrus* are in shape rather similar to the
Hydrobii. Their length varies from ⅛in. to ¼in., and their
antennæ are nine-jointed, the last four joints forming a pointed
club. Their bodies are long and convex, and in appearance
seem more like those of terrestrial than aquatic insects.

The Berosi are yellowish and very convex insects, and
are about ½in. in length. Their thoraces are ornamented
with a spot of beautiful metallic colour; their eyes are very
prominent, and their antennæ are eight-jointed, the last
three joints forming an obtuse club. The four species belonging
to the genus *Berosus* are *B. luridus*, *B. œriceps*, *B. spinosus*,
and *B. affinis*, most of which are fairly common. *B. spinosus*
possesses a short spine near the apex of its elytra; hence

its specific name. It is frequently found in brackish water.

The small beetles classified under the head *Hydrochus* are not more than ⅙in. long, but generally less. They have long, narrow bodies, seven-jointed antennæ, prominent eyes, and their elytra are very glossy and beautifully coloured. *H. angustatus* is perhaps the commonest of the four species of the Hydrochi, and is really a beautiful little insect, with its very glossy, greenish-black wing-cases. Its thorax, which is narrower than the elytra, is deeply punctured, and its legs and antennæ are reddish.

The little beetles belonging to the genus *Laccobius* are divided into the species *L. minutus* and *L. nigriceps.* They are rather less, most of them, than ⅛in. in length, and are yellowish-grey in colour. The Laccobii are by no means rare.

The very tiny beetles comprised under the head *Ochthebius* are frequently found crawling under or over stones which are half out of the water. Some of these insects are so small that they are not more than $\frac{1}{18}$in. in length. Their antennæ are nine-jointed, the five terminal joints forming a club. Their bodies are elliptical, their elytra of a glossy metallic colour, and their legs short. Of the ten species included in this genus, *O. pygmæus* is one of the commonest. It is about $\frac{1}{12}$in. in length, and of a bright metallic-brown colour. The thorax is deeply punctured, the legs are reddish, and the palpi and antennæ of a lighter colour with darker tips.

The beetles of the genus *Hydræna* have the same habits and habitats as those of the preceding. They are chiefly noticeable for the extreme length of their palpi, which almost equal in length half of the body. Their antennæ are seven-jointed, the last four of which form an oval club. The elytra, which are mostly of a bright black colour, do not cover all the abdomen. The thorax is broad across the middle, and gradually tapers towards the anterior and posterior margins; the legs are long. *H. riparia* is one of the most abundant of the six species of the Hydrænæ. It is a narrow, shining, black insect, having rather a long head, and the

s

thorax deeply punctured. The antennæ, palpi, and legs are dark brown. It is rather less than ⅙in. long.

The beetles belonging to the genus *Limnebius* are the tiniest of the *Hydrophilidæ*, some of them being less than ₁₀in. in length. Their bodies, which are black, are slightly depressed. Their antennæ are eight-jointed, the last six joints forming the club. The elytra are slightly truncate at the apex. These insects are divided into five species, some of which are very common.

The beetles comprised in the family *Parnidæ*, though very interesting, are not so suitable for the aquarium as those already mentioned, as they are generally found in swift-running water. The insects of the sub-family *Parnides* are covered with a kind of hair, by means of which they are able to carry with them sufficient air for their wants during the long time they are accustomed to spend beneath the water. *Parnus prolifericornis* is the commonest species, and is ⅛in. long. It is oblong in shape, and of a dark brown colour, its legs being reddish. The *Parnidæ*, as well as the *Hydrophilidæ*, are herbivorous.

The *Elmides*, which are also a sub-family of the *Parnidæ*, are chiefly remarkable for their largely-developed tarsi and claws, by means of which they are able to cling to stones at the bottom of very swift-running water. The longest feet and claws are possessed by *Limnius tuberculatus*, the one species of the genus. This remarkable insect, which is rare and local, is found in the River Trent.

Very often an aquarium is found to be made out of proportion—that is, its depth is too great for its length and breadth. This mistake of construction can be rectified by filling the vessel only half or three-quarters full, as the case may be. Such a tank as this will be very useful for keeping not only many of the smaller species of the *Hydrophilidæ*, but also some of the very beautiful and interesting beetles which live rather upon aquatic plants than in the water itself, such as certain of the *Donaciadæ*, *Chrysomelidæ*, and *Gallerucidæ*, and even one or two of the *Rhynchophora*, or Weevils. The tank for these insects should be covered with a sheet of glass cut to fit, and stocked with such aquatic plants as protrude in their growth above the surface of the water, choosing, if possible, those upon which the different species of beetles are accustomed to feed—*e.g.*, Water Plantain (*Alisma Plantago*) for the Weevil, *Hydronomus alismatis* and the Arrow-head (*Sagittaria sagittifolia*) for the *Galleruca sagittariæ*, &c.

The *Donaciadæ* are very beautiful beetles, and are divided into the genera *Donacia* and *Hæmonia*, the former containing nineteen species and the latter two. All of them are herbivorous, gregarious, and of more or less lovely metallic colours. They are nearly always found upon water-plants, in the stems of which their larvæ live, and at or near the roots their pupæ are inclosed in silk-like cocoons. The underpart of these beetles is covered with downy hair, and their legs and tarsi are very strong. Their bodies are generally elongated, their thoraces are narrow, and their elytra are rather flat. As a rule, these beetles do not take to the water unless it be to escape capture ; and their swimming under such circumstances is not much more than a struggle to regain the plant from which they fell, or its neighbour.

Donacia dentata (Fig. 162) is a species generally found upon floating leaves, such as those of the Water-Lily or Pond-Weed. Its

FIG. 162. DONACIA DENTATA.

strong hind-legs are furnished with two teeth or spines. The elytra are of a brassy colour, and the legs are reddish. There is a glossy pile beneath the body.

The *Chrysomelidæ*, or Golden Apple Beetles, are as beautifully coloured as the *Donaciadæ*, but are of a different shape, being very convex above and flat beneath. Their length varies from about $\frac{1}{6}$in. to $\frac{1}{5}$in. Their heads are not sunk in the thoraces, and their antennæ are rather short, gradually thickening towards the tips. *Chrysomela polita* is a common species, and is frequently found upon the Water-Mint (*Mentha aquatica*).   It is an ovate insect, having brightly-polished elytra of a greenish or bluish tint.   The legs are of a metallic green.

Besides the beautiful beetles just mentioned, there are many others, equally beautiful and interesting, which have similar habits and habitat.   As all these insects delight in the sunshine, it should be arranged that, as far as possible, the tank in which they are confined can receive the rays of the sun upon the parts of the plants which are growing above the surface of the water, but not upon the water itself.

In concluding this chapter, I venture to repeat that no one should attempt to keep beetles in an aquarium unless they can be properly and regularly fed. The little trouble necessary for this will be amply repaid.

CHAPTER XIII.

WATER-BUGS OR WATER-MEASURERS, WATER-SCORPIONS, ETC.

INSECTS are said to have a complete metamorphosis when their pupal, nymphal, or chrysalis condition is quiescent. For example, the larvæ of beetles are active and voracious; but when they become pupæ they pass their time without either moving or eating, until they arrive at the imago or perfect state. The Coleoptera have, therefore, a complete metamorphosis. But as the Heteropterous insects change very little, apparently, except in size, during their lifetime, and as they are always more or less active and ravenous, they are said to pass through an incomplete metamorphosis.

The *Heteroptera*, or Bugs, as they are not very euphoniously called, have beaks or rostra, and by means of these they are able to suck the juices which form their food. The holes, whether in the plant or in the animal, through which this liquid nutriment is extracted, are made by four very sharply-pointed bristle-like members which are inclosed within the rostrum.

These insects are divided into the two tribes, *Geocorisæ* and *Hydrocorisæ*. The members of the former are chiefly distinguished by the possession of long antennæ and three-pointed tarsi from those of the latter, which have antennæ hidden in a groove beneath the eyes, and two-jointed tarsi.

All the *Geocorisæ* are terrestrial with the exception of the *Hydrometridæ*, which are generally found upon the surface of the water.

Everyone who has been accustomed while in the country to spend any time by the water's side, must have noticed those curious insects which seem to have the wonderful power of walking or rather progressing upon the surface of the water. These creatures are commonly called Water-Measurers, and often, but erroneously, Water-spiders. Not a few of them are very abundant, and may be found almost everywhere and at any season of the year. They are gregarious, wary, and active. Some of them frequent both stagnant and running water, and others either the former or the latter. The *Hydrometra*, *Gerris*, and *Velia* are the principal genera of the *Hydrometridæ*, the different species of which may be treated while in confinement in almost the same way. Many of them will be content with house-flies killed and placed upon the surface of the water, and some of them after a time will suck the juices from a piece of raw meat suspended in the right position. As most of these insects possess wings, and those which do not have them are very agile climbers, the aquarium in which they are confined should be covered. It should be also remembered that they are carnivorous, and will be likely to feed upon each other unless they are properly associated and properly fed.

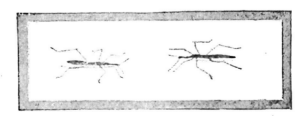

FIG. 163   HYDROMETRA STAGNORUM.

Hydrometra stagnorum (Fig. 163) is a very remarkable-looking insect, reminding one by its appearance of Euclid's definition of a line, for the creature has length, but seems to have no breadth to speak of. It is indeed the narrowest for its size of all British insects. It is about ½in. long and about half a line broad; its legs are wonderfully slender, and it is of a dark slate-colour. The portion of its head in front of its eyes is considerably elongated, and at the extremity of this curious elongation rather long and very fine antennæ are inserted. The eyes are prominent, and the under-part of the body has a hair-like covering. As *H. stagnorum* has no wings, the easiest way to tell the perfect insect from the pupa is to remember that the outer part of the body in the former is hard and in the latter soft. The soft covering allows for the necessary growth. To detect this curious creature, one must look very closely at the surface of the water upon which it walks. It is found upon both ponds and streams, and also upon their adjoining banks.

FIG. 164. GERRIS LACUSTRIS.

Of the genus *Gerris*, which contains about ten species, *G. lacustris* (Fig. 164) is the commonest member. It is not quite ½in. long, of a dark slate-colour, with yellowish marking at the sides of the body.

G. Najas, the largest and one of the commonest species, can be easily recognised by its great size, long legs, and want of wings. It is found upon running water, and is very difficult to catch in the net. The larva and the pupa of this insect may be distinguished by the size of the abdomen. When the former is just hatched, the abdomen is extremely small, but it increases in size as the animal grows older. The legs are very long from the first, and the full-grown *G. Najas* is known by the faint signs of wings. *G. thoracica* is smaller and less common than the preceding Gerris, and may be readily detected by a reddish mark upon the back of the thorax; hence the specific name. *G. gibbifera* is of the same size as *G. thoracica*, but is without the mark upon the thorax. It is also a rather broader insect, and is more abundant.

G. argentata is the smallest of all the *Gerridæ*, but it is by
no means common. All the members of this genus have a
fine, hair-like covering beneath their bodies. They use their
fore pair of legs for seizing their prey, their intermediate pair
for rowing themselves along upon the surface of the water,
and they steer by means of the last pair. Their antennæ are
four-jointed, and their wings are carried so close to their
bodies that there is some little difficulty in detecting them.
Their eyes are prominent, and their beaks, when not wanted,
are kept folded back beneath the fore-part of their bodies.
Most of the *Gerrid* æ hibernate in the winter-time beneath
some stone or piece of wood and the like close to the water's
edge, occasionally leaving these quarters upon any fine and
mild days which may happen during that season. The
smaller species of the *Gerridæ* are more gregarious than the
larger.

Velia currens, a common and very active little water-runner,
is exceedingly abundant, and more suitable for the aquarium
than any of the *Hydrometridæ* already mentioned. It seems
to be a very contented insect, and readily submits to captivity.
It is, however, a skilful climber, often astonishing its owner
by its adroitness in escaping from an apparently quite secure
prison. When it has been a short time in the aquarium, it
becomes tame, and eagerly attacks the food which is given to
it. Half-a-dozen of these insects will quickly extract all the
nutriment they can from the body of a bluebottle. Flies
seem to be their most suitable food while in confinement; but
if these cannot be procured, they will satisfy their hunger
with a piece of raw meat. This lively little insect is sometimes called the Water-Cricket, and may be found upon nearly
every pond or stream, and frequently at any season of the
year. It is not quite ½in. long, of a dark brown colour, with
two orange stripes along the back. It very seldom has wings.
In summer-time great numbers of these *Veliæ* are found
together, and they do not seem to care about choosing the
smoothest pieces of water for their meetings. Besides the
Hydrometridæ just mentioned, there are other interesting
members of the family which might be kept in confinement.

The two familes belonging to the tribe *Hydrocorisæ* (Water-Bugs) found in Britain are the *Nepidæ* and the *Notonectidæ*. The former include the genera *Nepa*, *Ranatra*, and *Naucoris*, and the latter *Notonecta* and *Corixa*.

All the members of the *Nepidæ* family (Water-scorpions) live for the greater part of their life in the water, and there feed upon other aquatic animals. They are not very active insects, trusting rather to stealth than to speed for the capture of their victims. The Water-scorpions have very powerful raptorial fore-legs, with which they seize and hold their prey while they extract all its juices. There are four other legs, which are chiefly used for swimming or crawling among aquatic plants. Their rostrum, which has three joints, is quite strong enough to pierce the human skin. They have wings and fair powers of flight.

The Water-scorpion should not be kept in the same aquarium with small fish, for it will kill them; nor with large ones, for they might kill it. Though this insect is so courageous and predaceous, it will quickly succumb to improper treatment. It is an interesting object in a small tank, where it ought to be the only occupant. The vessel in which it is confined should be covered, and should also be provided with something or other, such as a piece of cork, wood, or pumice-stone, which will float, and upon which the creature can climb when it wishes to leave the water for a short time. With care the Water-scorpion will live for a long while in captivity. For food it apparently prefers small fish and tadpoles, but it is content with almost anything of an animal nature.

Nepa cinerea (Fig. 166) is very common in ponds nearly everywhere. It readily escapes detection, however, owing to its colouring, which is similar to that of the mud upon which it is fond of resting. More than once I have thought that my Water-scorpions had escaped from their aquarium, on account of this facility of hiding, and only discovered my mistake by their change of position. This aptitude for concealment is very useful to the insect, for its prey comes unsuspectingly into its neighbourhood, and only realises its danger as it is seized by the cruel fore-legs, and pulled within reach

of the sharp beak. *N. cinerea* has great courage, or recklessness.
For example, I have taken a Nepa from its aquarium, in which
it has lived for a considerable time, and placed it with a tiny
minnow (Fig. 165) in a saucer before me ; but no sooner did the

FIG. 165. THE MINNOW (LEUCISCUS PHOXINUS).
(*From a Photograph by the Author.*)

little fish swim within reach of the fore-legs of the "scorpion,"
than it was seized by them and pressed against the hungry
creature's rostrum.   Yet this "water-bug" had not only been

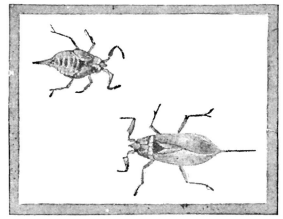

FIG. 166. LARVA AND PERFECT INSECT OF NEPA CINEREA.

moved from one vessel to another a minute or two previously,
but also from one room to another.

N. cinerea (Fig. 166) is very flat, elliptical, about 1in. long,
and of a dark brown colour, with a slight reddish tinge.
The upper part of the abdomen is a brighter red, and the

head is small and sunk almost to the prominent eyes into the thorax. At the end of the body there are two long and slender appendages, more than ½in. in length, which are used for breathing. These caudal appendages, when placed close together, have the appearance of only one appendage (Fig. 166): they have given the animal its familiar name of Water-scorpion, for, of course, it is no scorpion, but a bug. This insect respires by means of these filaments. The larva, with the exception of its size and want of wings, is very like the imago (Fig. 166); the pupa, just before it enters the perfect state, casts its outer covering, which, when shed, is so complete in shape, that it may be readily mistaken for the creature itself. *N. cinerea* lays very curious oval eggs, which have seven filaments or bristles at one end. These filaments, which are about as long as the egg itself, form themselves into a kind of receptacle for the egg which follows that to which they are attached.

Ranatra linearis (Fig. 167) is a much more curious and less

FIG. 167. RANATRA LINEARIS.

common insect than the preceding. It resembles the Nepa in its antennæ, tarsi, and its long respiratory apparatus at the extremity of its body, but it is unlike that creature in the great elongation of the thorax and abdomen—hence its specific name. The Ranatra measures 1½in. from the beak to the commencement of the two bristle-like appendages, and the appendages themselves are nearly 1¼in. long. The head is small, but the eyes are large and very prominent. The fore pair of legs, which are raptorial, are extremely curious and interesting. By means of an unusually long *coxa* they have great freedom of movement. The Ranatra moves slowly and stealthily through the water, either by swimming with a curious motion of the legs, or by crawling over the aquatic plants. Its manner of securing its victims is similar to that of the Nepa, and it is, if anything, more fearless and ravenous than that insect. The Ranatra has very beautiful wings, which it not infrequently uses. When this "scorpion" has been some

little time out of the water, it has difficulty in returning
beneath the surface, owing apparently to its small specific
gravity and to the dryness of its body.   The upper part
of the insect's abdomen beneath the wings is bright red,
and the rest of the body is a darkish brown.   The Ranatra
will sometimes breed in confinement, but the larvæ are difficult
to rear.   They will not hesitate, if they lack a sufficiency of
suitable food, to feed upon one another, the younger ones falling
victims to the older.   It is necessary for success to provide them
with a considerable variety and quantity of small aquatic animal
life.   The eggs are longer than those of *Nepa cinerea*, and are
furnished with only two filaments or bristles each instead of
seven.   These filaments are passed, pressed together, through
the leaf of some water-plant, such as that of the Frog-bit
(*Hydrocharis morsus-ranæ*), and immediately after insertion they
open, and thus the egg is fixed securely to the leaf.   Sometimes
as many as half-a-dozen eggs will be found hanging to the same
leaf.   The eggs, according to the temperature of the water,
batch in about a month.   The young *Ranatræ* from the first
are in shape very like their parents, but lighter in colour.
R. linearis will live a long time in captivity if properly cared
for.   It should be fed on the same kind of food as that recom-'
mended for its relative the Nepa.   The two Water-scorpions
must not be kept together in the same aquarium.   *R. linearis*,
which is rarer than the Nepa, can generally be bought for
about a shilling, during the summer, of London dealers in
aquarium articles.

The *Naucoris cimicoides* (Fig. 168)
is rather a rare insect.   It is about
½in. in length, oval in shape, and of an
olive-brown colour.   It is not provided
with respiratory filaments like those of
the Nepa and the Ranatra   It is able,
owing to its fringed hind-legs, to swim
very much faster than the two "water-

FIG. 168. NAUCORIS
CIMICOIDES.

scorpions" previously mentioned.   A little care is necessary
in handling this insect because of its power to inflict a
rather painful wound.   Its habits and habitat are similar to

those of its relatives, and while in confinement it should be treated in the same way.

The best known, but perhaps not the commonest, member of the family *Notonectidæ* is *Notonecta glauca* (Fig. 169), or Water-Boatman. This curious and interesting insect may very frequently be observed floating upon its back, with its oar-like legs extending at right angles to its body, just below the surface of nearly every pond or ditch. It is a little more than ½in. long; its body is convex and slightly keeled above and flat below, and its prevailing colour is yellow, with the exception of a black mark in the shape of a triangle upon the back; this black triangle is the scutellum. *N. glauca* has a broad head, very bold-looking eyes, four-jointed antennæ, and the tibia and tarsi of the hind-legs very flat and fringed on both sides with a kind of hair. The creature's fore-legs are raptorial, and its beak is so sharp and strong that it is able to inflict quite a painful wound on the human hand. The eyesight of the Water-Boatman is very acute, and he will dive quickly to the bottom of

FIG. 169. WATER-BOATMAN
(NOTONECTA GLAUCA).

the pond or ditch directly his would-be captor puts forth his net to take him. This insect looks well in the aquarium, for it is very lively and an expert swimmer. It always swims upon its back, and as it dives beneath the water it takes with it a store of air entangled in the hair with which parts of its body are covered. The air under these circumstances has somewhat the appearance of quicksilver, and makes the insect very attractive as he darts to and fro among the weeds of a well-arranged tank. But beauty, activity, and method of respiration, are about all that can be said in its favour; for it is extremely predaceous, and will quickly attack and kill most of the aquatic animals which are usually kept in an aquarium. It will even, unless properly and regularly fed, destroy its own species. Small fish seem to be its favourite food. It swims under and seizes its victim with its fore-legs, and quickly buries its beak deeply into the poor creature's body ; nor will the "boatman" relax its hold until it has extracted all the nutriment it can. *N. glauca* will also feed upon tadpoles, small frogs, and flies, placed upon the surface of the water. Sometimes it will content itself with a worm or a piece of raw meat suspended in the right position. As this insect is able and willing to use its beautiful and interest-ing wings, the vessel in which it is confined should always be kept covered. On no account should the Water-Boatman be placed in the same aquarium with fish. At night-time occasionally it makes a curious noise. The larva can be distinguished from the full-grown insect by its shorter body, its unseasoned-looking colour, and its want of wings.

Notonecta maculata is generally regarded as a variety of *N. glauca*. It may be known by a blackish band across the lower part of the body and by its spotted back ; hence its specific name.

The insects belonging to the genus *Corixa* are more abundant and less rapacious than the species of *Notonectæ*, and they are quite as interesting and ornamental in the aquarium. They are often wrongly called Water-Boatmen, from which they may be quickly distinguished, not only by their shape, but by their swimming with their backs upper-most. These creatures, unlike the *Notonectæ*, do not remain for any length of time near the surface of the water. They spend most of their life either hunting for food or clinging to the stones or weeds at the bottom of the pond or ditch in which they live. Of course, they frequently have to rise for the purpose of taking in a fresh supply of air. It is quite surprising how many insects of this genus one may sometimes capture with a single sweep of the net. They are not able to swim so quickly as the Water-Boatman. There are more than twenty species of *Corixa* found in British waters ; but some of them are taken only in Scotland, and others in brackish water, such as the ditches near

Gravesend. They are all more or less interesting in the aquarium, where they may be kept much more easily than the *Notonectœ*. The head of a Corixa is rather curious; it is convex in front, and very concave behind, and it is attached apparently so slightly to the thorax that there always seems a danger of the creature becoming decapitated. Indeed, I have not seldom found *Corixœ* in the aquarium floating about dead and minus their heads. The creatures take in a fresh supply of air by coming up to the surface of the water in such a way that the top of their heads and the upper part of their thoraces are slightly out of the water, and then, bending their heads downwards and upwards, they enclose some air, which is conducted to the breathing-holes beneath their bodies. During summer the bottoms of shallow ponds may be seen literally swarming with small species of *Corixa*, which are continually coming to the surface of the water for oxygen. *Corixœ* have wings, which they frequently use. The upper part of their bodies is flat, and in many of the species is ridged. While in the aquarium *Corixœ* are much more easily provided with food than the *Notonectœ*, for they will readily content themselves with garden-worms or pieces of raw meat. They are very good scavengers. I have kept a great many *Corixœ* for a long time, and I have never seen them attack fish, but I am not sure that they would not do so if starved. They will occasionally prey upon each other. The *Corixœ* make quite a distinct noise as they knock their heads against the side of the aquarium in which they are confined.

Corixa Geoffroyi (Fig. 170) is the largest and about the

commonest species of the *Corixœ*. It is about ½in. long, and the upper part of its body is a kind of dark brown, minutely spotted with yellow, with the exception of the thorax, which is marked with transverse black and yellow

FIG 170. CORIXA GEOFFROYI.

ones. These spots and lines cannot well be seen without the help of a magnifying-glass. The legs are also yellow with the exception of the lower parts of the posterior pair, which are about the same colour as the insect's back. *C. Geoffroyi*, like *Notonecta glauca*, has a fringe of hair round the extremity of its body.

C. Sahlbergi is more abundant than the preceding species, which it resembles in appearance, but it is about half the length, and less than half the width, of its greater relative. This insect will live for a long time in an aquarium, where it will give very little trouble.

Besides the above, *C. striata*, *C. moosta*, and *C. fossarum*, are the commonest members of this genus, the different species of which are very difficult to distinguish.

Besides the *Notonecitæ* and the *Corixæ*, there are other members of this family, such as *Plea minutissima*, closely related to the former, and the *Cymatiæ* and *Sigaræ*, allied to the latter, which may be kept in the aquarium, but which, I think, give more trouble to feed and to keep than most aquarium-owners would care to bestow upon them.

CHAPTER XIV.

LARVÆ OF WATER-FLIES.

CERTAIN rather fragile-looking insects may be seen in summer-time flying, apparently with difficulty to themselves, over the surface and in the neighbourhood of fresh water, or may be found concealed among the weeds and trees growing on its banks. These insects are commonly called Caddis-flies. They are very like moths, with unusually long antennæ. Their chief colours are either brown or black. Some of them are as much as 2in. across their expanded wings, and these (the large insects) generally fly at night. A few of the Caddis-flies are so much like moths that it is no easy matter to make a distinction. However, as a rule, the former may be distinguished from the latter by remembering that the wings of the Caddis-fly are covered more or less closely with a kind of hair, while those of the moth are adorned with powder-like scales; hence the one is a trichopterous (Gr. *thrix*, a hair, and *pteron*, a wing) insect, and the other a lepidopterous (*lepis*, a scale, and *pteron*, a wing). The Caddis-fly can also be known from a moth by its antennæ and mouth-organs. Its antennæ are proportionately longer than those of a moth, are carried more horizontally, and are filiform or thread-like, whilst those of moths are generally plumose or feathery.

The females of the Caddis-fly deposit their eggs upon stones near to, or half in, the water, upon aquatic plants, or even,

T

occasionally, under the water itself. The eggs are inclosed in
a gelatinous envelope, and hatch in a few days. The young
larvæ remain in the glutinous mass for a short time before
they venture to brave the dangers of their watery world.
They are elongated, and more or less cylindrical in shape, and
of a yellowish-white colour. Their bodies are soft, with the
exception of the head and the thoracic segments, which are
horny They have branchial filaments, placed either in bunches
or singly (according to the species) on the sides of their bodies,
six legs, and strong jaws. These insects, which are in themselves so defenceless, would soon fall victims to fish and other
aquatic animals were they not endowed with an instinct which
makes them about the most interesting inhabitants of the
fresh-water aquarium. Under the influence of this instinct,
they build for themselves houses portable in most cases, but
stationary in others, in which they are more or less secure
from the attacks of their numerous enemies. These houses
are formed in various shapes, and are made of various
materials, according as a rule, to the species of the larva
which constructs them. Sometimes the materials depend, to
a great extent, upon the locality. The caddis-cases, as they
are generally called, are made of pieces of stick, leaves, sand,
small stones, shells of molluscs, moss, rushes, seeds, and the
like. These cases are formed either of all one kind of substance or of two or more different kinds. But whatever
material is used, the larvæ generally manage to make these
places of refuge of the same specific gravity as the water, so
that they may have no difficulty in moving from place to place.
The insects fasten their building materials together by the
help of a viscous secretion, which on exposure hardens into
a kind of silk. The insides of the caddis-cases are also lined
with this silk-like substance. The larvæ are able to cling
most tenaciously to their tubes by means of small hooks placed
at the extremity of their bodies, by the third pair of legs,
which are often longer than the rest, and in many species by
the help of three smaller humps situated upon the first
segment of the soft part of their bodies. So firmly, indeed,
will these creatures hold to their cases, that to attempt forcibly

to drag them out would only end in their being pulled in half—or, at any rate, in their death. But they may easily be dislodged by inserting the stalk of a leaf or a very thin piece of stick into the end at which is the extremity of the insect. This part of the tube is generally of smaller diameter than the other, and the animal will nearly always, after a little tickling, evacuate its fortress. Sometimes the larvæ will voluntarily leave their cases; but whether they have been driven out of their homes, or have left of their own accord, they will generally return to them upon the first opportunity.

It is a very interesting sight to see these clever little architects and builders at work. Upon being taken from their cases and placed naked, along with suitable material, in a

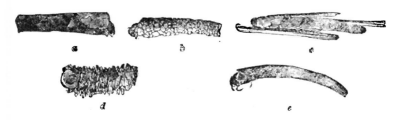

FIG. 171. LARVÆ OF DIFFERENT SPECIES OF THE CADDIS-FLY IN THEIR CASES.

saucer or other vessel, they will readily make new tubes. They can be persuaded to construct their dwellings of pieces of coal, bits of glass, beads, filings of metal, and other things of a similar kind. Some caddis-worms work much more quickly than others, but the speed of construction frequently depends upon the materials at hand.

There are in Great Britain about one hundred and sixty different species of Caddis-flies, which have been divided by Mr. McLachlan, the author of the "Monographic Revision and Synopsis of the European Trichoptera," into seven families. Of these families, that of the *Phryganeidæ* (Gr. *phruganon*, a bundle of sticks) contains the largest species; and that of the *Limnophilidæ* the most numerous. It will, of course, be impossible to refer in this chapter to anything like all the species, nor is it necessary, for reference to a few of them will be quite sufficient to remind those who do know, or to show those who do not know, how very interesting the larvæ of the Caddis-flies are.

The worm of *Phryganea grandis* makes a cylindrical case (*a*, Fig. 171) of almost equal diameter throughout, and forms it of portions of leaves and other vegetable matter arranged spirally. This larva and its case are generally found in ponds or very slow-running streams. The insect, in common with many others, has the habit of turning itself while within its tube, so that it can protrude its head at either end. *Phryganea grandis* (Fig. 172), about the largest British species, is a little more than $\frac{3}{4}$in. long, and its wings, when expanded, are at least 2in. from tip to tip. It is one of the commonest and handsomest of the Caddis-flies. It may be known by its ash-coloured

FIG. 172.　PHRYGANEA GRANDIS.

anterior wings, brown posterior wings, and yellow-ringed antennæ. Like all its relatives, it folds its wings alongside of its body when at rest.

The larvæ of *P. obsoleta*, *P. striata*, and all of the family, make the same kind of cases as that of *P. grandis*. *P. minor* is the smallest member of the *Phryganeidæ*. It is rather a handsome insect. Its anterior wings are spotted.

The larvæ of the large and well-known family of the *Limnophilidæ* make cases very varied in their construction. They may be found either in stagnant or quick-running water. The case of the *Limnophilus rhombicus* (Fig. 173) is rather common and cumbersome. It is made of pieces of vegetable fibre, pieces of stick or twigs of various thickness, bits of grass, and portions of moss. These are all cut about the same length

FIG. 173.　CASE OF THE LARVA LIMNOPHILUS RHOMBICUS.

and laid transversely, giving the whole case a bristling appearance.

The cases of the larvæ of the Caddis-fly *L. flavicornis* are very varied, and often uncommonly beautiful and interesting. Some of them are most regular in their construction and others exceedingly irregular. Occasionally they are made of the same kind of materials which are used by the larvæ of *L. rhombicus,* with the shell of a small species of *Planorbis* added here and there (*d*, Fig. 171). Not infrequently are

FIG. 174. (1) LARVA AND CASE, AND (2) NAKED LARVA (ENLARGED) OF LIMNOPHILUS FLAVICORNIS.

they constructed entirely, or almost entirely, of these shells, which are so closely and skilfully packed together, that as many as forty or fifty shells may be counted in a single case (1, Fig. 174). The larvæ of *Limnophilus flavicornis* (2, Fig. 174) will use other shells besides those of tiny Planorbes in the formation of its tube. Not only will it press into its service small univalves of any kind it may happen to meet with, but even bivalves, such as the *Sphærium corneum,* other *Sphæria,* or some of the *Pisidia.* It seems to be quite careless whether it makes use of the right or left valve, or both valves of one of these molluscs. Nor does it stop to find out,

before it "annexes" a shell, whether the owner of it has left
or not; for it is by no means an unusual thing to find a
caddis-case composed of shells in which the animals still live.
This is rather hard upon the poor molluscs, for they have
to be carried about as their captor wishes. It is a very
good plan for those who are collecting fresh-water shells to
examine the cases made by the larvæ of *L. flavicornis.* Of
course, it will be readily seen that the tubes formed of such
a variety of materials must often be very irregular, as well
as apparently cumbersome.

The larvæ of *L. lunatus* make a case of sand or vegetable
material, to which they attach long pieces of stick, which
project at either end (*c,* Fig. 171). These long bits of wood
seem to act as balancers. This case is generally found in
stagnant or very slow-running water.

The larvæ of *L. vittatus* make a curved case of fine sand.
It may be likened in shape to an elephant's tusk, and in
appearance it is somewhat similar to *e,* Fig. 171.

The larvæ of *L. pellucidus* make cases chiefly composed of
whole leaves, laid almost flat against each other. The "worm"
itself is inclosed in a tube within the leaves. This is by no
means an uncommon case in some parts of the country. It
is generally found in stagrant water.

The larvæ of the genus *Stenophylax* live in streams, and
make their tubes of tiny pebbles (*b,* Fig. 171). Sometimes
when the water is very swift, the cases are fastened slightly
to large stones. If the collector will take the trouble to
examine the lower part of large stones in quick-running
streams, he will frequently find bunches of very small gravel
attached to that part. So firmly are they fastened that it
requires quite a strong pressure of the finger or thumb to
remove them. These bunches are fixed cases of the Caddis-
worm. The larvæ of Caddis-flies found in quick-running
water are not suitable for the aquarium.

As the Caddis-worm grows, it enlarges its case by making
an addition to the larger end. When this is done, the case
is shortened at the other end. While the Caddis-worm is
moving from place to place, it protrudes its body just suffi-

ciently to use its legs, and when it is attacked by an enemy it withdraws itself deeply into its tube. Most of these larvæ may be considered herbivorous, though at times they are not unwilling to partake of a carnivorous diet. They will occasionally eat a portion of a worm, pieces of beef or mutton, sometimes very young fish. A few of the Caddis-worms are thought to be entirely carnivorous, feeding as a rule upon other aquatic larvæ. However, it is well to take for granted that the Caddis-worms which are suitable for the aquarium are herbivorous. These little creatures should not be placed in a tank in which choice weeds are growing, or they will certainly do a great deal of harm; and the best way to keep these very interesting insects is to place them in small aquaria, where they may be easily seen at their work, and in which small quantities of weeds may be put as required. Caddis-worms should not be kept together in great numbers, or they will interfere with one another. They will live for a long time in the aquarium, often apparently without eating anything at all. When they do not feed, the period at which they will enter the pupal state is considerably postponed. Caddis-worms of various species may be found at almost any season of the year.

As the time arrives at which it is necessary for the larva to enter the pupal-hood, it in most cases makes preparation for that change by fastening its tube to a stone or water-plant, and covering the open ends of it with a kind of sill or net, so constructed as to keep out all enemies, and let in the water necessary for respiration. Sometimes this grating is made with the help of pieces of stone or vegetable matter. Occasionally a larva closes up one end of its case in the manner just described, and with the head protruding at the other end digs a hole in the bottom of the stream, in which it almost half buries its tube vertically. When it has done this it is supposed to change its position in the case before it becomes a pupa. On one occasion I saw a Caddis-worm in an aquarium performing this act of semi-interment. I removed it to another vessel, and it soon reburied itself. A few days after the larva has closed up its case, it enters the pupal state. The insect's appearance as a pupa is very different from that which it had as a larva. Its wings, legs, and antennæ are then placed close to the sides of its body. The pupa's only movements while in the case are said to be oscillations from side to side. After spending a few weeks in the pupal state it breaks the covering at one end of its tube and swims very swiftly to the surface of the water; then it mounts some protruding stone or aquatic plant, and remains there while the pupal envelope splits, and it—a perfect insect —is free. Some pupæ, however, do not leave the surface of the water, but float there until they emerge fully-developed Caddis-flies.

Everybody knows a Dragon-fly when he sees it; but everybody does not know what an exceedingly interesting creature it really is, especially during that portion of its life which it spends in the water. The Dragon-fly, of which we have in England over forty species, is one of the most beautiful, and the most voracious, of all our insects. It is often called by country people the "Horse-Sting" or "Horse-Stinger," and sometimes also, I believe, the "Flying Adder." But it does not deserve such names, for it has no sting at all. That which is taken for a sting is an apparatus given by Nature to the male Dragon-fly for the purpose of carrying off a wife. This gay and gaudily-dressed courtier seizes his lady-love round the neck with the claspers situated on the last segment but one of his body, and leads her away as his own. Pairs of Dragon-flies thus united may be frequently seen in summertime making their flight together in tandem fashion. The female Dragon-fly deposits her eggs either singly or in bunches in the water or very close to its edge. Sometimes they are attached to the stems of water-plants, and sometimes also, it is said, they are inserted by females of some species, by means of an ovipositor, in small incisions made in aquatic weeds. Occasionally the Dragon-fly has been seen to go beneath the surface of the water, by crawling along the stalk of a suitable plant, for the purpose of laying her eggs.

Dragon-flies are divided into three sub-families, viz.: (1) *Æschnidæ,* (2) *Libellulidæ,* (3) *Agrionidæ.*

The *Æschnidæ* may be generally known by their large and almost hemispherical heads, by their exceedingly great eyes, which meet together above, and by their long and rather slender bodies. These insects keep their wings extended when at rest. The largest British Dragon-fly (*Anax formosus*) belongs to this sub-family, and is about 3in. long; and the *Æschna grandis* is nearly as large, measuring not much less than 4in. across its expanded wings.

The *Libellulidæ* have heads, eyes, and wings very like the *Æschnidæ*, but their bodies are generally broader, shorter, and flatter. They also keep their wings extended when not flying. The commonest representative of this sub-family is *Libellula depressa*. Perhaps this insect more than any other is called the "Horse-Stinger." It is about 2in. long, and its body is broad and flattened. The male is covered with a lovely violet-blue powder, and the female has a yellowish-brown abdomen, spotted with yellow upon the sides. Another well-known species belonging to the *Libellulidæ* is *Sympetrum vulgatum.* It is about 2in. long, and has a yellow cylindrical body and clear wings.

The *Agrionidæ* are the smallest, the most elegant, and the most delicate-looking of all the Dragon-flies. It is owing perhaps to their graceful forms that the French call them and all their relatives "Demoiselles." The English name, however, seems the more appropriate, for the *Libellulidæ* are certainly about the most predaceous and bloodthirsty of all British insects. The eyes of the *Agrionidæ* are separated from one another by a wide crown. The abdomen is cylindrical, extremely slender, and flattened a little at the extremity. These Dragon-flies when at rest place their wings close together over their backs. *Agrion puella* is about the best-known member of this sub-family. It is a little more than 1¼in. long. The body of the male is prettily spotted, or rather ringed, with blue, while that of the female is marked with brassy-black. *Calopteryx virgo* is also very abundant in certain parts of the country. The abdomen of the male is blue and that of the female is greenish. The former insect has beautiful metallic-blue wings, while those of the latter are of a pretty brown; hence the generic name.

As Dragon-flies have an "incomplete metamorphosis," their larvæ have more or less a resemblance to themselves, the full-grown insects. The resemblance is in shape, certainly not in colour, which is generally dark brown and very like in shade to the mud upon which the larvæ frequently crawl and hunt for their prey. They are nearly the most predaceous of all aquatic larvæ, and they are more ravenous still, if possible, when they become pupæ. Though they are so greedy, they have at the same time a wonderful power of fasting, and will live, seemingly in perfect health, without apparently eating anything at all.

One of the best ways of procuring the larvæ of Dragon-flies is to sweep the bottoms of ponds, or rather deep ditches, with the net, or to fish up with a hook, fastened to the end of a cord or a stick, the tangles of weeds which have sunk there, and lift them on the bank. After watching such dripping masses for a minute or two, most likely several larvæ, together with other insects of different species, will be seen crawling about the mud and the decaying plants which have been thus drawn out of the pond or ditch. Some of the larvæ will be exactly of the colour of the mud; others will be nearly black; while a few, perhaps, will be covered, more or less, with confervæ. They will be, if there are many of them, most likely of different shapes, sizes, and ages. In fact, some of them ought to be called pupæ rather than larvæ, for the signs of wings in their cases will show that they have arrived at their *nymph* stage.

On examining many larvæ of Dragon-flies taken from two or more pieces of water, one will conclude that they may be divided, on account of their various forms, into at least three groups. The first animal to be noticed, perhaps, owing to its strong and bold appearance, will be in shape like *a*, Fig. 175. This will be the larva of one of the *Æschnidæ*. Then there will be another insect, having much the appearance of the preceding, but stouter and clumsier. The eyes are smaller and further apart, and the head is more square; sometimes it will be more or less covered with foreign matter (*b*, Fig. 175). This larva is a representative of the *Libellulidæ*. And, lastly, there will be noticed an insect much slenderer than either of the former, and instead of the spine-like projections at the end of the body, there will be some beautiful leaf-like appendages—often of considerable length. This is the larva of one of the *Agrionidæ*.

All these larvæ, to whatever sub-family they belong, are extremely predaceous, and get their living by preying upon their weaker companions of the water. They occasionally do not hesitate, if food is scarce, to become cannibals. Unlike some aquatic carnivorous creatures, such as *Nepa cinerea*,

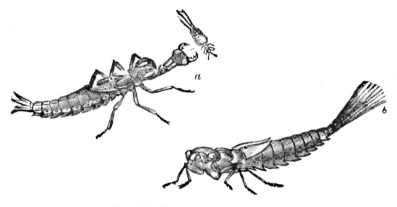

FIG. 175. PUPÆ OF DRAGON-FLIES.

they do not kill unless to satisfy hunger. Nor are they quarrelsome.

They obtain their prey in a most extraordinary manner. They are really hypocrites, for they wear a "mask." This "mask" is a deadly and very curious apparatus. It is a remarkable arrangement of the lower lip or labium, and consists of several joints. The first joint is about ¼in. long, more or less, according to the size and species of the insect, and it is also about one-third of its length broad, and very thin. One end of this piece is fixed, so to speak, under the chin of the animal, and at the other end there is attached a somewhat similar joint, but rather broader at its further extremity. At this extremity there are articulated two claw-like pieces, which open and close at the will of the insect. When this apparatus is in repose, the first joint folds backward under the head of the creature, the second folds forward, and the claw-like pieces, when placed together, form a kind of cup, which covers a portion (more or less, according to species) of the lower part of the face. So closely does this prehensile arrangement pack away, that its presence may easily escape unnoticed. When the animal wishes to seize any prey, it creeps very stealthily and slowly up to its victim, and when near enough shoots out with great rapidity the apparatus just described, seizes the victim with the claw-like part (a, Fig. 175), and drags it, firmly held, to within a convenient distance of its mouth. The limb is used so quickly and surely that one is reminded, while seeing it in operation, of the tongue of the frog, already referred to in Chapter VII. The creature does not often miss its mark. This "mask" has little or no lateral movement.

The larvæ and pupæ of Dragon-flies are not only very interesting in their manner of obtaining food, but they are, if possible, even more interesting in their method of respiration. Those, however, which belong to the two sub-families, the *Æschnidæ* and the *Libellulidæ*, differ somewhat in their breathing arrangements from those of the *Agrionidæ*. The former have at the extremity of their bodies five spines, two being much smaller than the other three. These spines, which can be opened and closed at the will of the animals, surround an opening which leads into the interior of the body, in which the tracheal, or air, tubes are situated. Through this orifice, thus guarded, these insects can draw water into the latter part of their bodies, and then having, by means of the respiratory apparatus which is placed there, extracted all the oxygen it contained, they discharge (b, Fig. 175) it through the same opening by which it entered. This water is generally expelled gently, but occasionally with great rapidity and force. When the latter is the case, the animals are driven through the water with considerable speed. Indeed, this forcible expulsion of water is the only way by which these creatures can travel with anything like celerity from place to place. Under such influence they progress with a series of jerks or plunges. Frequently, when a larva or pupa is suddenly removed from its aquarium, it will be seen to discharge a tiny stream of water into the air. The water in such circumstances is sometimes shot no little distance. I was once examining some of these insects which I had placed in a little water in an ordinary plate, and while lifting gently, with a pair of forceps, the tail part of one of the larvæ, some water was driven upon the globe of the lamp by the light of which I was working; and I do not think I shall be exaggerating when I say that, had not the water been stopped in this way, it would have been thrown nearly 3ft. The insect was not much more than 1in. long. Sometimes, when a larva or pupa is returned to its aquarium, it will shoot water into the air. In this case the creature seems so anxious to get quickly away from its captor, that it discharges its stream before it is fairly under the surface of the water. If one of these insects be placed upon its back in a little water contained in a plate, the expansion and contraction of its abdomen can be plainly seen as it takes in and discharges the water necessary for respiration. These animals are able to swim upon their backs.

The larvæ and pupæ of the *Agrionidæ* have three rather large leaf-like appendages at the end of their abdomens. These appendages, which are furnished with tracheal tubes connected with others contained within the bodies of the insects, extract the oxygen from the water and supply it to the internal tracheæ. The animals often use these gill-like plates in the same way that fish do their tails, and thus they swim somewhat slowly through the water.

As the larvæ and pupæ of Dragon-flies grow, it is necessary for them, from time to time, to change their skins. This change of skin is rather frequent, and very complete; so complete, indeed, that sometimes the aquarium-keeper will think that there are two larvæ in the same vessel where the night before there was only one. After a certain number of changes of skin, the wing-cases begin to appear, and then the creature has passed from the larval state into that of the pupal. As the time draws near for the nymph to become the perfect Dragon-fly, it ceases to eat, and begins to grow languid. It should now, if in captivity, be provided with some means by which it may leave the water. A piece of stick put slantingly in the gravel and sand at the bottom of the tank, and rising above the surface of the water, will answer the purpose very well. The pupa will creep slowly up this stick, and will remain at some little distance above the water, clinging with its claws (given it for this special purpose) to the under side of the stick, and will wait there its final change. In due time the skin at the back of the thorax splits ; through this split, after considerable effort, the head, thorax, and legs of the Dragon-fly slowly emerge, and then the creature, apparently quite exhausted with its struggles, hangs helplessly down, the remaining portion of its body still being within the old skin. When it has thus rested sufficiently, it gradually lifts itself up until it can grasp with its legs the forepart of its late covering, and with this purchase it is able to draw from the pupal integument the remainder of its abdomen. It has now, with the exception of the wings, all the appearance of a perfect Dragon-fly. Gradually, however, the wings expand until they are of the full size, and after a little hardening and drying they are fit for use. The development of the Dragon-fly from the pupa is a most interesting sight. I shall never forget my delight and astonishment when the first pupa I kept became a Dragon-fly. The change was made at night. (I believe these changes generally do take place at night, for the Dragon-fly is at this time of its life so helpless that if it were not for the darkness it would have little hope of escaping from its numerous enemies.) In the morning when I looked at my pupa I saw it, as I thought, in the same place that it had been the evening before, but on lifting the cover of the aquarium I found clinging to it a magnificent Dragon-fly of the species *Æschna cyanea*. I could not quite understand its presence at the moment, for to all appearance there was still the pupa. However, on a closer inspection, I discovered that it was only the skin of the former object of my care, though it was exceedingly like the insect itself. The larvæ and pupæ of Dragon-flies are very easy to keep in confine-ment, giving little or no trouble. They will eat various aquatic animals, such as tadpoles, water-worms, tiny fish, Corixæ, Notonectæ, &c.; and when these fail they will con-tent themselves with garden-worms. The water in which they live, if they are carefully supplied with food, will remain perfectly bright and clear. Several of these insects will agree together, and they will not be guilty of cannibalism unless they are starved. I have hardly ever known them die, though I have kept very many in confinement. The larvæ and pupæ of the *Æschnidæ* are, I think, the most suitable of their kind to keep in confinement. It is supposed that these insects live from one to three years, according to their species, before they become perfect Dragon-flies.

The members of the *Ephemeridæ* (Day-flies) family of the *Neuroptera* are chiefly remarkable for the extreme shortness of their lives when they attain the imago or perfect state. Some of them, when they have reached that condition, only live for a few hours—being born, so to speak, after sunset and dying before sunrise; while the longest-livers, the patri-archs of the family, exist but for a day or two as a rule, though in captivity it is said that they have been kept alive for a week or even more. Appropriately, then, are they named *Ephemeridæ*—beings whose length of life is limited to a day. The larvæ of these insects, however, live from one to three years, according to their species.

Day-flies, or rather May-flies, as they are commonly called, are very delicate-looking creatures, generally possessing four minutely-reticulated wings and two or three extremely long *setæ*, or tail filaments. The hinder wings are very much smaller than the former pair, and sometimes are wanting altogether. These insects, owing to the lack of development in the organs of the mouth, seem incapable of taking food of any kind whatever. Their antennæ are very short and awl-shaped, and their fore-legs are very often extremely long. The males are distinguished by two curious appendages affixed to the last segment but one of their body, by the great elon-gation of their fore-legs, and by the "up-and-down" manner of their flight. The females as they fly deposit their small oval eggs in the water, which sink and adhere to stones and aquatic weeds. The larvæ, which in due time are hatched from these eggs, do not bear much resemblance to the full-grown insects. Their bodies, which are flat and elongated, have three long feather-like appendages at the extremity of the abdomen. At the sides of the abdomen there are some leaf-like branchial organs attached in pairs to all the segments of the body except (according to species) the last three or four. The antennæ are long and bristle-like. The larvæ and pupæ have strong mouths, and feed by preying upon small aquatic animal life. For a long time it was quite a matter of doubt what was their proper food. Some authorities declared that because their bodies, when dissected, were found to contain mud, that they ate mud; while others supposed that they consumed vegetable matter. These larvæ construct no cases as do those of the Caddis-fly, but live either freely in the water or in curious burrows made in the banks of the ponds and streams which they inhabit. As a rule, it is the larvæ of the larger species of the *Ephemeridæ* which make the burrows. These burrows, which are formed somewhat in the shape of the letter U, are so arranged that the insect can go in at one end and out at the other, and so save itself the inconvenience of turning round within its narrow home. In making the burrows, these creatures seem, in some measure, to imitate the common earthworm by swallowing at least a portion of the mud or soil they are excavating. This habit accounts, it is thought, for the presence of mud within their bodies.

These larvæ change their skins frequently as they grow, and are said to have become pupæ when their thoraces show signs of bearing wings. After a certain time, according to species, the pupa leaves the water and develops into a fly, but, strange to say, not the perfect fly, for there is still another change before the imago appears. The sub-imago, as it is called, is the " Green Drake " of the fisherman. ' It is a slow and clumsy flyer, and soon settles upon some spot conveniently situated for getting rid of the pellicle which covers its whole body, and hides its true colour. It then frees itself in a wonderful manner from this very thin skin, and emerges a beautiful and active fly, with the filaments at the extremity of its body of about double their former length. Numbers of these filmy skins may be seen adhering to trees or weeds upon the water's edge.

The wings of the perfect Day-fly are so delicate and fragile, that it is almost impossible to preserve the insect in anything approaching a life-like condition without placing it in spirits of some kind. These insects emerge from their pupal envelope generally about sunset. They nearly always appear, when at all, in great numbers; the males assembling together in crowds, and attracting attention by their curious and graceful up-and-down flight. The swarms of these insects, though frequently very great in this country, are often far greater in the neighbourhood of rivers and canals upon the Continent. Indeed, their numbers there are sometimes so enormous that the bodies of these tiny flies are gathered and used as manure.

The larvæ and pupæ of the Day-flies can be easily kept in confinement, where they may be seen to go through their wonderful metamorphosis. They will live, apparently quite contentedly, in a small aquarium, whether its bottom is covered with mud or not. The best species for the tank is *Ephemera vulgata*, the larva (Fig. 176) of which is about an inch long. It will frequently change its skin, which forms a very interesting object under the microscope. It ought to be always provided with suitable food, which should consist of cyclops,

FIG. 176. LARVA OF DAY-FLY, EPHEMERA VULGATA (ENLARGED).

water-fleas (*Daphniæ*), and the like. These little fresh-water crustaceans may be easily bred in great numbers for this and similar purposes, directions for which will be given in another chapter. When the time draws near for the pupa

U

to become the sub-imago, a landing-stage should be prepared for it—one similar to that recommended for the pupæ of the Dragon-fly will do. And if the aquarium-keeper is fortunate, and has arranged matters properly, he will be able to witness not only the interesting sight of the pupa becoming the " Green Drake," but also the " Green Drake " developing into the beautiful and graceful Day-fly (*Ephemera vulgata*) (Fig. 177).

There are three other genera belonging to the family *Ephemeridæ*—viz., *Baëtis, Brachycercus,* and *Cloën*. The imago of the genus *Baëtis* is much like that of the Ephemera, with the exception that it has only two setæ instead of three,

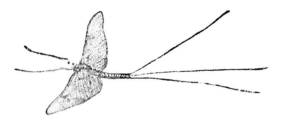

FIG. 177. DAY-FLY (EPHEMERA VULGATA).

but the larva of the former is very different from that of the latter. Its head is much broader, blunter, and more sunk in the thorax than is that of the larva of the Ephemera. The legs are also larger in proportion and placed more closely together than are those of the latter insect, and the antennæ are much shorter. There are some curious and interesting branchial leaflets attached to the segments of the abdomen, and at the extremity of the body there are three long bristle-like appendages. Its treatment, and that of the larvæ of the two genera *Brachycercus* and *Cloën*, while in confinement should be the same as that of their near relative the larva of the genus *Ephemera*. The imago of the genus *Brachycercus* has two wings and three setæ, and that of the genus *Cloën* has two wings and two setæ. The Day-fly of the genus *Baëtis* is the "March Brown" of the angler. The larvæ of the *Ephemeridæ* may be found, either in their burrows in the mud, or hiding under stones, in either stagnant or running water. It is hardly worth one's while to hunt for them specially, as they are so frequently found while searching for other fresh-water animals; but they certainly repay the trouble of keeping them when taken. They are generally seen crawling about the mud which is brought up with the hand-net.

The insects of the *Perlidæ* family of the *Neuroptera* are distinguished chiefly by the veins of their wings and by the formation of their thoraces. The longitudinal nervures on the disc of their wings are united by transverse ones; and the three segments of their thoraces are almost of equal size. These flies have four brownish wings, and long and tapering antennæ. The wings are longer than the body, and when folded, lie flat, overlapping each other, upon the creature's back. There are two, generally long, filaments attached to the last segment of the abdomen. The larvæ (Fig. 179) are very similar in appearance to the perfect insects (Fig. 178). They live in either stagnant or running water, but much oftener in the latter than in the former; do not make cases like the caddis-worms, or burrow like the larvæ of the Day-flies, but live freely in the water, crawling about aquatic plants or under stones; are carnivorous, and feed upon small animal life, especially upon the larvæ of other insects; and swim well with an undulatory motion of their bodies. The pupæ are known from the larvæ by the appearance of the wings in their cases. The aquatic life of the *Perlidæ* lasts for two or three years, and when it comes to an end, the pupæ climb up an aquatic plant or something else which will take them above the water, and then wait until the pupal skin bursts and they are able to emerge from it perfect insects. The females carry their eggs, for a time before they deposit them, at the extremity of the abdomen. The flight of these insects is slow and laboured, and some of the males do not fly at all. The larva of *Nemura variegata*, sometimes called by anglers the "Willow-fly," is the most suitable for the

aquarium, as it is found in stagnant as well as running water.
This species is one of the commonest of the *Perlidæ*. The
Perlidæ are frequently called "Stone-flies." Some fishermen,
however, only recognise the *Perla bicaudata*, a brownish insect
nearly 1in. long, as the "Stone-fly."

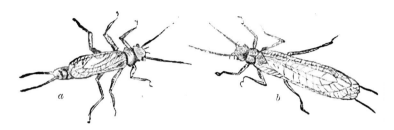

FIG. 178. STONE-FLIES. *a*, MALE; *b*, FEMALE.

While hunting for fresh-water animals, one not seldom comes
across an insect wrapped up in two or more green leaves or
pieces of leaves of some aquatic plant. The leaves and the
animal have somewhat the appearance of a caddis-worm in its
case: in fact, for a time before I knew what it was, I mistook
it (and I dare say others
have done so also) for a
caddis-worm. It does not
however belong to the
Trichoptera, but is a cater-
pillar of a small moth
commonly known as a
"China Mark." The "China
Marks" are remarkable for
being the only moths whose

FIG. 179. CREEPER, LARVA OF THE
STONE-FLY.

caterpillars are aquatic. There are only five species of
these moths in Britain, the largest of which is not
more than 1in. across its expanded wings. These moths
have white wings, with black, brownish, or yellowish markings. The females deposit their eggs upon aquatic plants,
and the larvæ generally seem to eat their way into the interior

of the plant upon which they are hatched, and then after a time proceed to make for themselves a case or home out of its leaves. The case is usually made of two pieces of leaves neatly joined together. The larvæ of some of the *Hydro- campidæ* use more than two portions of a leaf in the con- struction of their cases. For instance, the larvæ of the *Cataclysta lemnalis*, as its specific name implies, feeds upon duckweed, and of several of the leaves of this plant it makes its home or case. The larvæ of the "China Marks," as they grow, from time to time enlarge their cases, or, as the leaves forming them decay, repair them. They enter and complete their pupalhood while in their larval homes. These creatures are herbivorous, and feed generally upon the leaves of the plants on which they are born, and of which they make their cases. They do not always, however, confine themselves to the same weed either for food or for building material. One of the most beautiful of these "China Marks" is the *Hydro- sampa stagnalis*, and its larva is suitable for the aquarium. The vessels in which these larvæ are confined should be pro- vided with plenty of water-weed—such, for instance, as the Vernal Starwort (*Callitriche verna*), (Fig. 50), which ought to be placed in the tank according to directions given on p. 70.

There are many people, I believe, who look upon Gnats and their near relatives the mosquitoes as not only tormenting, but useless and uninteresting, insects; whereas, in fact, at least during the greater portion of their lives, they are both useful and very interesting. And to look upon all Gnats as tormentors is to err not a little in the matter of justice; for it is only the female members of the family which are guilty of what is commonly called "biting." The males are known by their plumed or feather-like antennæ, which have been compared to ostrich feathers on a very minute scale. The females are also plumed, but in a small degree when compared with the males, and there is no difficulty in distin- guishing the sexes. Sometimes, during fine weather, Gnats are seen flying together in such multitudes that at a distance they look like columns of smoke. It is only, as a rule, the males which thus assemble in the air. For food, Gnats extract the nectar from flowers; but the female Gnat is always ready to make an addition to this fare by sucking the blood of animals, not even omitting, alas! that of man.

The female Gnat's method of laying her eggs is exceedingly curious and interesting. She deposits them upon the surface of stagnant water. To do this, she looks about for some piece of floating grass, stick, or the like, upon which she settles. She then places her fore pair of legs upon her temporary raft, and her intermediate pair either just touching the water or else upon the extreme edge of the raft, while she crosses her hind-legs ready to receive the egg she is about to lay. This egg, which is oblong and narrower at one end than the other, she holds until she has brought forth a second and has joined it, by means of the sticky substance with which it is surrounded, to the first. She thus continues to lay her eggs and fasten them together until they number from 200 to 300. All the eggs are glued side by side with their narrower ends uppermost, and so a kind of unsinkable boat is formed, which is slightly concave above and convex below. This curious "boat" will stand a great deal of very rough weather without running any risk of going to the bottom. If it is pushed forcibly under the water, it will rise again to the surface in the proper position immediately upon the removal of the pressure. Neither a very heavy shower nor the pouring of a considerable quantity of water upon it will sink it: its buoyancy and self-righting power are remarkable, and quite worthy of the notice of makers of lifeboats. During favourable weather the eggs which form the "boat" hatch in a few days. A kind of small door opens at the lower end of each egg, which closes again after the exit of the young larva into the water.

The larvæ of Gnats are curious-looking little creatures (Fig. 180); they have rather large heads, very large thoraces, and elongated bodies, with a curious breathing arrangement near the extremity. This breathing arrangement consists of a small tube, which is fixed to the eighth segment of the body. When the creature wishes to take in a fresh supply of air, it protrudes the end of this tube above the surface of the water, and the bristles which guard the orifice open in a star-like fashion, admit the air, and close again, to prevent the ingress of the water as the larva, with its extraordinary motion, dives down again to the bottom of the pond, ditch, or tub. There are some curious bristle-like fins attached to the last segment of the body, which seem to assist it in swimming and sustaining itself near the surface of the water during the act of respiration. These larvæ are useful in helping to cleanse the water in which they live by devouring various decaying matters which they find there. The jaws of these creatures are fringed with bristles in such a way that they are able to cause a small current of water to set in towards the mouth, and so suitable food is brought within the insect's reach. If some of these larvæ are kept in a plate in which there is a little pond-water, this very interesting manner of feeding may be plainly seen through an ordinary magnifying-glass. These creatures swim by alternately straightening and bending their bodies. They never seem to make any journeys, except those between the bottom

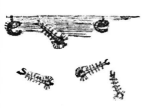

FIG. 180. LARVÆ AND PUPÆ OF THE COMMON GNAT (CULEX CILIARIS).

of the water and its surface. If one should go, during warm and sunny weather, cautiously to the side of some old tub or butt full of water, he will most likely see several of these larvæ busily taking in fresh supplies of air; but directly they notice any movement upon the observer's part, they will wriggle and jerk their way down to the bottom out of sight. They may be easily captured by placing under them, as they descend, a small hand-net made of very fine muslin. These creatures are useful for feeding small fish and other aquatic animals upon.

Before the larvæ of Gnats enter their pupalhood they change their skins at least three times. The pupa is in appearance very different from the larva. It seems to be top-heavy, on account of what may be called its head. This head is enormous (Fig. 180), in proportion to the size of the body.

That which is taken for the head is really the head, thorax, wings, and legs of the future Gnat, enclosed in a kind of envelope. The creature undergoes another great change when it leaves the state of the larva and enters that of the pupa, besides the apparent enlargement of the head, namely, the alteration of the position of the respiratory organs. The larva, when it needed to take in oxygen, floated head downwards, with the top of its breathing-tube just above the surface of the water; but as the pupa, on account of its large head, would have no little difficulty in taking up such an attitude, it is supplied with two horn-like members, which are affixed to the hinder portion of that part which is called the head, and which it can protrude above the surface of the water. The pupa, therefore, when it breathes, floats head uppermost. At the extremity of its abdomen there are two leaf-like appendages. Its motion when swimming is somewhat similar to that of the larva. It takes no food. As the time for the final change draws near, it comes to the surface of the water, and remains there perfectly still. Gradually its body seems to get lighter and lighter, and to rise higher and higher out of the water, until the skin between the respiratory organ splits; and soon the perfect Gnat is free. The imago uses its late pupal skin as a kind of raft during the time it is drying its wings and preparing for flight.

The aquatic life of the Gnat under favourable circumstances lasts for about a month. The "egg-boats" of these insects should be procured and placed in a suitable and portable vessel, and then their very interesting life-history may be observed from almost the beginning to nearly, if not quite, the end. The Gnat, I think, will not lay her eggs and build her boat while in confinement, but she may sometimes be seen going through the curious operations upon the surface of the water of some pond or tub.

In England there are nine different species of Gnats, the commonest of which are the House Gnat (*Culex ciliaris*) (Fig. 181), the Wood Gnat (*C. nemorosus*), and the Ring-footed Gnat (*C. annulatus*). The first and the last are those which generally enter dwelling-houses and torment their inmates.

C. annulatus is the larger of the two, and is able to inflict the more painful wound. The curious humming noise made by Gnats is caused by the exceedingly rapid vibration of their wings. It is said to be only the females who make this sound. It "has been calculated," says one writer, "that the Gnat vibrates its wings 3,000 times a minute," but another writer records that the sirene proves the vibrations to be 15,000 a second!

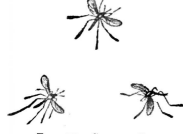

FIG. 181. COMMON GNAT
(CULEX CILIARIS).

The *Chironomidæ*, or Midges, are chiefly distinguished from gnats by their proboscis, which, instead of being long and horny, is short and fleshy. They are very gnat-like in appearance. Their antennæ are long and plumed, especially those of the males. The antenna is so plumed as to be of a triangular shape. The "bite" of a Midge is not nearly so painful as that of a gnat; and many of the Midges are altogether harmless. These insects, like the gnats, spend the larval and pupal portion of their lives in the water.

The members of the genus *Corethra* are the most gnat-like of all the Midges. One species, *C. plumicornis*, is very common, and its larva is one of the most interesting and decidedly the most extraordinary of all aquatic larvæ. This creature is sometimes called the "Phantom- Larva" or the "Glass Larva." It well earns such names, for it is so transparent that there is no little difficulty in seeing it in the water; and through the translucent sides of the animal the greater portion of its internal organisation is plainly visible. Its specific gravity seems to equal that of the water, so that, without any effort at all, it can remain at the top, middle, or bottom of the water in which it lives, as it thinks fit. This interesting larva is slightly more than $\frac{1}{2}$in. long, about $\frac{1}{16}$in. deep, and less than this broad. It gradually tapers towards the tail. Its head has somewhat the appearance of a rabbit's head when it has been skinned. Fig. 182 gives some idea of this curious larva to those who do not know it. At the extremity of the head there are two antenna-like members (*a*), each of which is terminated with four spines, or claws. The animal is supposed to use these claws in turning over the mud in search of food; but though I have kept a great many of these larvæ for a long time, and watched them closely, I have never seen them so hunt. Perhaps it is because they have always been provided with plenty of the insects upon which they feed. Next to the antennæ there is a cluster of ten needle-like bristles, or lancets (*b*), and just behind these bristles there are two little members somewhat like semi-circular saws. Posterior to these "saws" is a curious upper lip, or labrum, furnished with a kind of brush-like arrangement (*c*). The eye (*d*) is large and black. In the upper

FIG. 182. LARVA OF CORETHRA PLUMICORNIS (MUCH ENLARGED).

part of the deepest portion of the body there are two air-sacs (*e*). Some authorities consider that these air-sacs are very closely connected with the respiratory organs, but others look upon them just simply as "floats." The œsophagus, or gullet (*f*), leads into a curious and powerful gizzard (*n*), the use of which can be readily understood when one remembers that this larva, as a rule, feeds upon the smaller fresh-water crustacea. The gizzard is joined to the stomach (*g*) by a very narrow channel. The stomach may be seen by the naked eye through the very transparent sides of the creature, and its contents can be pretty plainly observed with the help of the microscope. The stomach is joined to the colon (*i*) by four very slender tubes or ducts. Between the stomach and the colon there are two posterior air-sacs (*h*), which evidently perform the same functions as the anterior ones. There is a curious fan (*j*) composed of delicately-plumed bristles attached to the under-part of the last segment of the body. With the help of this fan the larva forces and steers its way through the water. It is also connected, so it is supposed, with the tracheal system. Posterior to this organ there are two curious and much-curved hooks (*k*), the use of which I do not know. Dr. Carrington, in his very interesting article upon this larva in *Science Gossip*, for April, 1868, suggests that they are utilised during the creature's transformation. Several of these larvæ have become pupæ, and the pupæ have changed into perfect Midges, while in my possession; but I have never noticed the hooks made use of in any way. *l* represents four bronchial leaflets, and above them there are four more plumed bristles (*m*). Upon different parts of the body of the creature there are very curious hairs, which are simple at their root, but afterwards become compound. Sometimes as many as seven or eight branches spring from a single stem. The organs of respiration of this larva are very difficult to trace, owing to their minuteness; but the appendages at the extremity of the creature's body are so formed and so connected with the tracheal system that the animal, unlike most of the larvæ of the Diptera, seems to have no need of coming to the surface of the water for air.

I have given rather a long description of this larva, because of the unusually curious and interesting formation of its body, and I am sure that if anyone who does not know the animal will examine it carefully, he will be amply rewarded for his pains. A little trouble will certainly be required, for though the creature is so strangely transparent, it is by no means easy to investigate closely, owing to its restlessness. Frequently when one sees it conveniently near to the side of the vessel in which it is confined, and just as the magnifying-glass has been placed in position, the creature, with a powerful stroke of the extremity of its body, will shoot out of focus. A good plan, to simplify the examination, is to put two or three of the larvæ in a very clear glass bottle, of not more than 1in. and not less than ¾in. in diameter. One animal at least will be almost certain to be in the right position for the magnifying-glass. Under the microscope, the creature will be even more interesting, if possible, than when seen at liberty in the water through the magnifying-glass, though its condition will not, of course, be natural.

The larva has a curious habit of suddenly turning itself, so that its head and tail change places. Sometimes, instead of making only half a turn, it will make the whole turn, so quickly that the eye can scarcely follow it, as if in obedience to the drill-sergeant's command, "As you were!" In summer these larvæ may be taken from ponds of clear water in great numbers. Too many must not be kept in the same vessel: three or four in one which will hold about a quart of water will be quite sufficient. If such a vessel is provided with some healthy aquatic plant, and a quantity of water-fleas and the like, the phantom larvæ will give no trouble whatever. The Crustacea and their offspring will always provide them with plenty of suitable food. These larvæ often live for a long time before they become pupæ. I have had some for eight months. During that time only a very small proportion of those I first captured developed into the perfect Midge. But others which I had taken earlier in the year (about June) entered the imago condition much more quickly.

The pupa of *Corethra plumicornis* is somewhat like that of the gnat. The change from the larva to the pupa is very great indeed. Professor Rymer Jones, in reference to this change, says that "the air-sacs, situated both in the thoracic region and in the hinder portion, burst and unfold themselves into an elaborate tracheal system, and a pair of ear-shaped tubes, of which not the slightest trace could hitherto be discerned, make their appearance upon the dorsal aspect of the thorax; two long tracheæ seem to be thus simultaneously produced, occupying the two sides of the body, and constituting the main trunks, from which large branches are given off to supply—in front the head, the eyes, and the nascent limbs; while posteriorly they spread over the now conspicuous ovaries, and terminate by ramifying largely through the thin lamellæ (plates) that constitute the "caudal appendages." The vessels in which the larvæ and pupæ of *Corethra plumicornis* are confined should be covered with glass, so that the insects, when they become perfect, shall not escape before they have been seen and examined. If a piece of flat wood is allowed to float upon the surface of the water, the imago will be sure

of finding a resting place when it has emerged from the pupal envelope. The perfect insect (Fig. 183) is about ¼in. long, and of a brown colour. The antennæ are lighter in colour, the plumes on those of the male being almost white. Both the wings and the plumed antennæ look unusually beautiful under the micro-scope. There are two dark stripes upon the sides of the thorax. The inner edges of the wings are fringed.

FIG. 183. MALE MIDGE, CORETHRA PLUMI-CORNIS (ENLARGED).

The genus *Chironomus* includes about 195 British species, of which *C. plumosus* is by far the commonest. The larva of this species is the "Bloodworm" of anglers, and the "Red Wriggler" of the schoolboy. These larvæ can be found in stagnant water almost anywhere; e.g., in rain-water tubs, ponds, ditches, pools, and the like. The life-history of these insects is very similar to that of the gnat already mentioned. These larvæ are much more worm-like than those of the gnat. They are of a blood-red colour. The pupa has five long hairy bronchial appendages on each side of its large thorax. The perfect insect is about ½in. long, and of a light yellowish colour. There are three dark bands on its thorax.

One of the commonest species of the family *Stratiomyidæ* is the beautiful fly known as the *Stratiomys chameleon*. The female insect deposits her eggs upon the under-side of a broad-leafed aquatic plant—generally the Water Plantain (*Alisma plantago*). The eggs are arranged so as to overlap each other, like the slates on the roof a house. The larvæ which are hatched from these eggs are very curious and interesting. They are elongated in shape, tapering much towards the tail; and they have small heads. At the narrower end of the body there is an extremely interesting breathing apparatus, which partly consists of thirty feathery hairs surrounding a small orifice connected with the tracheal system. These hairs can be opened and closed at the will of the animal. While expanded they are very star-like. When the creature wishes to take in a fresh supply of air, it ascends to the surface of the water by means of a wriggling motion, and there it spreads out its bronchial plumes : these act not only as a float to support the animal in the water, head downwards, but are also so constructed as to repel the water and to admit the air into the orifice which they surround. As soon as the larva has obtained sufficient air, it folds the plumes, which then inclose a small globule of air, and this is carried by the animal to the bottom of the water. This larva obtains its food in the same way as does that of the gnat. A current of water, owing to the formation and the movements of parts of the head, is made to set in towards the head, carrying with it the minute animals and particles of matter which form the creature's food. The pupalhood of this animal is passed within the larval skin. The pupa only occupies the broader and anterior portion of this envelope, and in it floats until it changes into the perfect insect. The imago is a little more than $\frac{1}{2}$in. long, and it has a broad flat brassy-black body marked with yellow.

An insect belonging to the family *Syrphidæ*, known as the Drone-fly (*Eristalis tenax*), has a very curious larva; or, rather, is a very curious creature during its larval state. This larva is called the "rat-tailed larva," and is very common in stagnant water. The late Rev. J. G. Wood, speaking of these larvæ, says: "The largest assemblage of these creatures that I ever saw was in Wiltshire. A tub had been sunk in the ground for the reception of water, and had gradually become half-filled with dead leaves and other *débris*, which decomposed into soft mud. This mud was so closely packed with the larvæ of the Drone-fly that the water was quite choked with them." This larva is shaped somewhat like a "maggot," with a long tail. The tail is composed of two segments, one of which fits inside the other after the manner of the joints of a telescope. The respiratory organs pass through this curious tail, and the creature is thus able to breathe atmospheric air while lying at the bottom of very shallow water. When the larva is about to enter the nymphal state, it buries itself in the ground, and becomes a pupa while still within its larval envelope. The perfect insect may be often seen flying about gardens and the like. It is a little more than ½in. long, is black and hairy, and is very active in its movements.

There are, of course, many other aquatic larvæ and pupæ, besides those I have mentioned in this chapter, which are suitable for and very interesting in the aquarium; but I hope I have said sufficient to give a novice in aquarium matters some idea what kind of creatures to look for, and how to keep them in a manner satisfactory to both the captor and the captives when found.

CHAPTER XV.

WATER-SPIDERS AND WATER-WORMS.

THE Water-spider (*Argyroneta aquatica*) is an exceedingly interesting inmate of the tank: its intelligence and ingenuity have long made it a great favourite with aquarium-keepers. It is about ½in. long, and is therefore rather a large spider. Its abdomen is ovate in shape, and of an olive-brown colour, and the rest of its body, including the legs, is a dark reddish-brown. Its first and last pairs of legs are of greater length than the other two pairs. The females of most spiders are larger than the males, but in regard to the Argyroneta the reverse is the case. Water-spiders may be found in the ponds and ditches of many parts of England, especially in those of Cambridgeshire and Norfolk; but when the aquarium-keeper is not fortunate enough to be able to catch them in his own neighbourhood, he can always buy them in London at prices ranging from 3d. to 1s. each. The abdomen of the Water-spiders is covered with a kind of hair, which repels the water and prevents the creature from getting wet. Sometimes, however, when these animals are being carried in water from the pond in which they have been taken or from the shop where they have been bought, to their new home (the aquarium), they will be found at the end of their journey to be nearly if not quite drowned. The splashing of the water in the can in which they have travelled has so thoroughly saturated the hairs which cover the abdomen that they (the hairs) can no longer do their duty in connection with the respiratory organs. When a spider is found in this condition it should be placed upon some blotting-paper and under a tumbler until it is perfectly dry. As a healthy spider goes beneath the surface of the water. the latter part of its body looks as if covered with silver, owing to the air which has become entangled among the abdominal hairs.

Though these spiders can live upon land, they spend the greater portion of their time under water, where they construct most ingenious and curious homes, or nests. It is quite an interesting sight to watch one of these very intelligent creatures make its nest. First of all, it begins by weaving a web between the branches of an aquatic plant, or between a stone and one side of the vessel in which it is confined, or in some similar position. When the web is completed, the Argyroneta ascends to the surface of the water, and protrudes above it the extremity of its abdomen, and, with a jerky movement, obtains a bubble of air, which it holds between the latter part of its body and its crossed hindermost legs. The spider then descends with the bubble of air, and discharges it within the web which it has woven. In this way many other bubbles of air are brought beneath the surface of the water and placed inside the web, which, after a time, owing to the accumulation of air within it, assumes the shape and often the size of a lady's thimble (see Fig. 184). In making these journeys for air, the spider climbs up and down a thread which it has stretched between the nest and the surface of the water. The journeys are long or short, according to the depth at which the Argyroneta constructs its nest; for they are sometimes placed quite close to the surface of the water (an example of such a position is seen in the illustration), occasionally very near to its bottom, but more frequently midway between these two positions. In one of these subaqueous homes the Argyroneta spends the greater part of the winter. I have had several spiders which have remained in their nests under water for three or four months, without either moving or taking food.

x

When the female Argyroneta wishes to lay her eggs, sne either enlarges her old nest or builds an entirely new one. The enlargement is effected by spinning an addition of web to its lower part, which she fills or inflates with air as soon as it is completed. The male Spider often makes a new nest for himself near to the one which his lady-love has constructed or enlarged for her eggs. The eggs are enveloped in a kind of cocoon, which is fastened to the inside of the nest. The young Spiders appear, according to the temperature of the water, in about a fortnight. Almost directly they leave the nest in which they have been born, they begin to construct

FIG. 184. WATER-SPIDER (ARGYRONETA AQUATICA) AND NEST.

small homes of web and air for themselves. Water-spiders feed either upon terrestrial or aquatic animals; and for the former they often leave the water. The Argyronetæ while in confinement may be provided with house-flies and small aquatic insects. Their appetites, however, are very uncertain; sometimes they will eagerly seize flies which have been thrown to them, and drag them within their nests, soon to turn them out again, sucked dry of all their juices; at other times they will disregard all food, however tempting it may be. I am sorry to say that these intelligent little creatures are occasion- ally guilty of cannibalism. More than once I have noticed that when several of them have been confined in the same carefully-covered aquarium, their numbers have gradually diminished, until only one or two of them have been left. One sex is not more guilty than the other of this unnatural practice.

Vallisneria spiralis is about the most suitable plant to place in an aquarium which is to contain these Spiders. If possible, there should be no other animals associated with the Argyronetæ except those which are intended for their food. A large snail is very likely to disturb the subaqueous nests and set free the air which they contain ; while a fish would be greatly tempted to devour a spider. If the small tank which is set apart for the Argyronetæ is properly situated in regard to light, little or no confervæ will interfere with the clearness of either the glass or the water; and the interesting habits of these animals cannot, of course, be satisfactorily watched unless both the glass and the water are perfectly transparent. This transparency is easily maintained. For example, the water of the aquarium in which I had some Spiders was not changed for nearly, if not quite, a year, and it seemed to be just as clear then as it was upon the day I first introduced it. This aquarium was covered with glass in such a way that air could be freely admitted, and it was placed about 6ft. from a window which faced due east. In this position the light was quite good enough to allow all the movements of the Spiders to be seen, and not sufficiently strong to cause the growth of the sight-impeding confervæ. Other aquaria were in the same position, and all were as perfectly clear as this one, and gave little or no trouble. These circumstances are mentioned here in order that novices in aquarium matters may not think that it requires any skill to preserve the water of small portable tanks in a perfectly clear and bright condition. A little care is the only thing necessary to attain this end.

Argyronetæ often remain above the surface of the water, especially when first placed in an aquarium. However, after a day or two, if they are healthy, they will enter the water and begin to construct their nests. The vessels in which these animals are confined should be covered, or they will escape. When flies are not taken by the Spiders after they have been upon the surface of the water for a day, they should be removed.

While hunting for specimens for the aquarium, one frequently notices some curious little spider-like creatures less than ½in. long. They are often called "Water-spiders." This, however, is not a correct name to give them, for though they are members of the order *Acarina*, of the class *Arachnida*, the title "Water-spider" properly belongs to their larger relatives the Argyronetæ, which have just been described. These Hydrachnidæ, or "Water-mites," are pretty, active little creatures of various colours, and very suitable for small aquaria. Some of them are able to swim freely about the water, while others spend their time crawling over its bottom or the aquatic weeds. The Water-mites are not found in any great number, only two or three being as a rule taken at one time; but they are by no means rare. The Hydrachnidæ, when mature, possess eight legs, affixed to a body which may be said to be without segments or division of any kind. The female Hydrachna lays her eggs upon the stem of a water-plant. The young Mites which come from these eggs are very different in formation from their parents. They have six legs, and not eight, and what appears to be a large head, but which is better described as a large suctorial apparatus. By means of this apparatus the larvæ are able to cling to larger aquatic animals, upon which they live as parasites. They are not seldom found attached to the upper part of the abdomen (beneath the elytra) of the water-beetle (*Dyticus marginalis*) or to the long caudal filaments of the water-scorpions (*Ranatra linearis* and *Nepa cinerea*). After living for a certain time as parasites, the larvæ become pupæ, and pass then through a period of inactivity before they make their final change and emerge as perfect eight-legged Mites. The colours of full-grown Mites are various, but generally they are of bright red, marked with black or brown spots. A magnifying-glass is necessary to see the markings plainly. Hydrachnidæ should be kept in small glass vessels, in which there is a healthy aquatic plant. They are very predaceous, and ought to be provided with cyclops, water-fleas, and the like, as food. The Mite's manner of seizing its prey is interesting.

Aquatic Worms are not, as a rule, considered either ornamental or desirable in an aquarium. Some of them, however, are very useful there, and by no means uninteresting. For instance, the *Naidæ* are active and graceful little creatures. They seem to be nearly always in motion, spending the greater part of their time either in crawling over weeds or swimming through the water. Their movements are assisted by small bristles, which are distributed over various portions of their bodies. Their average length may be said to be about ½in.; and they have great powers of elongation and contraction, especially with regard to their head, which can be easily distinguished from the rest of the body. They are both oviparous and multiply by spontaneous division. Their food chiefly consists of water-fleas and other minute animals. These restless little Worms can generally be found near or among the roots of aquatic plants. A Naid Worm is a very interesting object under a microscope—its bristles, of which there are two kinds, being beautifully transparent.

As one goes about the country during the spring and summer months, he will be almost certain to notice, if at all observant of nature. patches of red at the bottom of shallow pools of water. These red patches are caused by the congregation of many small, interesting, and useful Worms (*Tubifex rivulorum*), known commonly as the River, or Summer, Worm. If the water above them is disturbed, they will immediately disappear by withdrawing themselves into their burrows in the soft mud. They soon, however, recover from their fright, come out again, and at once recommence the restless movements which, with their numbers and bright colour, attracted the attention of the passer-by. It is the tail-end of the animal which is protruded out of the mud. The skin of these Worms is so thin and transparent that not only can the blood be seen through it—hence the title of "red"—but also the internal arrangements of the creatures may be plainly observed. The life-history of *T. rivulorum* is very similar to that of the common earth-worm, to which it is closely allied. It is not only found in ponds and pools, but also in the Thames and other rivers.

River Worms are exceedingly prolific and very gregarious. As they breed so quickly, they are useful in supplying fish and other carnivorous animals with excellent food. These Worms are often sold by aquarium-dealers, at so much a mass of them. But as they quickly die, unless properly treated, a little care is necessary in buying them, or else the purchaser will perhaps find that he has bought many dead ones among the living, and these will be sure to cause not a little mischief if introduced into the tank. The dead Worms may be detected by their being of a lighter colour than those which are alive and healthy, and by the unpleasant smell which will most likely proceed from them. It is prudent to refuse to buy any Worms, if all do not seem to be alive and well, for it is a difficult matter to separate the living from the dead. In shops these Worms are generally kept in running water, or in that which is frequently changed; or in a running stream during the night, and out of water altogether, but covered with a wet cloth, during the day. But I find from experience that they will not live in health for long under any one of these conditions, though perhaps long enough to answer the dealer's purpose. It is not natural for these Worms to be kept in tangled masses, either in water or out. Of course, the condition most conducive to their health while in confinement, is that which is most similar to that out of which they were taken; this may be attained by placing them in soft mud, over which there is water to a depth of from 2in. to 4in. They must not be too crowded. When the Worms are required for the aquarium, a small quantity of mud containing a number of the animals may be taken by the help of a small hand-net and placed in a shallow vessel, such as an old soup-plate. The mud, which has been placed with the Worms in the plate or other receptacle, should then be washed away with a stream of water made to run from a pump, tap, or siphon. The current of water should be strong enough to remove the mud, but not so great as to carry off the Worms. If the flow of water is carefully arranged, a small bunch of healthy Worms, free of mud, will soon be ready to be dropped into the aquarium, where those which are not immediately devoured by fish and other animals will live and thrive until their turn comes, at some future day, to furnish a meal for their fellow-captives.

I believe, from experiments which I have made, that these Worms may be easily bred in confinement, either in a large, shallow tank, or in such a vessel as an ordinary washing-tub, sunk a foot or two in the ground of a garden. The bottom of either tub or tank should be covered to the depth of about 6in. with mud taken from such pools as those in which these animals are naturally found. The water above the mud in the receptacle prepared for the Worms should not be more than 6in. nor less than 3in. The most convenient way, however, to insure a constant supply of these very useful animals is to place a quantity of them in a natural pool in the neighbourhood (if not already there), and there they would be almost sure to breed successfully.

A small hand-net, made of strong muslin or milk-straining material, of about 4in. in diameter, is very useful for taking the Worms from their native waters. The net should be thrust into the mud a little beneath the red patches, and the Worms and mud so obtained may be conveniently carried home in an ordinary can and treated in the manner already recommended.

I have written at some length concerning *T. rivulorum,* because it is so exceedingly useful for feeding fish and other carnivorous animals of the aquarium; because it forms one of the most suitable foods for the fry of trout and salmon; and because it is not likely, if not devoured immediately by the inhabitants of the tank, to die and corrupt the water. In conclusion, however, I venture to warn novices in aquarium matters against using either dead or unhealthy Summer Worms.

Leeches are by no means uninteresting in an aquarium. Some of them are handsomely marked, and others are more or less graceful swimmers. As they are carnivorous and greedy, they should be kept in a tank entirely given up to their use. Many people who sell Medicinal Leeches crowd them together in a large stone bottle nearly full of water. A cloth is tied tightly over the mouth of the bottle to keep the unhappy captives from climbing out of their prison. They are thus kept in the dark as well as in an unhealthy condition. The water, however, is occasionally changed. Nevertheless, it is a cruel and unwise way of keeping Leeches, and no wonder the sellers of them complain that they are delicate animals.

Those who wish to possess Leeches should place them in a large, well-arranged, and securely-covered aquarium, where they will thrive and be seen to the best advantage. They, of course, must have no companions besides those of their own

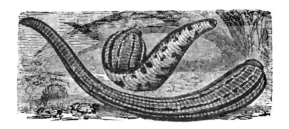

FIG. 185. MEDICINAL LEECH (HIRUDO MEDICINALIS).

species, and even of their size; for not only will they feed upon fish. frogs, and the like, but also, at times, upon one another.

The Medicinal Leeches, of which there are said to be three species, are the best known. They were formerly frequently used in medicine, but now only rarely. At one time there was such a demand for these creatures that they were with difficulty procured, until some Frenchman started what may be called leech-farming; and his venture was so successful, that leech-breeding became on the Continent quite an industry. The commonest Medicinal Leech (*Hirudo medicinalis*) (Fig. 185) is of a dark green colour, marked with six reddish-yellow bands along the back, and the under-part of the body is greenish and spotted with black. Leeches are oviparous, and live, when at liberty, in ponds and small lakes. The eggs are enveloped in cocoons, which are deposited upon the weeds or banks of the water. These Leeches are said to be five years arriving at maturity, but before this age they may be used for medicinal purposes. Leeches have no branchiæ: they respire by means of their skin. The mouth of a Leech is curious and interesting. It has three teeth, somewhat like circular saws, which make three small cuts, all inclining towards the same point. A Leech is both gluttonous and abstemious; that is, it will either make such a meal as to cause it to swell to more than double its ordinary size, or it will live for months, or even years, with no other food than that which it can obtain through a constant change of river or pond water. The number of eyes which a Leech has varies according to its genus: some have as many as ten. As these creatures frequently rise or sink in the water, according to the state of the atmosphere, they are regarded by some people as useful "weather prophets." The Medicinal Leech is from 4in. to 7in. in length, and is able to take at one meal from 1dr. to ½oz. of blood.

The Horse Leech (*Hæmopsis sanguisuga*) is about 4in. long and ½in. broad. Its body becomes rather wider towards the tail end, and its mouth is large and protruding above. It is greenish-black upon the back, and yellowish-green underneath. This Leech is a graceful swimmer, and lives very well in an aquarium. It is found in ponds and lakes, where it may be seen occasionally swimming near the surface, when it can easily be taken in a hand-net.

The Glutton Aulostome (*Aulostoma gulo*) is not a suctorial animal: its teeth are not strong enough to make the necessary wound for the extraction of blood. It is, however, an exceedingly greedy creature, as its name implies. It feeds readily upon garden-worms, snails, fish, leeches, and other aquatic animals. This Leech is common in ponds and lakes, and as it is bold and active, it is rather an interesting inmate of an aquarium, of which it should be the only occupant.

The Eight-eyed Leech (*Nephelis octoculata*) is an active and hardy little animal, and quite ready to adapt itself to a life in confinement. It lives in stagnant water, through which it swims quickly in a graceful and undulating manner. It often fastens itself to a stone or the like by means of its sucker, and while in captivity it can frequently be seen thus fixed to the sides of its aquarium, and waving its body to and fro. It swallows most of its prey whole, and it may be fed upon tiny garden-worms and small aquatic animals. The Eight-eyed Leech is about 1½in. long, and is of a reddish-brown colour, sometimes marked with yellow or other spots.

Besides the Leeches previously referred to, there are others which will live readily in confinement, where they will be interesting to those who care for them.

While hunting over the weeds or mud taken out of stagnant or slow-running water, one not seldom finds some curious worm-like creatures, of various lengths, which swim in an eel-like manner, and which, when at rest, frequently anchor themselves, by means of a sucker situated at the extremity of their body, to any hard substance such as the side of an aquarium or to a stone. These animals are called Nematoids, and they live chiefly upon vegetable matter. They have a habit, while holding on to anything with their sucker, of swaying themselves backwards and forwards until they recommence swimming in the graceful undulatory manner which has given to them the name of "eels."

Among the Nematoids is sometimes classed the interesting animal known as the Hair Worm (*Gordius aquaticus*). This curious creature has, at different times, given rise to some extraordinary theories in regard to the origin of eels. I have, more than once, in common with many others, heard it gravely stated that when the hair from a horse's tail falls into a pond, it will, after a certain amount of soaking, become endowed with life, and take the form of the Hair Worm, which, in time, under favourable circumstances, develops into the ordinary eel. *G. aquaticus* is so long—being sometimes as much as 10in. in length, and not half a line in thickness—and it has a habit, when being held between the fingers, of becoming perfectly rigid, after it has tied itself into an apparently unravellable knot, that the rustic seems to have

some excuse for imagining it to be an animated horsehair.
The male Hair Worm may be distinguished from the female
by its forked, or bifid, tail. The head-end of both the sexes
is round. These creatures seem to have no mouth, and
appear to obtain what nourishment they require by absorp
tion through the skin. Their power of resisting the ill-effects
of drought is so great that they may be taken out of the
water and exposed for some hours to the scorching rays of
the sun, until they look as if they were quite dead and dried
up into almost nothing, and then when returned to the
aquarium or pond they will soon regain both the life they
seemed to have lost and their former activity. They swim in
a most graceful eel-like manner. Hair Worms are oviparous
and deposit their eggs in strings.

G. aquaticus is an entozoon : that is, it spends some portion
of its life within some other animal. When a beetle, for instance
has fallen by accident into water, or has been driven there
by instinct, a Hair Worm will sometimes be seen emerging
from the unfortunate creature, having been for long its
unwilling host. Hair Worms may occasionally be seen in
great numbers swimming about the shallowest parts of rivers
and ponds, or entwining themselves among the aquatic weeds
growing there.

The aquarium-keeper, during his hunts for aquatic animals,
frequently finds certain little fluke-like creatures, crawling
over or clinging to the mud, weeds, or stones of the water.
These animals are known as Planarian Worms. They may
be found during any season of the year and in nearly every
pond, lake, or slow-running stream. They are of various
colours. There is, for instance, a white species (*Planaria
lactea*). a brown (*P. brunnea*), and a grey (*P. torva*); but the
commonest of all is the Black Planarian (*Polycelis nigra*).
These worms have soft and gelatinous bodies, which quickly
decompose after death. The Planariæ are both interesting
and useful in the aquarium. They are interesting principally
because they have the power of reproducing lost parts of
their bodies, and also because even their number may be
increased by cutting them in half, and they are useful

because in feeding upon dead animal matter they perform the duties of excellent scavengers. They are able, in common with some of the univalves, to support themselves in the water by what may be called a muccus thread. These creatures are oviparous, but the young remain affixed to their parent's body for some time after they are hatched. Planarian Worms will live for a long time in the aquarium, where I have never known them do any harm. They will sometimes, however. attack a diseased fish. The largest of these animals is, perhaps, *P. lactea,* which will sometimes, when well extended, measure nearly 1in. in length. The Planariæ, on being touched, either contract and harden themselves, or let go of that to which they are clinging and sink in the water. They progress by gliding evenly over the stones, weeds. or mud.

CHAPTER XVI.

FRESH-WATER CRUSTACEANS.

THE fresh-water Crayfish (*Astacus fluviatilis*) (Fig. 186) is a very interesting creature in an aquarium. The aquarium, however, should not only be arranged especially for it, but it must also be given up to the animal's

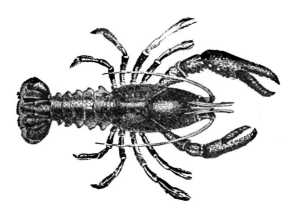

FIG. 186 COMMON RIVER CRAYFISH (ASTACUS FLUVIATILIS).

use entirely. Any companion, except one of its own species, it would be almost certain to either eat or hurt. A tank intended for a pair of Crayfish ought to be about 2ft. long by 1ft. or more broad. The bottom of this vessel should be covered with well-washed gravel and large stones, the latter so placed that there will be an island on to which the Crayfish can climb, and retreats into which they can retire. The water need not be more than 4in. deep. It will not be wise to introduce any aquatic plants, for the Crayfish would destroy them all. These creatures, while in captivity, will eat raw meat, tadpoles, dead fish, molluscs, garden-worms—in fact, almost anything of an animal nature. No food should be left in the aquarium which the Crayfish have refused to eat; but, notwithstanding all care in this respect, the water will require changing from time to time.

It is a very interesting sight to watch these creatures cast their shells. This exuviation is necessary, for the armour of crustaceans does not stretch as the animals grow. For some days previous to this important operation, Crayfish lose their usually very keen appetites, and appear to take no food at all. This fasting causes the body to shrink, and thus the moult is facilitated. The casting of the shell takes about half an hour, and after it is cast the animal is very exhausted—so much so, indeed, that occasionally it dies, especially when the exuviation takes place while the creature is in captivity. The moulting is particularly complete, even to the eyes, antennæ, and the lining membrane of the stomach.

Crayfish will sometimes breed in confinement. Unlike most of their relatives, the young, when they leave the eggs—for Crayfish are oviparous—very much resemble their parents. Crayfish inhabit the rivers of different parts of England, particularly those which have unusually gravelly and rocky bottoms, and are fond of hiding in holes in the banks or among the rocks and stones. They are generally caught by means of nets, in which pieces of raw meat have been placed.

A Crayfish may be described as a small fresh-water lobster of a green colour. When taken out of the water and held in the fingers, it flaps its tail with great vigour. Astaci should not be carried from place to place in water, but in damp water-weeds. Crayfish are very destructive to fish spawn.

The little crustacean sometimes called the "Fresh-water Screw," or Shrimp (*Gammarus fluviatilis*) (Fig. 187), is a useful and interesting inmate of the aquarium. It may be found in almost every clear and not very quick-running stream,

FIG. 187. FRESH-WATER SHRIMPS (GAMMARUS FLUVIATILIS) (ENLARGED).

but especially in those brooks in which the watercress or the Vernal Starwort grow in anything like profusion. A good way to obtain Fresh-water Shrimps is to take a handful of aquatic weeds out of the water in which these crustacea abound, and shake it over a newspaper or a piece of macintosh. After the first shake or two, several Shrimps, among other animals, will fall upon the surface prepared for them, and commence at once, as they lie helplessly on their sides, those curious twisting movements which have given them the name of Fresh-water Screws. These animals are very similar in appearance to the common sandhopper, to which, indeed, they are closely related. They are frequently found in pairs, the female being known by her smaller size, and they resemble fish in their habit of keeping their heads facing the stream. Fresh-water Shrimps are most useful, for not only are they excellent scavengers, but they also in their own bodies supply trout and other fish with the very best of foods. They may be kept in either large or small tanks, where they will do good by consuming any animal matter, which, if allowed to remain in the water, would certainly become a source of mischief. For example, should a snail die, they will quickly devour its body and make a home of its shell. Of course, in a large aquarium which is stocked in the usual manner, these Shrimps are almost sure some time or other to be eaten by the fish or other animals. The Gammari are very interesting in a small tank which is given up entirely to their use. They are by no means ungraceful as they dart swiftly about the water, hunt its bottom in a very dog-like fashion, or cling quite motionless to the weeds, with the exception of the rapid movements of their respiratory organs. Their shells, which from time to time they shed, are often so life-like as to be not infrequently mistaken by the novice for the animal itself. These crustaceans may be fed upon raw meat, a piece of dead garden-worm, or almost anything of an animal nature. They also feed occasionally upon aquatic weeds. They will breed very readily in an aquarium which is kept expressly for them, which should be stocked with plenty of aquatic plants and water-snails, and at the bottom of it there should be several large stones under which the Shrimps can hide. The females carry their eggs attached to the under-parts of their bodies, and there the young also remain for some time after they are hatched. The young of these crustaceans are pretty and active little creatures, and form excellent food for many kinds of fish. They are of a very much lighter shade than their

parents, which are, as a rule, of a dark reddish colour, but sometimes, owing to the locality in which they are found, nearly
black. When one considers what excellent scavengers, how
prolific, and how suitable as food for fish, these Gammari are,
one will naturally come to the conclusion that they are quite
worthy of encouragement in those waters in which trout and
other fish are preserved.

The Water-louse (*Asellus aquaticus*) (Fig. 188) is a very
common crustacean. It is so like in appearance to the wood-
louse or "garden-pig," that no description is necessary. It
does not swim, but is found crawling about the bottom or
weeds of ponds and ditches. *A. aquaticus* is a useful scavenger
in the aquarium, for it lives principally upon decaying vegetable matter. I have, how-
ever, seen it apparently
feeding upon animal food.
It will eat fish ova. The
female carries her eggs
in a membranous sac
attached to the under-part
of her body, and there the
young remain for some
time after they are hatched.

FIG. 188. WATER-LOUSE
(ASELLUS AQUATICUS).

The period which elapses
between the laying of the eggs and the young Aselli leaving
their mother's care is generally about six weeks. The young
are of a very light colour. The male is much larger than the
female, and is about ½in. long. These creatures breed freely
in captivity, and thus provide fish and other inhabitants of
the aquarium with suitable food. They are easily obtained,
for they are nearly always found crawling about the mud or
weeds which are taken from either stagnant or slow-running
water. The vessels in which Aselli are kept must be securely
covered, or their inmates will be certain to escape, and, as
a consequence, die.

The tiny crustaceans which are well called *Entomostraca*,
or " shelled insects," are all more or less covered with a shelly
envelope. They are both very interesting and very useful in

Y

the aquarium. In a natural state they do good service, by
helping to ventilate stagnant water by the means of their
almost constant movements; by (many of them) acting the
part of scavengers; and by, owing to their very great prolificacy, supplying fish and other animals with most nutritious
food. They may be found in either stagnant or slow-running
water during the greater portion of the year. They will
breed freely in captivity, and their presence should always
be encouraged in the aquarium. It is a good plan to keep
a small tank especially for them, and so they will be always
at hand for supplying food to interesting carnivorous
aquatic animals. Entomostraca can easily be obtained from
their native waters by the help of a very simple contrivance,
as explained on page 37. Though they are very small, they
can, as a rule, be readily seen with the naked eye: but a
microscope, or at any rate a magnifying-glass, is generally
necessary for observing their different parts. The commonest,
and perhaps the most interesting and useful, of these small
crustaceans, are the *Daphniæ*, the *Cyprides*, and the *Cyclops*.

The *Daphniæ*, owing to their curious antennæ, belong to
the order *Cladocera* ("branching horned"). Their jerky or
jumping movements in the water have given them the common
name of Water-fleas. Of these Water-fleas, *Daphnia pulex*
is by far the commonest. Its body, and that of all its near
relatives, may be said to be divided into two parts: the
smaller part is the head, a portion of which is produced in
front to a kind of beak; and the larger part, which consists
of the thorax and abdomen, is inclosed in a shelly envelope.
All the *Daphniæ* possess five pairs of legs, which by the
help of a microscope may be seen in almost constant motion
through the transparent shell. The female Water-flea carries
her eggs for a time between her shell and the back part of
her body. These small crustaceans are frequently found in
stagnant water in great numbers, especially where there is
plenty of duckweed. I have sometimes caught what appeared
to be thousands of them with one dip of a large bottle in
that part of a pond where they seemed to be the most
numerous. Dr. Baird, in his "British Entomostraca," in

speaking of the profusion of these creatures, says: "I have frequently seen large patches of water in different ponds assume a ruddy hue, like the red rust of iron, or as if blood had been mixed with it, and ascertained the cause to be an immense number of *Daphnia pulex*. The myriads necessary to produce this effect are really astonishing, and it is extremely interesting to watch their motions. On a sunshiny day, in a large pond, a streak of red a foot broad and ten or twelve yards in length, will suddenly appear in a particular spot, and this belt may be seen rapidly changing its position, and in a short time wheel completely round the pond. Should the mass come near enough to the edge to allow the shadow of the observer to fall upon them, or should a dark cloud suddenly obscure the sun, the whole body immediately disappears, rising to the surface again when they have reached beyond the shadow, or as soon as the cloud has passed over."

The male Water-flea is rarely found, and then only during the latter part of the year. It may be known by its smaller size and its larger superior antennæ, which are situated beneath what may be called the beak. In the female these antennæ are very small. It has been calculated that a Daphnia may have three broods during a month, each brood numbering from forty to fifty. No wonder that these tiny crustaceans are so numerous in our ponds! The *Daphniæ* are said to eject ephippia, or "winter eggs," which are said to be protected with an envelope of extra hardness, so that they will be able to bear without damage a degree of cold which would prove fatal to the crustaceans themselves. The food of these Water-fleas consists, for the most part, of minute infusoria. Dr. Baird enumerates at least six other species besides the one just described. The Parrot-beaked Water-flea (*D. psittacea*) receives its name from the formation of its beak, which is shaped somewhat like that of a parrot. The margin of its shell at the back is serrated. The Large Water-flea (*D. schœfferi*) is the largest British species, and has its shell almost circular. Dr. Baird speaks of it as having a heavy, tumbling sort of movement in the water. It is not very common. However, from its size it is certainly worth the trouble of procuring, for its interesting habits will be more easily observed than those of its commoner relative, *D. pulex.* The Spineless Water-flea (*D. vetula*) is without the tail-like spine which is possessed by all the species just mentioned. It has also a small head and hardly any "beak." This creature is fairly common. The Reticulated Water-flea (*D. reticulata*), as its specific name implies, has its shell covered with a net-work, the mesh of which is hexagonal. The spine is short, and is inclined backwards. This animal is by no means rare. The Rounded Water-flea (*D. rotunda*) receives its name from the fact that its shell is almost circular. It is not uncommon. The Long-spined Water-flea (*D. mucronata*) may be readily recognised by the straight edge of the front part of its shell and by its long, pointed spine. The whole creature is of a dark grey colour. The different species of these Water-fleas may be easily identified; and they can all be readily kept and bred in captivity. The vessels in which they are confined should possess plenty of vegetation, and ought to be placed in a light position, but not within reach of the rays of the sun. Water-fleas will give no trouble at all, and will be both very interesting and very useful to those who care for and keep aquaria.

The small and active crustaceans known as *Cypridæ* are placed in the order *Ostracoda* (from the Greek *ostrakon,* "a shell," their bodies being inclosed in a bivalve shell). Indeed, their outward appearance is so like very tiny bivalve molluscs that they have been mistaken, when at rest, for young mussels. The *Cypridæ* are divided into the two genera *Cypris* and *Candona.* The former genus contains about seventeen different species, all the members of which are rapid swimmers; and the latter not more than six, all of which spend their time in crawling over the mud or weeds of the water in which they live: they cannot swim, because they lack the hairy antennæ which their near relatives possess. The *Cypridæ* have two pairs of feet, two pairs of antennæ, and one eye. They are found in almost every piece of clear stagnant water, where they may be easily seen with the naked eye. They live chiefly upon dead—not putrid—animal matter, and they lay

their eggs in masses upon stems of plants and sides of stones.
The eggs hatch in about four days. The young *Cypridæ*
shed their shells frequently as they grow, the exuviation each
time being very complete. The eggs have great vitality,
and will survive the drying up of the ponds in which they
have been deposited.

The members of the genus *Cypris*—of which *C. fusca*
(Fig. 189) is one of the commonest—are, on account of their
swimming powers and active habits, much more interesting
in the aquarium than are those of the other genus, *Candona*.
The *Cypridæ* can be obtained from their native pools in the
same way as that recommended for procuring the *Daphniæ*.

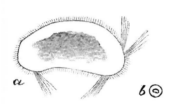

FIG. 189. CYPRIS FUSCA (*a*, MUCH
ENLARGED; *b*, NATURAL SIZE).

They may be fed while in captivity
upon a tiny piece of a garden-
worm or a small portion of raw
meat. If food is not given to
them, they will devour one another.
These little Entomostraca are very
interesting under the microscope.
While viewing them in this way,
it will be seen how they protect
themselves upon the appearance
of any danger, by withdrawing
their legs and antennæ within the shelter of their pretty
shells. And when they think that there is nothing further
to fear, the watcher will notice how cautiously they protrude
their limbs and make preparation for continuing their journey
in the drop of water which has been placed with them upon
the stage of the microscope. As they are securely inclosed
within their shells, their resemblance to tiny mussels will be
readily observed. The shells are often prettily marked and
coloured, and covered with fine hairs. The aquarium-keeper
may take it for granted that all the *Cypridæ* which he captures
are females, for the males, I believe, have never been found.
These crustaceans are larger than the water-fleas.

The curious, interesting, and useful Cyclops may be found
in ponds, ditches, and slow-running streams, almost everywhere. *Cyclops quadricornis* (Fig. 190) is shaped somewhat

like an "Indian club," or an elongated pear, and it is quite large enough to be easily seen without the help of a magnifying glass. It has received the generic name of Cyclops, from the fact that it possesses only one eye, which is situated in the centre of the fore-part of the first and largest segment of its body; while the specific name of *quadricornis* ("four-horned") has been given to it on account of what may be called its double antennæ. The male Cyclops differs from the female in the formation of its antennæ. The superior or upper antennæ of the latter are long, tapering, and gracefully curved, while those of the former are rather shorter and thicker, and slightly swollen near their tips, which terminate in a kind of hinge-joint. The lower pair of antennæ of both the male and female are not nearly so long or so slender as their upper pair. All the antennæ have numerous articulations, and are fringed with very fine filaments. Cyclops possess five pairs of legs, two pairs of foot-jaws, and at the end of their bodies two elongated lobes, to each of which are

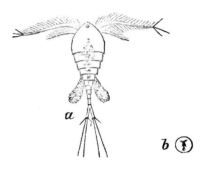

FIG. 190. CYCLOPS QUADRICORNIS
(*a*, MUCH ENLARGED; *b*, NATURAL SIZE)

attached four setæ of different lengths; these setæ, like the antennæ, are also finely and beautifully fringed. The females are about three times as numerous as the males, and may very frequently be seen swimming about with their eggs hanging to each side of the lower part of their bodies. The eggs can easily be detected with the naked eye, but under the microscope they look very like bunches of grapes. In each cluster there are sometimes as many as thirty or forty eggs. M. Jurine is said to have made careful observations and calculations in regard to the increase of these Entomostraca, and he came to the conclusion that one female would lay, or rather produce, her eggs at least eight times within three months, and at each laying there would not be less than forty eggs; and from these 320 eggs there would come by the end of a year (supposing, of course, that all were hatched and no enemies attacked the young) 4.442.189,120 Cyclops; that is, considerably more than four thousand millions. As one tries to comprehend this vast number, he need feel no surprise that these crustaceans, notwithstanding their numerous foes, can nearly always be found in such profusion. They supply fish with excellent food, and some authorities say that the trout frequently owes the delicate flavour of its flesh to these little creatures. The young Cyclops is so unlike its parent that it frequently has been mistaken as belonging to a different genus. Dr. Baird considers that it takes these crustaceans from seventeen to twenty days to complete their growth, and during this time they moult three times. At every change of shell the little creature becomes more and more like its parent. Cyclops can endure extreme cold much better than drought, for it has been proved that while exclusion from all moisture for five-and-twenty minutes is sufficient to kill them, they will survive continuous freezing for twenty-four hours apparently without any evil consequences. The Cyclops feed upon both animal and vegetable matter, but principally the former. and they are most readily kept and bred in confinement. As they not only act the part of efficient scavengers. but also supply the best of living food to fish and the like, they should certainly be encouraged as far as possible in the aquarium. They seem to increase most rapidly in those tanks in which carnivorous animals are kept. They swim in a very jerky fashion. C. quadricornis varies in both size and colour, this variation being chiefly due to locality and food. It is often white, but sometimes of a greenish or reddish tinge.

Besides the Entomostraca thus briefly described, there are, of course, many others which are just as interesting and nearly as useful in the aquarium. Those just referred to are the commonest and the most easily obtained, and, perhaps, owing to their great prolificacy, the most useful in the tank.

There is, however, one other Entomostracon, which I think
ought, though rather rare, to be mentioned here, owing to its
beauty, viz., the Fairy Shrimp (*Chirocephalus stagnalis*). It
is about 1in. long, and nearly transparent. The tail is a bright
red, and the back of the female is blue. It is found in
stagnant water, and, according to Dr. Baird, in ditches and
deep cart-ruts on the edges of woods and plantations. I
believe that it is nearly always to be seen in a pond on
Blackheath. Dr. Baird, in writing of the Fairy Shrimps,
says that "they swim upon their backs, and in fine warm
weather, when the sun is not too strong, they may be seen
balancing themselves, as it were, near the surface by means
of their branchial feet, which are in constant motion. On
the least disturbance, however, they strike the water rapidly
with their tail from right to left, dart away like a fish,
and hasten to conceal themselves by diving into the soft
mud, or amongst the weeds at the bottom of the pool. It
is certainly the most beautiful and elegant of all the Entomostraca. The male is especially beautiful: the uninterrupted
undulatory, waving motion of its graceful branchial feet,
slightly tinged as they are with a light reddish hue, the
brilliant mixture of transparent bluish-green and bright red
of its prehensile antennæ, and its bright red tail, with the
beautifully plumose setæ springing from it, render it really
exceedingly attractive to the view. The undulatory motion
of its branchial feet serves another purpose in addition to
that of keeping the animal suspended in the water. The
thorax, or body, of the animal has been described, when
floating on its back, as like the cavity of a little boat, the
feet representing oars. When these are in motion, they cause
the water contained in this cavity to be compressed, and to
mount up as along a canal, carrying in the current the
particles destined for its food towards its mouth. It seems
to be constantly, when in this position, employed in swallowing
and digesting its food, its masticatory organs being in
perpetual motion."

The food of this beautiful little crustacean consists of
animal and vegetable matter—chiefly, however, the former.

It is said to lay its eggs, during March and April, loosely in the water. Though they are very small, they can be seen by the naked eye. They are covered very thickly with "sharp spines." These spines, which can, of course, only be seen by the help of a microscope, are for the purpose, it is supposed, of causing the eggs to adhere to any solid substance against which they may fall, and also to act as some slight protection from the attacks of small aquatic animals.

CHAPTER XVII

HYDRÆ.

THERE is nothing in connection with the fresh-water aquarium more extraordinary and interesting than the Hydræ. These polypes were first noticed, I believe, by Leeuwenhoek, in 1703; but M. Trembley, of Geneva, about 1740, was the first to describe their life-history. The three species known in Britain are the Green Hydra (*Hydra viridis*), the Orange-brown (*Hydra vulgaris*), and the Brown (*H. fusca*). These interesting creatures, of which *H. vulgaris* is about the commonest, may be found in ponds or slow-running streams nearly everywhere. They are generally taken adhering to such plants as the duckweed or water-crowfoot. The best way to procure Hydræ for the aquarium is to gather a little of the weed among which these tiny creatures are supposed to live, and take it home. Then fill a few tumblers, or other transparent glass vessels, with clear water, put them in a sunny window, and in each of these receptacles place a small portion of the weed. If there are any polypes at all, their presence will be easily detected in less than an hour. When startled or frightened in any way, these creatures contract themselves until they assume the appearance of minute lumps of jelly, which are not likely to be noticed by an inexperienced eye; but under the influence of quiet and sunshine they will soon begin to extend themselves in such a way that even a novice will be easily able to see them. Their bodies may be likened in size and shape to a piece of horsehair of about $\frac{1}{4}$in. long. One end of this body has a sucking-disc, by means of which the animal is able to affix itself to any foreign substance; at the other end there is a mouth, which is surrounded by very fine tentacles, varying in number from three or four to twelve. These tentacles are capable of great extension, so much so that in some species they may be stretched several times longer than the length of the creature's body. The mouth, which is very elastic, has the food brought to it by the tentacles. Dr. Hogg says that "the organ of prehension, which is called the *hasta*, consists of a sac opening at the surface of the tentacle, within which, at the lower portion, is placed a saucer-shaped vesicle supporting a minute ovate body, which again bears a sharp calcareous piece called the '*sagitta*' arrow. This can be pushed out at the pleasure of the animal, serving to roughen the surface of the tentacle, and afford a much firmer hold of the living prey."

The tubercles, which more or less cover the tentacles, possess extremely fine threads, called "urticating threads," by means of which the Hydra is able to sting its victim to death. These "urticating threads" are so deadly in their action that none of the smaller aquatic animals, upon which this polype feeds, ever seem to recover from the consequences of coming in contact with them. It is a most curious sight to watch a Hydra fishing, as it were, for its food. Its tentacles are extended and swaying to and fro, and directly a water-flea, larva of a gnat, little redworm, or any such creature comes within touch of one or more of them, the victim seems to be paralysed, for after a few faint struggles it either dies, or resigns itself to its fate as the long and pliant tentacles slowly entwine themselves around the poor creature, and gradually draw it towards the mouth which they surround. Sometimes a Hydra catches at the same time more victims than it feels disposed to eat. It will, in such a case, devour sufficient to satisfy its appetite and relax its hold upon the rest: for the latter, however, there is no escape, as the "urticating threads" will have done their work, and the unfortunate animals just released from captivity sink down to the bottom of the water to die—that is, if they were not already dead before the polype allowed them to become disentangled. A redworm or small larva seems immediately to succumb to the powers of the Hydra's sting, but a Cyclops or Daphnia will, with a few struggles, make some show of resistance, the shell, or carapace, of the tiny crustaceans in their case affording a slight protection against the effects of the captor's poison.

While in confinement, the Hydræ may be fed upon such Entomostraca as the Cyclops and Daphniæ, which can be bred in a separate vessel for the purpose. The polypes expel the indigestible parts of these small crustacea. Though the Hydræ very often kill more animals than they are able to eat, the dead bodies of the victims need not be removed from the water, for the Entomostraca, if present in the tank in any numbers, will act the part of scavengers, and help

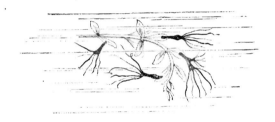

FIG. 191. HYDRÆ ATTACHED TO A PIECE OF ANACHARIS PLANT.

to keep the water pure. A clear and thin glass tumbler makes a very suitable little aquarium for the Hydræ, which of course should have no other companions than those they feed upon. They ought to be provided with some aquatic plant, to which they can affix themselves (Fig. 191) if they choose. A little duckweed, or a small spray of the water-thyme (*Anacharis alsinastrum*) will answer the purpose very well. The Hydræ, however, frequently fasten themselves to the sides of the aquarium, thus much facilitating the observation of their habits. Hydræ increase both by germination and by being hatched from eggs. The former manner of reproduction seems to be commoner than the latter. The budding takes place on any part of the creature's body except the tentacles. When a polype is about to produce offspring by germination, a small lump or tubercle will be seen upon some portion of its body, and this gradually grows and lengthens out until the small tentacles of the young Hydra appear, which it begins to use for obtaining food almost immediately. The young sometimes remain attached to their parent's body until they are quite full grown, and occasionally, indeed, until they themselves have also produced children by germination. It not infrequently happens that mother and daughter, though still closely united by family ties, will both begin to devour the same unhappy worm, and in a little time the relatives meet face to face near the middle of their victim's body, which, however, generally breaking in half, frees the captors from an awkward dilemma. It does happen, though rarely, when two Hydræ have attacked the same worm, that the worm is too tough to be broken, and the stronger polype swallows the weaker one and its prey until the prey has been digested, and then the vanquished Hydra is rejected, or returned to its watery world to fish and fight again, and none the worse, apparently, for its rather unpleasant experience. Polypes increase very rapidly during the summer time by budding.

Other lumps grow upon the body of Hydra besides those which are to bud into young polypes, and these are called sperm-cells or ovisacs. Both sperm-cells and ovisacs appear upon the same Hydra. When the former are ripe, they burst and discharge that which they contain, and thus fertilise the ovum. After a time the ovum is extruded, and sinks to the bottom of the water, where it remains for a long or short time, according to the season, until it is hatched. The parent Hydra dies after producing her egg. It very rarely happens that a polype discharges more than one egg. The ova are about $\frac{1}{60}$th of an inch in diameter. The young Hydra, when first hatched, possesses only two tentacles, which gradually increase in number. Mr. James Fullagar, who has written in *Science Gossip* from time to time some very interesting articles upon these creatures, says that the young Hydræ have the power of stinging their natural prey to death before they are old enough to devour it. Hydræ which have been kept in captivity during the summer apparently disappear about autumn, but reappear again in the spring from the ova which during the previous summer had been deposited at the bottom of the aquarium. According to Mr. Fullagar "the reproduction of *Hydra vulgaris* from ova takes place in the autumn, and that of *Hydra viridis* in the spring."

There is another way by which Hydræ may be increased besides being produced from eggs and by budding, and this is by artificial division. This extraordinary power on the part of this polype has given it the generic name of Hydra, and well is it deserved, for it does seem to rival in this particular that monster which, according to the ancients, was conquered by Hercules. If a Hydra is cut in half, it apparently suffers little or no pain; for the half containing the tentacles will sink to the bottom of the water, because it has no disc by which it can adhere, but will, if it has an opportunity, immediately seize and devour prey. The other half will remain clinging to the spot to which it was affixed when the operation took place, and gradually develop a new mouth and new tentacles. Should a polype be divided into four or more pieces, it will, in all probability, produce in time the same number of perfect Hydræ; or, if it be slit from top to bottom, the cut portions of each piece will slowly unite, and two Hydræ will take the place of the original one. It has been said that a fresh polype will grow from a small portion of a tentacle, but this is very doubtful. It has been generally noticed that those Hydræ which have been the result of artificial division are stronger and finer animals than those which have sprung from eggs or have been produced by germination. M. Trembley has recorded that he was successful in turning some of these polypes inside out, and that even under this unnatural condition they were able and willing to capture their prey and feed upon it and thrive.

Anyone who carefully studies these wonderful fresh-water Hydræ will be sure to be amply rewarded for his trouble, for nothing can be more extraordinary than their habits and life-history.

CHAPTER XVIII.

RECAPITULATION, ETC.

 THINK it wise in a very short chapter to recapitulate, in a rule-like form, some of the suggestions and warnings which I have given in the previous chapters to novices in aquarium matters.

1. No one should think of keeping an aquarium who does not make up his mind to bestow upon it a little daily attention. This necessary attention will involve hardly any trouble. Sometimes all that will be required will be just a glance to see that nothing is wrong. As a rule, however, there will be little to do but to supply some of the inhabitants of the tank with a small quantity of food. If the aquarium is attended to at a stated time—such as always before breakfast or before lunch—the giving of this necessary attention will become a habit, and therefore, then, is not likely to be omitted. An aquarium properly arranged and properly looked after is certain to be a source of pleasure and instruction; but if neglected, or only noticed by fits and starts. It is sure to become an eyesore and a nuisance.

2. An aquarium will run a great risk of being altogether a failure unless it be correctly proportioned; that is, the breadth of the vessel should always be greater than its depth. The strength of the tank ought to be considered before its elegance, though the latter quality should by no means be entirely disregarded.

3. An aquarium cannot do well, without a great deal of unnecessary trouble, unless it be properly situated. The sun should never be allowed (except under special circumstances, which have already been referred to) to shine directly upon the water of it: and a north aspect is the best.

4. Unless it be very small, an aquarium should be placed, before it is filled with water, in the position in which it is intended to remain. Any attempt to remove a fairly-sized tank when full of water will be certain to do some, if not great, harm to the vessel or its contents.

5. Everything, whether gravel or sand, or water or weed, which is placed in the aquarium should be perfectly clean.

6. The aquarium ought, if possible, to be filled with water by means of one or more small siphons.

7. All aquaria, with very few exceptions (which have already been mentioned), should contain aquatic plants. These plants ought, of course, to be healthy, of the right kind, and set in the right way. *Vallisneria spiralis* is one of the best of all plants for this purpose.

8. All aquatic animals should be wisely associated. No fish or any other animal ought to be allowed to molest its companions.

9. No strange fish, especially a fish purchased, should be introduced into a tank unless it has been for some time in quarantine. The introduction of an unhealthy fish is almost certain to be the cause of considerable loss. All gold-fish procured for the aquarium should be those known as "cold-water" fish.

10. Aquatic snails ought to be judiciously chosen; that is, those univalves which feed upon confervæ and decaying vegetable matter should be preferred to those which eat healthy and growing plants. The Planorbes, as a rule, are the best for aquarium purposes.

11. Carnivorous and herbivorous beetles should never be kept in the same vessel.

12. No animals should be expected to live without food; nor ought animals to be tempted to prey upon each other through lack of a sufficiency of food.

13. The different foods should be kept conveniently near the aquarium or aquaria: the animals will then run less risk of being starved.

14. No discarded food ought to be left in the tank. If allowed to remain, it will be certain to corrupt the water, and so considerably interfere with the welfare of the whole of the inmates of the aquarium.

15. All garden-worms should be killed (as already suggested) before they are given to carnivorous fish or other carnivorous animals. It is neither a pleasant nor a profitable sight to see a worm struggling with its captor, even if the creature suffers no pain. Worms should also be dipped in water before they are placed in the aquarium: they will not then be the cause of the introduction of impurities into the tank.

16. A dead animal or plant or any decaying matter should at once, upon discovery, be removed from the aquarium. A small glass tube is very useful for obtaining certain things from the bottom of the water. The tube should be about ½in. in diameter and a few inches longer than the water in the tank is deep. It ought to be cut perfectly square at both ends. Almost everything which is small enough to enter the tube may be removed by it from the bottom of the aquarium. The tube is used in the following way: One end of the tube is hermetically closed by means of a finger, the other end is placed over the object required, the finger is then suddenly removed from the upper end of the tube, and the object desired shoots up immediately into the tube; and if the finger be returned to its former position, and kept carefully there, so that no air can enter the tube, the object now contained within the pipe may be readily removed from the aquarium. This operation is very simple, and may be easily and quickly performed. The tube should be kept conveniently near the aquarium.

17. Every aquarium should be covered with glass in such a way that the necessary air may be able to come in contact with the water, that none of the inhabitants of the tank can escape, and that no dust can fall upon the surface of the water.

z

18. No aquarium is likely to do well unless the representatives of the vegetable and animal world which it contains are properly balanced : that is to say, that there is a sufficiency of oxygen-yielding weed. This balance may be known by the growth of the plants, by the health of the animals, and the brightness of the water.

19. The water of a properly-balanced aquarium need never be changed—except, of course, under the special circumstances which have already been referred to. A little water must be added occasionally to make up for the loss by evaporation.

20. Aquatic animals should never be crowded together in an aquarium. It is always wiser to have too few animals than too many. When fish are swimming with their heads close to the surface of the water, it may be taken for granted that there are too many in the tank, or that the temperature of the water is higher than it should be. Under these circumstances, some of the fish should be at once removed, or one of the artificial means of aëration previously described should be resorted to, or the method (which has also been described) of reducing the state of the water to its proper temperature should be employed.

21. Directly a fish or any other animal is seen suffering from the dreaded fungus, it should be removed from the aquarium. If a cure is wished for, the sufferer should be placed (as already described) in running water, or in water in which chloride of sodium has been dissolved, in the proportion of a tablespoonful of the salt to half a gallon of water. A fish should be kept in this solution until it turns upon its back, when it ought to be at once placed in fresh water. This operation should be repeated once or twice every day until a cure is effected. A beetle might be kept in the solution for at least half a minute.

22. All the animals and plants which can be kept in an aquarium are interesting and instructive; some, no doubt, more so than others. Nothing, however, should be discarded as useless or uninteresting, for everything has a duty to perform in the world.

23. All who keep aquaria should be on their guard against giving the animals which they may contain any suffering, but should, instead, learn to have the same consideration for their feelings (whether they be sensitive or not) that a reasonable and properly-disposed person is expected to have for those of his fellow-creatures.

24. Conferva, when tenacious, may be easily removed from the glass of a tank by means of a pad of thick brown paper dipped in salt, or by gently rubbing the glass with the finest "glass-paper." The latter may be used while the tank contains water.

25. When it is necessary to fill an aquarium with water, and no small siphon is at hand, the water may be kept clear by spreading a thick piece of paper over the gravel and planted weeds, and pouring it (the water) into the aquarium through the fine rose of a watering-can. After the filling of the tank, the paper can be easily removed without disturbing either the plants or water.

26. The pleasure of keeping an aquarium is very much enhanced if the person who owns it has some definite object in view ; e.g., the thorough investigation of the life-history of some particular plants or animals. There is very, very much still to be learnt in this direction.

The series of chapters which it has given me so much pleasure to write, is now completed; and I venture to express the hope that what I have said in them will be of such use to novices in aquarium matters as to save them from some failure and disappointment, and not a few aquatic animals from unnecessary suffering.

I here repeat, that a properly arranged aquarium which is well cared for is always ornamental, interesting, instructive, and, in a sense, elevating.

INDEX.

I.

Ilybius, 235, **243**
 ater, 243
 fuliginosus, 243
Implements for collecting, 34
Insect aquaria, 18, 27, 30
Italian Water-weed, 59
Ivy-leaved Crowfoot, 72
 Duckweed, 88

J.

Japanese Goldfish, 185-188
Jars for cabinet aquarium, 27
Jeffreys, Dr. Gwynn, quoted, 217, 224
Jesse, Mr., quoted, 154
Jet for fountain, 52
Jones, Mr., quoted, 113, 127
Jones, Prof. Rymer, quoted, 300
Jurine, M., quoted, 326

K.

"King Carp," **178**

L.

Labelling aquaria, 32
Labyrinth-gilled Fishes, 166
Laccobius minutus, 257
 nigriceps, 224, 257
Laccophilus, 235. 245
 hyalinus, 245
 minutus, 245
Lamellibranchiata, **221**
Lampern, 158
Lamprey, River. 158
Large-mouthed Bass, **171**
Large Water-flea, 323
Larvæ of Water-flies, 273
Leather Carp, 120, 177
Leech. Eight-eyed, **313**
 Glutton. 313
 Horse, 313
Leeches, Medicinal, 312
Lemna gibba. 88
 minor, 88

Lemna polyrhiza, **88**
 trisulca, 88
Lesser Duckweed, **88**
Leuciscus cephalus. 123
 erythrophthalmus, **125**
 orfus, 135
 phoxinus, 126, 266
 rutilus, 122
 vulgaris, 124
Libellula depressa. 280
Libellulides, 280, 281, 282
Light, effects of, 48, 336
Lily, Cape Fragrant Water, 84
Lily-like Villarsia, 72
Limnæa, 205, 212
 auricularia, 196, 214
 glabra, 217
 glutinosa, 217
 palustris, 215
 peregra, 215
 stagnalis, 196, 198, 200, 213
 truncatula, 217
Limnæidæ, 205
Limnebius, 258
Limnius tuberculatus, 258
Limnophilidæ, 275, 276
Limnophilus flavicornis, **277**
 lunatus, 278
 pellucidus, 278
 rhombicus, 276
 vittatus, 278
Limpets and snails, 195
Livingstone, Dr., quoted, 140
Loach, Pond, 135, 181
 Spinous, 135
 Stone, 133
Lobelia Dortmanni, 72
 Water, 72
Long-spined Water-flea. 324
Looking-glass for cave, 44
 Fish, 120
 for shading and effect, 49
Louse, Water, 321

M.

Macropodus viridis (Polyacanthus viridi-auratus), 160, 161
Making aquaria, 8

Lightning Source UK Ltd.
Milton Keynes UK
UKOW051803091011

180027UK00001B/12/P